ECHOES *of the* ORIENT

ECHOES of the ORIENT

The Writings of William Quan Judge

VOLUME IV

Cumulative Index

Compiled by Dara Eklund

THEOSOPHICAL UNIVERSITY PRESS
PASADENA, CALIFORNIA

Theosophical University Press
Post Office Box C
Pasadena, California 91109-7107
www.theosociety.org
(626) 798-3378 tupress@theosociety.org
2011

Second and Revised Edition

The paper in this book contains 30% post-consumer recycled content, is acid free and FSC certified.

Library of Congress Cataloging-in-Publication Data

Judge, William Quan, 1851-1896.
Echoes of the Orient : the writings of William Quan Judge / compiled by Dara Eklund. — 2nd and rev. ed.
p. cm.
Includes bibliographical references and index.
ISBN 978-1-55700-195-5 (cloth., v.1 : alk. paper) — ISBN 978-1-55700-196-2 (cloth., v.2 : alk. paper) — ISBN 978-1-55700-197-9 (cloth., v.3 : alk. paper) — ISBN 978-1-55700-194-8 (pbk., v.4, cumulative index : alk. paper)
1. Theosophy. I. Eklund, Dara. II. Title.
BP525.J77 2008
299'.934—dc22

2008042215

Cover design by Patrice Hughes

Printed in the United States of America

Foreword

This Cumulative Index to Volumes I-III of *Echoes of the Orient* has been expanded and revised for the new edition. For providing the additional entries and co-editing of the original indices I owe my husband, Nicholas Weeks, much gratitude.

Our main entries are arranged alphabetically, ignoring personal titles such as Count or Saint. Individual books of the Bible are found under their titles, but entries about the Old and New Testaments are included under the general heading, Bible.

Subentries are also alphabetized, ignoring initial articles, prepositions, and conjunctions, as well as people's initials and titles before surnames such as Dr., Rev., Mr., and Mrs. Numerals and initials such as 7th, E.S., T.S., and *S.D.* are treated as if spelled out.

We again thank David and Nancy Reigle for the correction of Sanskrit terms, using a modified International Transliteration System. Certain terms however, which would not appear hyphenated in Sanskrit today, are kept as Judge used them, for the purpose of clarity in distinguishing compound terms as adopted in Theosophical literature.

Finally, we are indebted to the press staff at the T.S. Pasadena mentioned in each prior volume of the *Echoes* series for their continued diligence and support. Without their perseverance this series could not have been expedited so quickly.

Dara Eklund
March 21, 2011

Cumulative Index

Abbott, Dr. Lyman (1835-1922)
  gave sermon on Theology of Evolution, I 509
Abnormal
  nothing, under Karmic law, II 268
  a relative term, II 268
Abraham
  Jewish sage, I 441
  trial of, on Mt. Moriah, III 227
Absolute
  See also Parabrahman
  abstract space, II 296
  affirming all is the, absurd, I 137
  human monad a ray from the, II 226
  incapable of limitation, III 326
  inherent law of, I 158
  Life & Consciousness as aspects of, III 368-9
  man attains Oneness with, III 234, 404
  not understood by Dhyāni-Chohans, II 225
  relativity and, I 241
  Spirit & Matter co-exist in the, II 238, 310, 360, 406
  Spirit & Matter differentiations of, II 310
  Spirit as 1st differentiation of, II 238
  on spirit "returning" to, II 406-7
  Theosophy has knowledge of, III 53
  Unknown and Unknowable, II 296
  as unmanifest, II 310, 360, 407
  world diagram, III 332
Abstract
  qualities are also "objective things," II 339
  Space & Motion, II 296
Abstraction
  of motion & color, II 296
  Spirit as unconscious, II 232
Action
  See also Karma
  all, for sake of humanity, II 9
  bad karma of self-seeking, II 351
  centers of force confused with centers of, III 406
  and inaction, II 284; III 356
  motive for good, II 462-3
  perform, without concern for results, II 464
  sacrifice in, II 463
  Theosophy a guide for, III 72
  thought causes, II 162
  three kinds of, II 109
Acts
  on possessed woman, I 289
Adam & Eve
  allegorical, II 112, 268
  "Fall" of, II 268
  Garden of, allegory, III 189-90
Adam Kadmon ['Ādām-Qadmōn] (Heb)
  and Fohat, III 336
  interlaced triangles &, I 14
Adept(s)
  See also Initiate(s); Mahātma(s); Master(s); Messenger(s)
  accused of selfishness, I 113; III 23
  on Ākāśic influence, III 8
  all, married in some life, I 20
  altruism fostered by, III 92
  ancient college of, in Ireland, I 231
  archaic evolutionary scheme of, III 9, 10, 21-2
  are conscious mediums, I 355, 395
  are incarnated Spirit, II 255
  are Karma just as we are, II 284

bogus messages from, I 469-70
can transfer thought to another brain, II 95
cannot alter evil, I 314, 400
cannot alter Karma, II 284; III 17, 59, 126
cannot pander to Science, I 376-81
cipher of, I 392
Circle of, and T.S., III 419
on collective hallucination, I 400
a colony from the gods, I 121-2, 127
come in last quarter of each century, II 9-10, 301; III 283-4
communication between, III 27
conscious on all planes, I 80
constant communication with, not needed, I 116
crave no honors, III 24, 30
on craving for phenomena, III 94q
cycle of 1897 and, III 203
declaration of belief in, I 339-42, 376
as Deva becomes lesser god, III 66
Deva state of some, II 375-6; III 66, 126
Devachan of others can be entered by, II 382
on Devachanic time period, I 337-8
did not desert the T.S., I 201-3, 270-3
each man connected to one of, I 140
efflorescence of age, II 95, 257
feats of, compared to fakirs, II 307
forfeits progress if powers are claimed, II 446
founding of U.S. and, II 77-8
fraternity of, III 27-8, 29, 379
guard astral & spiritual records of man, III 9
heirs of, influenced by, I 273
help moral progress of man, I 202, 360
hierarchies of, & Dhyāni-Chohans, III 14-15
higher flowers of human race, II 135, 414
higher T.S.degrees held by, II 258
how, assist humanity, I 315
imitation of, not wise, II 405
imperishable secret records of, III 5, 9
influence history behind scenes, III 23-4, 28-9, 283-4
influence not withdrawn, II 433
as Jīvanmuktas, II 272, 415
keepers of Wisdom-Religion, II 135
know future & what is best, I 69
laws of nature by-laws of, III 27
legacy in ancient Ireland, I 544-5
liṅga-śarīra of, III 382
live on inner planes, II 433
living men, not Gods, III 15, 23, 29
Māyāvi-rūpa of, III 449
mediums of a high order, I 53, 308-9, 355
modify only minor currents of cycles, II 259q; III 17, 24
Nirmāṇakāyas, I 127
not subject to Devachan, II 382
objections to, refuted, I 313-14, 340
only, recognize their chelas, II 440
only true scientists, III 11
past initiations obscured, I 127-8
powers acquired naturally, II 464
powers of, not gifts, I 103
precipitation of messages from, I 391-8
projects consciousness into Nature, III 356
protect man from true sun, I 141
reasons for not proclaiming themselves, I 315
refined Kāma Rūpa of, III 385
refuse to display powers, I 106-7
Ṛishis who protect the race, I 141
science not helped by, I 245
scientific scheme of, III 11
and screen of time, I 548-50; II 234
service to Humanity ideal of, II 60, 135-6, 259-60
shrines of India have resident, III 29
some, greater than others, II 441
St. Paul an, I 103
telegrams or letters claimed from, II 445-6

testimony to existence of, I 313-14; II 328
T.S. influenced by, III 28, 283-4
T.S. not only channel for, I 270-5
on thoughts & beliefs of man, III 8
Tree of, and Padmapāṇi, III 358
triumph of the best in man, II 414
use of Principles by, III 347, 417
voluntary incarnation of, III 364
White, cp. with master musician, III 347
of White Path vs. Black, II 256-7, 414; III 379

Adeptship
See also Initiation(s)
all experiences understood before, III 396-7
forging ahead in, to benefit race, III 379
Nirmāṇakāyas and, III 66
no easy road to, III 379, 396
on pretensions to, III 30

Adhémar, Count & Countess d'
Enghien phenomena and, II 22-4
H.P.B.'s visit to, II 21-4

Aditi (Skt)
divine Voice a form of, III 359
higher than ether as Vāch, III 359

Adyar
alterations of shrine at, by Coulombs, I 264, 265
description of T.S. Headquarters, I 142, 263-7
formation of T.S. Hq. at, I 67
library, I 68, 189
Oriental Library, I 263

Æ. *See* Russell, George Wm.

Age
Ego connects with body, II 302
limit in Occultism, III 461
what is old, II 309

Age(s)
See also Cycle(s); Yuga(s)
Adept is efflorescence of, II 95
Azoic, of Science, II 238
of darkness & transition, III 429, 455
of man in palmistry, II 100
of mankind, III 31-2
New Order of, II 78-9
reverence paralyzed in our, II 62
succession of the, III 31
what current, needs, I 245

Agnishvātta Pitṛis (Skt). *See* Solar Pitṛis

Agnishvāttas (Skt)
a class of Fire Lords, III 465

Agnosticism
T.S. faced the scorn of, I 217

Airplanes
known to ancients, I 447, 565-6

Aiyar, T. A. Swaminatha (1868-?)
biographical sketch, II 518-19
worker for T.S., I 443

Ākāśa (Skt)
See also Astral Light; Ether
Astral Light is lowest division of, III 297, 407
central impulse within Atoms, III 360
circular motion, III 46-7
compared to astral light, II 232
as "ether," II 237; III 45, 359-60
fifth Cosmic Principle, II 224
and 5th element in 5th Round as its gross body, II 237
as first Tattva, III 359-60
images persist for centuries in, III 8, 46q
Logos acts through, III 359
Logos, and Sound, III 60 &n, 359
manas proceeds from, II 224
mantras and, I 90
mystery concerning, II 239
new element visible when Manas fully developed, III 365
occult phenomena through means of, III 45
permeates every atom of globe, III 46
projected from the eyes, II 72
recorder of acts & thoughts, III 8, 45, 60
records in Auric Egg, III 364
resonance of Aum is, III 360
silent during Pralaya, III 360
source of all Tattvas, III 359-60
spooks of dead float in, III 45

substratum of Auric Egg, III 403
a subtle form of matter, I 236
Third Principle in Nature, III 319
useful function of, III 47, 60
as vibratory motion, III 359-60

Ālaya (Skt)
Spiritual Soul whose Ray is Buddhi, III 367

Ālaya-Ākāśa (Skt)
Archetypal World of cosmic ideation, III 333
basis of astral world, III 337
corresponds to Auric Egg in man, III 333

Alchemists
and lure of gold, I 60

Alchemy
affinity with lower agents in, III 436
may lead to black magic, III 436, 447
as self-transformation, III 446-7
study of, can transform into selfishness, III 435-6
use of "red powder" in, III 447

Alcohol
effects of, II 278, 377
Jesus and Buddha on, III 106
morphine more degrading than, II 377
use and abuse of, II 377
use of, II 248

Alger, Rev. William R. (1822-1905)
reincarnation and, III 110
——— *A Critical History of the Doctrine of a Future Life*
a text used in all denominations, II 159

Allāhābād (or Prayāg)
See also Prayāg Letter
Master's letter conveyed by H.P.B. to T.S. in, I xlv

Allegory
of the Gem, III 267-9

Alternation Theory
of incarnation, II 299

Altruism
achieves goal of Esoteric Section, III 284, 293
Adepts inculcate, III 92
aim of life must be, I 341; II 416-17
appeals to Higher Self, II 261; III 64
disease and, I 297
does not interfere with Karma, II 245
essential to man's destiny, II 235
frees one from Māyā, III 452
impulses toward, must be acted on quickly, I 104-5
lifetimes needed to develop, I 215
main goal of T.S., II 277, 416-17
on occult path, I 19-22; II 264-5, 277
opens door to soul, I 18
or Philanthropy is actively beneficent, III 70
pledge to Higher Self demands, III 438
practice, & study philosophy, I 179
saves one from danger, II 265
vegetarian diet without, is vain, I 101-2
virtue &, bases of Rāja-Yoga, I 78

Ambition
killing, doesn't justify apathy, II 352-3

America
See also United States
ancient race had home in, I 206-7, 524
ancient wisdom to be championed in, I 150
Atlantean connection of, III 18
black magicians sprouting in, II 258
cataclysms will split up, II 25
dangerous psychic powers growing in, II 305
destined to be civilized, I 109, 150; III 18-19
education in, II 82, 86
"Fifth Continent" acc. to *S.D.*, I 150
germs of 6th sub-race in, II 25, 425
glorious civilization of, to return, III 18-20
H.P.B. on future of, II 24-7
memories of past glories vie for space, I 109
"new order of Ages" in, II 27

new race forming in, I 479, 524-5; II 153, 422, 425; III 19-20, 176
nursery for coming great Root-Race, II 24-7, 422, 425
in perpetual ferment, III 19
portion of the 6th continent, II 24-5
poverty & materialism of, III 19
theological shackles broken in, II 86, 169
T.S. work in, II 44-5
why T.S. founded in, II 26; III 156-9
Amida Buddha
See also Amitābha Buddha
in Japanese Buddhism, I 86-8; II 157
Amitābha Buddha
and Pure Land doctrine, I 86-8
salvation by faith in, III 109
on vow of, I 86-8, 438-9
vow of, wins salvation, I 438
Ammonius Saccas (ca. 175-245 CE)
as agent of Adepts, II 301
had same platform as T.S., I 244, 274
mission of, I 244
term Theosophy from, III 233
Amṛita (Skt)
battle over vase of, I 15
as spiritual wisdom, I 15
Analogy
Law of, II 367-8
Law of Correspondence and, III 312
Muṇḍaka-Upanishad & OṂ, I 10
in this & other worlds, II 367-8
Ānanda
gave up govt. job to aid T.S., I 68
Ānandamaya-Kośa Document
lists T.S. representatives at World's Fair, II 122-3
Anarchy
how nations can prevent, III 8
Anaxagoras (ca. 420 BCE)
taught palmistry, II 98
Ancestors
can't blame, for our Karma, II 180
we are our, II 182
Anderson, Jerome A. (1847-1903)
biographical sketch, II 477-9
Angel(s)
astral light as Recording, III 60
fall of, in Boehme's philosophy, II 108
Anger
destroys inner man, I 76; III 286, 424
as distinguished from indignation, II 455
occult results of, III 61-2
OṂ never to be said in, III 286
overcoming, a step in initiation, II 451
"righteous," I 76; II 254, 455
Anglo-Indian T.S.
Master K.H. on, I 63
Animal(s)
on antediluvian, III 31
defenseless, & moral law, II 71-2
dwell in mental plane, II 317
fate of the anthropoids, II 230
from man's matter, II 322, 420-1
influenced on astral plane by man's eidōlons, II 420
location and meaning of soul, II 458-9
Man before, in 4th Round, II 321-2
man influences Karma of, I 117
Manas is dormant in, II 317
monads progress to other globes of earth-chain, I 428
rebirth of man as, II 419-21; III 318
reincarnate, II 247
reparation for suffering of, II 247
seldom seen in séances, I 427
as "Soulless" in *S.D.*, I 427q
and vegetarians, I 247-8
wanton killing of, I 117-18, 247
Annihilation
in 5th Round of those who choose evil, II 321
Antaḥkaraṇa (Skt)
action & interaction of, III 374-5
as aspirations of Lower Manas to spiritual state, III 374
as bridge to Higher Self, III 302, 395

at death destroyed as a Bridge, III 366, 374
definition, III 365
on destruction of, III 395-6, 406-7
Judge, between East & West, I xxxix; III 414, 439-40
kāma-rūpa and, III 352
links Higher & Lower Manas, III 365-6, 374-5, 395
as mode of consciousness, III 366, 374, 395-6
Antardhānan (Skt)
disappearance by deception, I 411
Antaskaraṇa. *See* Antaḥkaraṇa
Anthony, St. (ca. 250-350 CE)
temptation of, I 98
Anthropoid Apes
karmically rewarded in a future Round, II 230
liberated monads of, II 230-1
Antinomians
attitudes of the, II 337
Anugītā
quoted, I 24, 31
Anupapādaka [aupapāduka] (Skt)
parentless & eternal space, III 15q
Anxiety
astrology relieves, II 76
freedom from, II 465
an insidious foe, II 76
Aphrodite (Venus)
born of the sea, III 318-19
and companions when symbol of earthly love, III 319
earlier, personified pure love, III 319
Apocalypse. See Revelation
Apollonius of Tyana (1st century CE)
accepted no money for magic, II 275
an Adept, II 353
apportations of, I 399
insulated from astral currents by wool, II 392
Apportation
by astral hand, I 356, 394; II 313
depolarization of book in, II 313
phenomena of, I 399
powers requisite for, II 307
Arabia
had her men of science, II 92
Arabian Nights
stories echo Lemuria and Atlantis, II 92-3
Archery
analogy in Upanishads, I 163
bow of Ulysses, I 163
symbolizes concentration, I 162-3
Archetypal
Man on Globe A, II 228
models in astral light, II 225
Architects
appear when materials ready, II 451
Arena (Boston)
Judge's reply to Conway in, III 195-202
Argument
avoid, I 23
belongs to intellectual plane, III 244
convinces no one, III 244
Plato's, on immortality of the soul, III 244
Arjuna
typified as Nara or man, III 357
Arnaud, M.
ed. of *Le Lotus*, III 143
Arnold, Sir Edwin (1832-1904)
——— *Bhagavad-Gītā* [trans.]
on cyclic Dawn, I 123
on Kṛishṇa's descent among men, I 122
——— *Indian Idylls*
on Yudhishṭhira & dog, I 101
——— *Light of Asia*
I 24q, 25q, 93q
gave currency to the term Buddhism, II 428
verse discussed, II 374-5
Arpentigny, Casimir Stanislas d' (b. 1798)
on palmistry, II 98-9
——— *Le Science de la Main*
on Chirognomy, II 97 &n, 98
on palmistry, II 98-9
Arūpa-Loka (Skt)
Rūpa-Loka & compared, II 394

Ārya Samāj
founded by a Brahman, II 51
Āryan(s) (Skt)
astronomical views, III 118-19
on evolution of universe, I 7-9
investigation of, culture by T.S., II 189-91
meaning of "M" sound for, I 7-8
Mercury represents OṂ, I 9
West needs philosophy of, I 245
wisdom of, in man's quest, II 84
Āryan Literature
devotion to, I 36
what it offers the West, I 5
Āryan Lodge
first T.S. "branch" formed, II 456-7
headquarters for American T.S., II 45, 456-7
Mr. Judge presided over, II 439
secrecy rule in, II 454
summary of, discussions, II 439-67
Āryāsaṅga
on Man & Kosmos, III 435q
Āryāvarta
restoration delayed by caste system, II 113
Asceticism
and concentration, I 410-11
dangers of extreme, I 91-3
responsible use required for, I 412
Ashburner, Rev.
says Hindus abandon Theosophy, III 129-30
Aspiration(s)
antaḥkaraṇa and, III 395-6
form antaḥkaraṇa, III 375
great, yield great success, III 398
heat of spiritual, uplifts soul, III 446-7
Higher Manas responds to, from Lower Manas, III 375
more valuable in despondency than when elated, II 443
towards Higher Self is needed, III 374
Astral
after-death state of slain warrior, II 276-7
atoms, II 42-3
bell sounds follow H.P.B., II 23; III 141
communication, II 353
currents, as Iḍā & Piṅgalā, I 236-7
danger of, matter, I 356
degraded, attracted to séances, II 420
Divine, as Mānasic World, III 334
dreams made in, sphere, II 391
form came first, III 9
hand, I 75, 356, 394; II 313
intoxication, I 49-50, 154; II 29
matrix in precipitation, I 354-5
memories, I 453-4
mental life impressed on, II 397
mesmerism awakens, man, I 255
monad does not reincarnate, II 333-4
music, II 23
phenomena no proof of spirituality, I 49-50
protection from, II 392
prototype of man, II 225
rising above the, II 397
senses in sleep, II 431
soul must free itself from, II 391, 397
spine & brain, II 38-9
Spirit of cometary matter, III 334
substance in mesmerism, II 33
travel, II 356
travel in dreams, II 402-3
travel is passive, II 391
travel most difficult feat, I 74
Astral Body
See also Liṅga-Śarīra
Adam as, before "coat of skin," III 190
alters little until death, II 37-8; III 383
anger influences, I 76-7
Auric Envelope contributes to, III 383
automatic action of medium's, I 453
brain has hold on, when awake, II 431-2
can develop unevenly, I 75-6
on changes in, & disintegration, III 383, 424

concentration develops, I 75
control of, II 395
currents in ethereal or, I 296
danger of anger, vanity, & pride to, I 76-7; III 424
dangers of travel in, I 74-5
as demon to the real man, III 447-8
Design body, III 189-90, 297, 320, 390, 444-5
disentangles itself before death, III 384-5
dissipates after death, III 44, 445
as ethereal form not confined to spleen, III 462
as ethereal inner person, III 444
even clothes have, III 390
explains mesmerism, II 35
explanation of, I 353-4, 415-16
governed by solar orb, I 76
hindrances to coherence of, I 75-6
joins with Kāma after death, II 338
Kāma acts through, III 383
Kāma-Rūpic spook and, III 385
or Liṅga-Śarīra, III 44, 189-90, 446
made at conception, II 302
man's accountability for, II 420
man's outer senses and, III 190
on many layers of, III 462
may be used for more than one life, I 453
in mediumship, III 190
model of its outer case, II 137; III 320
permeates physical, II 34-7, 137
purification of, III 446-7, 447-8
resurrected if odic chord to, not cut, III 140
séance may attract a dying, III 445
as seat of emotions, III 382-3
seven great divisions of, III 444, 445-8
a sheath of Soul, II 41
solidity destroyed by anger, III 424
study of, not profitable, I 4
sub-divisions of, II 41
transformed by fire, III 447
use in mediumship, I 453-4; III 190
use of, or hand, I 352-3, 356, 394

Astral Light
See also Ākāśa; Ether
Adepts can uplift, III 60
Ākāśa and, III 45, 60, 136, 297, 407
as *anima mundi*, III 46
beyond our control, III 8, 60-1
condensation by Yogi, III 48
confusion in, I 109, 154-5
darkness of Ineffable Light is, II 399
deceptive nature of, III 334-5, 408
deleterious currents in, III 47
Divine Uplifter if purified, III 49
in dreams, II 263, 390-1
Earth's, diffused in upper & lower portions, III 407
electricity a shadow of, II 399
elementals and, III 60-1, 136
elementals exist in, II 72
fading of images in, I 116
Flammarion describes, III 46
good fades in, evil stays, III 9
grosser type of matter than in body, I 154
H.P.B. could gaze into, for teachings, I 342-3
hypnotizes mankind, III 47-9
ideal prototypes in, II 225
illusions of, I 154; III 143-6
images persist for centuries, III 8, 45-6, 62, 136-7
influx of pictures in, II 263, 412
Kabbalists describe, as Satan, III 297
on karmic alterations of, I 96
Liṅga-Śarīra of our globe, III 297, 317, 334
looking into, not profitable, I 4, 153-4
as magic screen of time, I 550
in magnetizing, II 72
matrix of the earth, III 317
mediumistic phenomena in, III 46, 47-8, 136-7, 143-6, 334-5
medium's relation to, I 453; III 334-5
morals and, III 8-9
mystical creatures of, III 45
not inherently "good," II 232

not "light" as we know it, III 46
photographs of past & future in, I 49, 197, 407-8, 409
picture gallery of Earth, III 45-7, 60-1, 136-7, 334-5
as plastic medium, III 136-7
preserves every thought, II 346-7
qualities of, III 45-9, 60-1, 136-7, 143-6, 297, 407-8
"radiant matter" of science, III 46
as Recorder, I 52, 154, 197, 199-200, 553; II 263; III 47-8, 60-1, 136-7, 145, 297, 317
reflects beliefs & acts of man, III 8
reflects images from above & below, III 297, 407-8
remains of dead in, III 45, 60-1, 136-7, 144
retains matrix in precipitation, I 393
reverses all things, II 232
S.D. partly written from, I 342
Spiritualism creates delusions in, I 108
subconscious impressed by, III 49, 62
symbolized by the eye, I 115-16
symbols in the, II 413
teaches nothing of itself, I 154-5
vehicle for Karma, III 62

Astral Plane
cannot teach, I 154, 455
is dangerous, I 50
divine, of Nature, III 333
lingering on, II 276-7
of man's double, II 137
and our psychic senses, I 50
is wholly material, I 49, 455

Astral Soul
or Kāma-rūpa, III 44

Astral World
black magicians live in, II 353
character of man seen in, I 427
corresponds to astral body of man, III 334
delusion of, II 357, 359
executed criminals affect society from, I 488-90
lunar body and, III 334-5
plane of astral light, III 334

Astrologers
ancient Indian, II 103
of today much at sea, I 424

Astrology
ancient and modern, cp., II 15
disasters predicted by, I 422-4
Genethliacal, Mundane and Atmospherical, II 73
horary, & correspondences with planets & metals, III 290-1
horary, examples of, II 74-6
horary, the most reliable, II 73-4
ignore predictions of, I 424
Karma not negated by, II 273
Mundane, re nations, etc., II 73
of Nāḍīgranthams, II 101-3
nativities in, II 74
not soothsaying or divination, II 273
planetary influences in, II 273
planetary influences are only foci, II 15
President Garfield's death &, II 75
Ptolemy's *Tetrabiblos* influenced by Eastern, II 76
relieves anxiety, II 76

Astronomy
ancient Indian, I 451

Atlantean(s)
antiquity of, II 352
Avatāras among, II 345-6
civilization & America, III 18, 19
date of last destruction of, I 128
degraded spiritual things, III 19
Greeks & Romans an appearance of the, II 352
H.P.B. on Karma of, I 128
Ireland once the abode of, I 231
legend about destruction of, I 566-7
resurrection beginning, III 19-20
sorcery of, darkened skin of, III 20-1
weighty karma of, II 224
were ourselves, I 128-9, 131; II 224, 352; III 362

Atlantis
one of "five great Continents," II 24
remains of, & other Continents, II 24
Ātma(n) (Skt)
as Auric Egg in E.S., III 367
contains all, I 163
Gītā on, I 143
illumines its vehicles, II 276
indivisible spiritual identity, III 44
informing spirit, II 236, 274-5
Masters united with, III 430
meditation subject, III 454
never incarnated, II 275
not individualized, III 44, 96
not subject to change, II 236
the one principle, II 274
the ONE REALITY, III 294
one, shines on all, III 44
principles are vehicles of, II 274
substitute for Auric Egg, III 319
synthesis of whole, III 96
Universal Spirit, III 44, 168, 191, 296
of upper triad in Devachan, II 281
white magician's talisman is, II 94
Ātma-Buddhi (Skt)
Mānasic entity completes Trinity with, III 296, 365
not of this plane, III 397
senseless on this plane, III 296
universal & eternal, III 296
Ātma-Buddhi-Manas (Skt)
becomes a god, I 212
Monad now evolving as, III 409
reincarnating principles, III 364
as returning entity, I 279; II 330-1; III 448
Atmospheric
changes & upheavals, II 279
Atom(s)
agents of Karma, II 226-7
astral, and embryonic development, II 423
atomic lives or jīvas and, III 335, 350
cellular, influenced by higher mind alone, III 349
education of lower, I 329
eternal change of, III 11
"fate"of an, II 228
Gods, Monads, and, III 351
heat of, II 226
as hypothesis, I 173, 464
impressions given to, by man, II 297, 420-1
an independent entity, III 348
inform the molecules, III 351-2
infused with life or spirit, III 234, 318, 350
interchanging of, II 145-7, 319-20, 421
on interstellar, III 351
Leucippus on, II 223
man influences evolution of, II 420-1; III 318, 349-51
no inorganic, I 208, 211
occult definition, III 350
of occultism differ from science, I 212
"physical," proceed from mineral monad onwards, III 350
physical, reincarnate, II 42-3, 319-20
principles of the Gods, III 350-1
psycho-spiritual not physical, III 349
recombination cycle of, II 320
subject to Karma, III 350
transmigration of life, II 420-1; III 318
vibration rates of mineral, give illusion of solidity, I 466
Augoeides (Gk)
Inner God or Higher Self, I 432
Seventh aspect of Auric Egg, III 403
Aum. *See* OṂ
Aura
in mesmerism, II 33
Auric Egg
aroma of spiritual aspiration preserved in, III 368
and Buddhi-Manas, III 364
on color of, III 337
corresponds with the "Egg of Brahmā," III 400, 403
at death & after, III 363-4, 403

on duration of, III 403
emanation of Ātmic Ray, III 403
or "Envelope" as a principle, III 319, 337, 403
Esoteric 7th Principle, III 337, 358, 403, 405
as invisible magnetic sphere, III 403
as Karmic record, III 321, 353, 364, 403
as kingdom of heaven & light, III 337
Lunar Pitṛis absorbed into essence of, III 463-4
Māyāvi-rūpa of Adept and, III 363, 403
no one life can express all karmic atoms in, III 353
origin of astral form, III 364, 367, 403
Paśyantī Vāch and, III 337
sphere represents the, III 417
Third Eye and, in E.S. diagram, III 400
Thread Soul or Sūtrātma and, III 337, 364, 403
unphilosophical statements on, III 288

Auric Fluid
forms invisible plastic Substances on our plane, III 334
inheres in kāma-rūpa after death, III 334
use in magnetism, III 334

The Austral Theosophist
Judge article on T.S. in, III 216

Authority
man is final, in this cycle, I 36
Wisdom-Religion uses reason for, II 135

Avalokiteśvara (Skt)
leader of Hierarchy, III 357-8
Logos in divine regions, III 356, 358
Padmapāṇi, the Initiator, III 357
7th Universal Principle, III 359

Avatāra(s) (Skt)
Kṛishṇa and Christ, I 439-40
may be born to a common mother, II 379
Planetary Spirits as, III 402
reincarnation of an, II 347

Āveśa (Skt)
or Tulku defined, I xxxiv

Avīchi [avīci] (Skt)
Kāma-loka and, III 236
kāmic soul in, III 353
Naraka, or "hell," I 439
not Hell in Christian sense, III 63
refusal to work with Nature for Good and, III 328
the "second death," III 63, 236-7

Avogadro, Law of
Prof. Crookes and Neumann on, I 208-9

B

Babajee
assisted Olcott at Adyar, I 68

Baltimore American
on T.S. & its teachings, III 153-5

Barborka, Geoffrey A. (1897-1982)
——— *H. P. Blavatsky, Tibet & Tulku*
Tulku & Āveśa in, I xxxiv-v n

Barhishad Pitṛis (Skt)
See also Lunar Pitṛis
Lunar Ancestors, III 361

Barker, A. Trevor [compiler, *The Mahatma Letters to A. P. Sinnett*]
See Sinnett, Alfred P.

Barrett, Prof. Wm. F. (1884-1925)
on thought transference, II 95

Barrows, Rev. John Henry (1847-1902)
——— *The World's Parliament of Religions*
chairman at Chicago in 1893, II 125
at Chicago in 1893, II 119
gathered chief dissenting sects there, II 172
opening speech ref., II 169

Basket Trick
explanation of Hindu, III 170-1

Battachārya, Benee Madhab
President of Prayāga T.S., I 470

Beasts
ferocious, man's responsibility, I 117

Beausobre, Isaac de (1659-1738)
——— *Histoire Crit. de Manichée . . .*
on pre-existence of souls, I 430
Beecher, Dr. Edward (1803-1895)
Rev. Alger and, saw logic of rebirth, II 159
saw logic of rebirth, III 110
——— *The Conflict of Ages*
claims reincarnation is Christian, II 453
on reincarnation in Christian scheme, III 155 &n
reincarnation needed in Christianity, II 159
Beecher, Henry W. (1813-1887)
brother of Edward, II 159
famous orator on Evolution, I 509
preached reincarnation, III 176
Behmen. *See* Boehme, Jacob
Being(s)
inner man not spiritual, II 36
many great, I 125
men are cells within, I 125
in other spots of cosmos, II 350
spiritual, pervade universe, II 298
Bellamy, Edward (1850-1898)
Judge letter to, ref., II 152n
Bellary Branch [T.S.]
aided by "Hindu Revival," I 443-4
vernacular work of, I 425
Bengtsson, Sven (1843-1916)
carver of H.P.B.'s bronze urn, II 196 &n
Berosus [Berossos] (3rd century BCE)
astrological prediction of, I 424
Besant, Annie (1847-1933)
accused Judge of creating discord between East & West, I 476
assisted in London by Jasper Niemand, II 503
believed in Brahmanism, II 57
Blavatsky Lodge and, I 298
calls Judge "the greatest of exiles," II 502
carried H.P.B.'s ashes to India, II 196n
changes mind about Earth-Chain, I 498
claims Prayāg letter false, I 476; II 53, 217
delegate of European Section to World's Fair, II 133
draws huge crowds, II 171; III 201
H.P.B.'s praise for, III 209
Inner Group Recorder of Teachings, III 340
on Judge, re. Olcott's resignation, I xlii
on Judge's occult status, I xlviii
London T.S. Hq. given by, I 190
Olcott's message read by, II 134
represents Eastern division of E.S.T., III 273, 391
reviewed *S.D.*, III 209
suggested Judge for T.S. president, III 392
——— *The Case Against W. Q. Judge*
Judge's reply to charges, I lvii
——— *Seven Principles of Man*
on apportation, II 313q
Bhagavad-Gītā
on action, II 464
Adepts & night of Brahmā, II 415
all worlds subject to karma, III 36
on Arjuna's bow, I 163
on Ātman, I 143
on battlefield of Karma, I 27 &n
on Brahmā's Day and Night, I 157-8; II 108
Buddhists with key to, driven out of India, III 251
condenses highest ethics, III 96
on control of emotions, I 219
for daily thought, III 277
on descent of God, I 122, 127
on destiny of worldly men, I 147
on "Devachanic" state, III 252
on devotion through action, I 54; III 39q
on difficulty of unmanifested path, I 86
on divine dependence, I 534q
doctrine of, once lost to world, I 147
on Duty, II 371, 463-4
on duty of helping evolution, I 15
on effort & study, II 467-8

on equality of matter and spirit, I 119
esteemed by Buddhists & Brahmans, III 251
evolutionary history of human race, I 161-2
on fall from Indra's realm, III 41
on fortunate birth, I 79
on future birth, II 107q
and Gnostic cross, I 14
on Haṭha-Yoga, I 72-3
ideas of today found in, I 221
on Īśvara the Ego, II 364-5
on Karma Yoga, III 39q
on Karmic bondage, II 445
key to, lost, I 162
knower & known & guṇas in, II 317 &n
on lawful war, II 376
on Lord within heart, II 110
on many births, III 178 &n
on moderation, I 92
on moment of death, II 448-9
on morality of, I 57
on motive for action, II 464
names for Supreme Spirit, I 71
on obtaining Brahm, I 534q
on organs of body, III 347
pleasures contrasted in, II 378-9
on power of self-ideation, II 274
on rarity of reaching perfection, II 267
on real man, I 17
on reincarnations of an Avatāra, II 347
on self as both friend & enemy, I 537q
Self vs. self of, discussed, III 82-4
on self-control, I 219
seven points of view on, II 109
sheaths of soul in notes on, II 459 &n
on spirit & matter, I 159, 229
spiritual cultivation of white adept, II 414
stresses inner light over practical occultism, I 4
study of, revives good seeds from past lives, III 134
Subba Row's notes on, II 104; III 96, 333, 336-8
Supreme One in us, II 9
Supreme Soul not polluted by body, I 71
and symbolism of interlaced triangles, I 13, 251
on union with Supreme, I 72
on Universal Spirit and rebirth, I 35, 71
why 18 chapters in, I 125
youths should study Upanishads, *S.D.* and, for years, I 151

Bhārat Dharma
Indian Convention of 1893, I 425

Bhashyacharya, N.
first director of Adyar Library, I 68

Bhāskara
Brahman's caste name, III 165

Bhūta(s) (Skt)
obsession by, in ancient India, I 288
or Piśācha in Ākāśic substance, III 45-6
worshiped in India, I 57

Bible
See also books of
on holding to good, I 49
on moon, I 432-3
mystic story based on, verse, I 276-7
reincarnation and/or Karma in, I 305-7; II 139, 140-2, 444, 453
reincarnation in, I 418-22
Theosophy in, II 140

Billing, Mrs. M. J. Hollis- (1837-?)
on materialization acc. to "Jim Nolan," I 406-8
séances with "Jim Nolan" &, I 198ff, 404-10; III 136-7
spiritualist, I 198ff
unusual mediumship of, II 69

Bismarck, Otto von (1815-1898)
divine impulse in destiny of, III 23-4

Black
lodge encourages psychism, II 11
represents lower self, II 414

Black Magic
See also Magic; White Magic

America the future theater of, II 257-8, 345-6
of Atlanteans, II 231, 346
in Bhutan, II 94
dangerous knowledge can lead to, III 293
disregard for ethics leads to, III 465-6
distinction between White Magic and, II 256-8, 290
Fourth Race dabbled in, II 94
greatest protection against, II 415, 417
as literary theme, II 180
in mental healing, I 227, 229-30; II 290
motive determines, I 45, 47
motive determines White or, III 290
origin of, II 231, 256-7
on racial destruction by, II 11, 345-6
seeds for, among Westerners, II 417
self & disruption as, II 257
taking pay in, II 275
talismans in, II 94
triumph of selfishness, II 256
use of magnetism is not, III 290
use of OṂ for material gain is, III 310
Black Magician(s)
See also Magician; White Magician
accept pay, II 275, 450
deify the body, III 290
on destruction of, II 94, 345-6, 415
devoid of love, though brilliant, III 329
fate of, II 375
fate of aspiring, I 45-6
Higher Ego divorced from, III 382
opposite pole to White Adept, II 414
a potential, within, II 414
prostitutes wisdom to selfish ends, II 450
psychic powers and, III 92
a rarity in our age, II 256-7, 414-15
reaps hell of Avīchi, III 63
seeks for self alone, III 92
treatment of, II 256-7, 414-15
on U.S. as theater of, II 345-6
use of elementals by, II 353
vegetarianism and, I 100
Blavatsky, H. P. (1831-1891)
See also The Theosophist; *Lucifer*
abuse & vilification of, I 139
on Adepts behind T.S., I 270-4
aim of, I 194
altruism encouraged by, III 174
an American citizen, III 159
on ancient Indian technology, I 447-8
appeal of her phenomena, II 59-60
ashes divided between 3 lands, II 194-7
ashes now in America noted, II 196n
ashes placed in Ganges, II 196n
astral bells heard around, III 141, 239
on atom, I 208, 209, 211
attacked by Dr. Coues, II 183-4, 200
on authenticity of Mahātmas' theories, I 395
biographical sketch, III 204-12
Blavatskyism not Theosophy, III 174
a Brahman Yogi's support of, III 418-20
a Buddhist, I 475
Cairo experiment of, III 207
came to America to reform Spiritualism, I 350
changed name of Esoteric Section, III 370
as Chela, I 366-7
Christ Jesus denied by, II 266
on "closing cycle," II 9-10
common sense in E.S. urged by, III 288
compared with Cagliostro, III 208
compassion of, III 139
on concentration, III 455
a conscious messenger, II 366
in constant communication with Masters, III 141-2, 241
Coues-Collins attack on, III 150-1
daily life of, I 257-63, 267-8

on dangers of Black Magic in healing, I 227
debt owed to, by T.S., I 58-9
demonstrated precipitations for Judge, I 310
description of homes of, I 256ff
deserving our loyalty, I 514
disappeared at Darjeeling, III 139
discarded phenomena later, II 356
disposal of, ashes a problem, II 194-5
early visit to America, III 206
Esoteric Buddhism teachings surprised, I 382
expenses for urn solicited, II 194
farewell tribute to, II 16-21
fearless & selfless, III 101, 212
focused on yellow with sacred "Word," III 457
Foulke's claims &, II 28-30
founded working girls' club, III 210
freezing room phenomena of, III 239-41
goes to India, I 175, 193
grandest being Judge knew, II 156
had few friends, II 20
Hindus' gratitude for, III 209
Hodgson report &, II 408
income & copyrights of, III 152
Ireland an Atlantean abode, I 231
on Judge as Antaskaraṇa, I xxxix
on Judge as channel for Nirmāṇakāya, I xxxiv
on Judge as resuscitator of Theosophy in U.S.A., I xxxix
Judge defended by, I xxxix-xl
Judge first meets, I 192; II 16
Judge taught rebirth by, II 334
Judge urged by, to help with *S.D.*, III 238-41
Judge's view of, I 58-9, 192-4
Karma of Theosophists taken on by, I 59
Keightleys first meet, II 482, 486
knew of her future abuse, I 193
laid down lines of force for Work, II 19
last words about the T.S., II 510; III 340
libel suit dropped, II 200
life objective of, III 210
on Life-atoms and reincarnation, II 319-20
London life of, III 138
loyalty to, II 63
Mahātma & a Chela's view of, III 419-20
marriage to old Blavatsky, III 206
Masters' 1st messenger to us, II 216
Masters and, III 411-12, 418-20
Masters are facts to, I 385-6
Masters' messages astrally impressed by, I 394
Masters' messages received after death of, I 201-2, 269-70
Masters stand by, I 63-4, 366-7
never asked for money, III 210
never claimed authority, II 62
never disavowed reincarnation, II 333-4
no fear of dying before work done, III 139
no "successor" to, II 28
not dogmatic, I 386
not infallible, II 59, 380
not possessed by elementals, I 512
Olcott accused, of fraud, II 215-17
Olcott carried Indian portion of, ashes, II 196
over-zealous worship of, II 60-1
phenomena at Enghien &, II 22-4; III 239-41
phenomena held back by, I 193-4, 462
phenomena of, I 307-10; III 93, 140-1, 206-7
on phenomena of teacup, III 198
place in the T.S., II 59
post of Corresponding Secretary to remain vacant at death, I 194
power of lions & sages in, II 19, 21
predicted Conway's attack on T.S., III 196
prediction about modern skepticism, I 146
private seal of, I 249, 321-3
prophecies of, I 243-4, 302-4, 462

on psychic powers growing in America, II 305
on psychological fraud, I 356
read astral light, II 223
on real H.P.B., II 320
on release of K.H.'s name, III 200
remains Head of E.S. after "death," III 344
reply to attack on, III 195-202
on right use of psychic powers, II 356
shared ticket with poor woman, III 139
shrine for ashes of, cited in *Harper's* magazine, I 299
on solar & Universal Cycles, I 123
on Spiritual Sun, III 447
on spiritual wickedness, III 328
Spiritualism investigated by, III 207
Spiritualists' view of, III 22
supposed after-death messages from, I 269-70
suspected as Russian spy in India, I 67
teachings of, deserve first consideration, I 223
T.S. fees do not go to, III 152
T.S. founding by, III 207-8
T.S. founding by, and Mahātmas, III 419-20
T.S. sustained by strength of, I 176, 298, 321-2
on Theosophical work, I 204
on Those who sent her, II 135
Tibetan training of, II 333
Tibetan training of, verified, II 335
tributes to, I 191-4; III 101, 419-20
trying to be a Theosophist, III 156
urn for, ashes described, II 194-7; III 101
utter devotion to Master, II 19
values Brotherhood more than T.S., I 486
visits Count and Countess d'Adhémar, II 21-4
warning for future of E.S., III 340, 343, 344
warns against astral messages, III 288
Washington D.C. branch named for, III 7
on Western teachers, III 444
——— *Collected Writings*
on aim of *Lucifer* magazine, II 15n
animals and man compared, I 211
bio. of A. Keightley in, II 487
bio. of B. Keightley in, II 485
bio. of C. F. Wright in, II 497
bio. of Dr. H. Coryn, II 487 ref.
bio. of G. R. S. Mead in, II 493n
bio. of Isabel Cooper-Oakley in, II 513
bio. of J. M. Pryse in, II 509
bio. of Julia Keightley in, II 503
Book of Rules, III 399
on chelaship, III 275 &n
consult, III 6, 24, 41 &n, 131, 191, 200, 328, 377
consult, Vol. XIV, Appendix II, I 409n
"Conversations on Occultism" ref., I 62
on daily meditation, III 373
diagram of 7 worlds & man, III 335
on disease, II 291q, 294q
on Double-page Diagram, III 416-18
on E.S. evolution, III 273 &n
E.S. Intro. by B. de Zirkoff, III 273
on E.S. "orders," III 345q
on E.S. rules, III 316n
on Fire, Motion, etc., III 358
on Hypnotism, III 334
on inorganic vs. organic, I 211
on Kāma-rūpa & Māyāvi-rūpa, III 334, 353
on karma & selfishness, III 345-6
on Lunar Pitṛis & Kumāras, III 462-3q
on man, God, & Nature, III 433, 435
on mantra and geometry, III 380
on Masters' handwritings, I xlix-l
Māyā defined, I 213
on meditation with color & sound, III 455-6
on medium & astral light, III 334-5
on Mind-cure, III 410

on motive, III 89q
Nirmāṇakāyas in, III 387
Occultism defined by, III 261
on physical body, III 289
on "Psychic & Noetic Action," III 348-9
ref. to Collins' "fraud," II 254n
ref. to J. D. Buck in, II 472
ref. to Wachtmeister in, II 492
on "Reincarnations in Tibet," II 347 &n
Table of Vibrations, III 309
on "Transmigration of the Life-atoms," II 319 &n

——— *Isis Unveiled*
Adepts inspired, II 254n
ancient secrets rediscovered, I 129, 146
denied reincarnation of personality, II 333-4
diagram on Vāch & Virāj in, III 359
Earth's evolutionary period and, III 400
on elementals, III 400
forerunner of T.S. literature, I 298
house where, written, I 268
on interlaced triangles, I 251
Judge drew up contract for, I 192
Judge, *S.D.*, and, II 21
Judge witnessed writing of, I 192
on length of Cycles, I 124
Paracelsus on "Sidereal force" in man, III 334
propositions from, I 403
on secret revelations of future cycles, I 129
study revives past knowledge, III 134
taught reincarnation, II 333 &n, 334
topical study of, in E.S., III 331-2
on triune Nature, III 430-1
on writing of, III 208

——— *The Key to Theosophy*
Adepts have no Devachan, II 381
on after-death states, II 281
on Ātman, III 367
on close of cycle, III 283
on Cycle of Life, I 123
on cyclical effort of Adepts to help humanity, II 301
on Devachan, III 365
on Devachanic time period, I 337
on E.S. & T.S. Messenger, III 284-5
on future of T.S. & vision of mankind, I 195, 244; II 10; III 95-7q, 283-5, 344
hints on study of, III 87, 331-2
messenger cycle of 100 yrs., I 270
on proper study of, I 132
on Theosophical books before T.S., I 274
T.S. warned on dogmatism, I 222
written in London, I 192; III 209

——— *Lucifer*
on "Genius," II 263
H.P.B. founded, II 15

——— *The Secret Doctrine*
on 20th century prediction, I 210
absolute abstract space in, II 296
acme of Theosophical Movement, III 148-9
aim of, III 148
animal has no Ego-Soul, I 427q
Anupapādaka is parentless & eternal space, III 15q
on Archangels & "The Fall," II 268
astral man before physical, III 31, 464-5
astral man models physical, III 295
on Atlantean Karma, I 128
on Atlanteans & cycle of avataras, II 346
on Atoms & nature spirits, III 350
basis of, Stanzas of Dzyan, III 149
careful study needed, III 322
certificate about, I 343-6
Consciousness as conceived in, II 304; III 368
consult, III 108n
on correspondence of Earth-Chain and man, I 369; III 335
on death & karma, III 41
on descent into matter, II 345
on Dhyāni-Chohans, Lipikas, & Space, III 14-15q
on Divine Mind's source, I 209

on door to human kingdom closed, II 314, 419
early private teachings of, I 382n
on Earth-Chain, I 324-6, 368; II 286, 424
on Earth-Chain & its companions, I 370q
"Elementals" chapter put aside, III 241
enormous success of, III 141, 148-9
on Eros as divine desire, III 333
Esoteric Buddhism corrected by, I 325-7, 368-70, 382-3, 512-13; II 265; III 95
on evolution of man's vehicles, II 274
facsimile of K.H. letter to Judge on, I 348
on fate of moon, I 434
on fiery Breaths, III 333, 463-4
on Fire & Water deities, III 358
on five great continents, II 24-6
full revelation not given in, III 241
on geometrical figures, III 416-17
on Gods, Monads, & Atoms, III 351
great cycles & eras in, II 266
on H.P.B.'s rescue from death, III 140q
on Heart & Mind of Universe, III 368
on Heart & plexuses, I 388-9
Hermetic teaching discussed by, II 331
home where, finished, I 262-3
how Atoms propel their molecules, III 350-1
introduction to, should be studied, I 216
on Kali-Yuga of Atlanteans, I 459
on Kwan-Yin, etc., III 358
on Logos, III 357-8, 359
on Lunar & Solar Pitṛis, III 294-5, 361-3
on Lunar Pitṛis & Fire Lords, III 463-5
on Mahat, III 334
on Mānasaputras & Dhyāni-Buddhas, III 362-3
on man's evolution, I 331-2
on Mars, Mercury, & Earth, I 513q
on Mars, Mercury, Venus, & Earth, I 370 &n, 383-4, 434
Masters dictated, I 343-4; II 10, 323; III 412, 416
Masters inspired, II 254n
on meaning of need for "all experience," II 380-1
method of study, III 312, 331-2
on Monad, II 315-16
on Monadic Essence, III 350-1
on moon as deserted planet, II 423
on Moon's dissolution, I 434
no inorganic matter, I 208
no new "egos" or monads for this planetary chain, II 419, 424-7
not based on pretended authority, I 218
not produced by elementals, I 512
originally an archaic MS, II 223
on Padmapāṇi, III 356-60
preparation of, III 138, 209-10, 238-41
on proper study of, I 132
prophecy concerning, II 223
prophecy concerning Adepts, I 302
prophecy on reascension of old facts, I 146
on Pythagorean doctrine of Numbers, III 338
R. Hunt article on the sun, I 135n
recordings of dictation of, III 141
reviewed by Besant, III 209
"Rootless Root" proposition of, II 323q
on septenary nature of Universe, I 330q
on serpent, I 250
seven forces in man & nature, II 270q
on Seven Hosts projecting men, III 465
on seven worlds, III 332-5
on seven zones & Root-Races, III 20q
study of, I 217-18
synthetic view needed to master, I 218
teachings about comets in, I 481-2

teachings highlighted, II 223-39
teachings of, antedate Vedas, I 303
theogony defined, III 96
on third eye, III 380
on thorough study of, I 151
on three classes of Elementals, III 335
Tibetan adepts aid in, III 150
triple evolutionary scheme in, III 294-5
triple production of H.P.B., K.H., and M., I 343-4; II 323
unifies science & religion, III 149
on Vāch & its aspects, III 335-8
Vishṇu-Purāṇa quoted, I 429
on Water, III 319
writing of, I 192-3, 342-4, 382-3

——— *The Theosophical Glossary*
on Mesmer, II 31

——— *Transactions of the Blavatsky Lodge*
everything is organic, I 211
on Fire, Light, Motion, III 358q

——— *The Voice of the Silence*
on antaḥkaraṇa, III 366, 375
antaḥkaraṇa after death, III 352
on Bird of Kwan-yin as Aum, III 359
doctrine of renunciation in, I 526q
on eternal man, III 186
on "heresy of separateness," III 316
on inaction, III 356q
on Karma, III 246
a key devotional work, II 355
ladder of the mystic sounds, III 337
on lunar body of disciple, III 335q
quoted on the Way, I 142
reading of, at E.S. meetings, III 311
satiation of craving opposed in, I 495
on self-sacrifice, III 25 &n
on service, I 316
study of, recommended, III 277
topical study of, III 331-2
writing of, I 192-3

Blavatsky, Nikifor V. (1809-1887)
on H.P.B.'s marriage to, III 206

Blind
clairvoyance in the, II 288

Blind Tom [Wiggins] (1849-1908)
the musician, II 160, 312

Blood
cells transmit sensations, II 41
circulation of, cp. with solar system, III 313
circulation of, long known in East, I 389
two aspects of, I 313

Bodhidharma (460?-534)
brought Buddhism to China, I 85

Bodhisattvas (Skt)
at dawn of evolution, II 225

Body
ancient view of, II 301-2
blood flow cp. with global circulation, III 313
disappears when consciousness leaves, III 289
Ego connects with, at age 7, II 302
ganglions of, register memory of sensations, II 41-2
gestation period of, is shortening, II 423-4
an illusion, III 289
invisible parts of, II 301-2
kept intact by astral body, II 38
killing, easily justified, III 218-9
law of correspondences seen in, III 313-14
lower self does not include, III 304, 367
magnetic & electric ties of mind to, II 288
man's, millions of years old, III 32
matter of, used by other egos, I 119
not a principle esoterically, III 368
not object of student's care, II 405
only affinities on lower plane, III 290
partially paralyzed by mesmerism, II 33, 37
personality belongs only to, I 84
physical, constantly changing, II 309
primordial substance is, of Spirits, II 239
in reality does not grow old, II 309
in sevenfold division of man, III 43

a sheath of Soul, II 41-2
yoga practices die with, III 304
Boehme, Jacob (1575-1624)
Adept influence on, I 273
and Esoteric Christianity, II 107
German mystic & shoemaker, II 106-12
idea of Brahm in works of, II 108
major works of, II 107n-8n
as messenger of Masters, II 365-6
obscured adept, I 128
on sun & planets, II 110-11
system of classification of, II 109-10
a Theosopher, I 273-4; III 156 &n
Theosophical movement and, I 486
——— *Forty Questions on the Soul*
disturbed priests of his day, III 156
Bombay (India)
Judge lecture in, II 80-2
Bonney, Charles Carroll (1831-1903)
accepts T.S. for Parliament of Religions, II 125-6
Book(s)
new students given only 3, I 151
of polished stones hidden, I 161
reading of, vs. thought, III 132-4
real, and archaic truths, III 133
suggested list of Theosophical, III 237-8
Book-Knowledge
lifeless, III 101
path of, I 43, 151
superficial skimming, I 151
superstition and, III 101
useless for occultism, I 78
Book of Rules
on chief aim of E.S., III 421
H.P.B. on importance of rule five, III 316
Judge present when H.P.B. formulated, III 316
numbering altered, III 316n
remained in force after H.P.B.'s death, III 441
Book of the Dead
on after-death state, III 41
Egyptian symbols in, I 252-3
Job based on, I 252
Boston Convention
split of branches at T.S., II 430-1
Boston Index
letter to, on S.P.R. report, III 123-5
Bow, Arrow & OṂ
analogy, I 10, 163; II 391
Boyd, Ernest (1887-1946)
——— *Ireland's Literary Renaissance*
editor of, II 3 &n
Bradlaugh, Charles (1833-1891)
disciples of, in India, II 90
Brahma (or Brahman) (Skt)
Adepts absorbed into, II 257
body as city of, I 61
idea in Boehme's work, II 108
karma does not apply to, III 36, 245
nothing is but, III 55
OṂ and, I 10, 163
rootless root, III 55
the Unmanifested, III 55
unmanifested, cp. with Brahmā, III 55, 335
Brahmā (Skt)
Brahma the unmanifested cp. with, III 55, 335
Breath of, II 225
consists of Sat-Chit-Ānanda, III 251
Days & Nights of, I 8-9, 122-3, 157-8
First Cause, III 55
four bodies of, overlap as Day does Night, III 326
Karma applies even to, III 126
life of, and yugas, I 116
manifested Logos is, III 55, 335
Parabrahma and, III 55
-Prajāpati caused 7 Ṛishis to issue, III 338
Vishṇu & Śiva, I 7
Brahman(s) [Brāhmaṇa] (Skt)
Allāhābād, & message to, II 215-17
can set example for other castes, II 250
false ideas of, towards T.S., II 51-2
immortality of soul taught by, III 109
initiated with *Gāyatrī*, I 311
Judge sympathetic to, I 361-5

on Mahātmas during Kali Yuga, III 131
miracles of, & Indian yogis, III 170
must set example for other castes, II 113
neglect of, and their MSS., I 425-6
no, missionaries, I 429
opposed H.P.B., I xlv
Prayāg letter to, I 470-6; II 54
prayer bell, III 108-9
promoted caste & idol-worship, I 478
religion of, in India, II 50, 250
religion of, prevails in India, I 361-2
respond to Judge's letter, I 424-5
sons of Āryāvarta, I 362
spiritual pride among, II 113, 372
suspect T.S. partial to Buddhism, I 361-5, 470-5

Brahmanical Thread
Olcott invested with, I 68, 363

Brahmanism
See also Hinduism
attitude towards Buddhism, II 51-2
the Bridge Doctrine in, I 438
Chakravarti represented, at World's Fair, II 122, 124, 489
compared to Christianity and Buddhism, I 438-40
confused with Buddhism, I 372
corruption of pure, II 250
crystallized & exclusive, I 477
Dāmodar gave up practices of, I 470
esoteric, and Buddhism, II 54, 430
idolatry as corruption of pure, II 430
idolatry of exoteric, II 430
India's dominant religion, I 361, 437
influence of T.S. in its spread, II 428
must be born into, II 428
must restore harmony, II 113
nearest the truth, II 56
priesthood of, & T.S., II 51
as proclaimed by Vedāntins, II 50-1
religion of India, III 173-4
theological dogmatism of, I 478
Theosophy is not, III 174

Brain
cannot be altered at once, III 95-6
carries out orders of the soul, II 457
concerned with present lifetime, II 161
daily impressions on, recur in sleep, II 34, 431
during sleep, I 152
effect of mesmerism on, II 34
fatigue and dreams, II 431-2
ganglia of, used for psychic work, III 303
as generator of Cosmic power, I 506
how AUM sound is conveyed to, III 304
impressed by Heart, III 349
medulla oblongata of, III 323
reversed images and, II 232
seat of the soul not in, II 457
on soul ganglia within the, III 303
third ventricle of, & pineal gland, III 303

"Bridge Doctrine"
of Brahman caste, II 157

Bṛihadāraṇyaka-Upanishad
aspiration for light, I 436q
on Brahman within all, I 115
on knowledge beyond Brahman caste, I 428-9
on Kṛishṇa as a Kshatriya, I 428-9
path of sages, III 133-4

Brotherhood
See also Universal Brotherhood
aim of Theosophy, II 373
Brahmanical faith on, II 250
and charity, I 46
community of T. L. Harris, II 192
a fact in nature, II 143; III 89
fearless reliance on, I 36
and forgiveness, II 253
freedom of thought leads to, II 86
of hate, I 508-9
of humanity aided by Adepts, III 103
includes everything, I 520-1
mechanical Theosophy negates, I 493
more valuable than T.S., I 486

not aided by Universal language, I 457-8
one-sided if selective, I 508
perfection and, identical, II 12
practice of, & helping lower classes, II 373
prime object of T.S., II 81-2, 151, 373; III 329-30
public work vs. private, I 463
real object of Inner Lodge, I 380
sentimentality is not, III 356
spirit of, at World's Fair, II 131, 171-2
talk of, not enough, I 148; III 83
Theosophic code is, III 168-9
T.S. a nucleus for real, II 20; III 103, 329-30
as toleration yet freedom of speech, III 103
Universal, II 143-8, 151-2; III 54-5, 89
Universal, goal, II 139
Universal, realization of, I 218-19
Work is expression of, I 505
The Brotherhood
See also Lodge
accidental discoveries &, I 304
almoners of the divine, I 210
a call from, I 245
cares not for name or glory, I 275
cause MSS. to be rediscovered, I 304
cipher used by, I 392
colony from the gods, I 122, 127
concerned with soul of man, II 135-6
constantly helps humanity, I 273; II 259
fosters Heart Doctrine, I 318
gods among, II 147
governs world, II 147
great function of, III 64
helped found T.S., I 131
of Mahātmas, III 22
members in all nations, III 15
Messengers from, I 303
modern science as seen by, I 376-81
moved by universal love, III 329-30
T.S. & next Messenger from, II 44
Theosophy proved by, I 179-80
unknown philanthropists, I 380
Brothers
all men are, II 156
appeal to live as, II 147-8
Elder, direct forces of salvation, II 21
letter to Brahmans, I 470-5
of T.S. examine all faiths, II 154
Buchanan, J. R. (1814-1899)
axiom on "Hindu-Theosophy" proved shallow, III 265-7
psychometry and, III 265-7
Buck, Dr. Jirah D. (1838-1916)
biographical sketch, II 471-2
chairman of Theosophical Congress at World's Fair, II 164
invited to speak at San Francisco, I 435n
on Theosophical books before T.S., I 274
tribute to Judge, I lx-lxi
——— *A Study of Man . . .* II 472
Buckle, Henry T. (1821-1862)
——— *History of Civilization in England*
on cyclic rise & fall of nations, I 515
Buddha Fields
described, I 140
Buddha, Gautama (643?-543? BCE)
Adepts' great Patron, I 478
the "Being of Tathāgata," II 325
Brahmanical lineage of, I 440
came to reform Hinduism, II 347
conscious on all planes, I 80
efflorescence of ages, I 33
forbade reading of "novels," I 506
on hatred, II 254
H.P.B. cp. with, III 420
and Japanese Buddhist sects, I 85
Jesus cp. with, I 526; II 378, 430; III 106
Karma of disciples not interfered with, II 442
luxury of, in early youth, I 92
and middle path, I 92
on Nirvāṇa, II 375

practical teachings of, I 281
renunciation of, I 440, 526
resisted Māra, I 440
Śaṅkara reincarnation of, II 347-8; III 420
as Savior, II 157
a secret doctrine taught by, I 440
on shunning drugs, II 277q
taught forgiveness, II 253
teachings of, I 91-3, 440
T.S. must follow advice of, II 11
on thought, II 347, 378
Tsong-kha-pa as reincarnation of, II 347-8
urges diligence for salvation, II 62
Wheel of the Law, III 45
works for salvation of world, I 33
Zen-Shiu sect and, I 85-6

Buddha-Gayā [Bodh-Gayā]
Olcott tries to restore, I 363; II 428

Buddhavaṃsa
mentions Buddhist perfections, III 305n

Buddhi (Skt)
in after-death state, II 281
color of, Principle, III 456
compared with Manas, III 296, 365, 367
endures Mahā-manvantaras, III 296
Fohat as universal prototype of, III 333
inspires spirit of Brotherhood, III 326
as intuition of Oneness, III 326
Madhyamā Vāch and, III 336-7
Manas gravitates to, II 281
"material" when cp. to Ātman, II 226
meditation as centering in, III 452, 456
in Padmapāṇi legend, III 360
sixth round related to, I 430
Soul, III 168
Spiritual Soul, II 137; III 44, 191, 367
Spiritual Soul as vehicle of Ātma, III 333

Buddhi-Manas (Skt)
Divine Consciousness when united with Ātma, III 365
the Divine-Ego, III 367
is Self-Consciousness, III 365

Buddhism
in America, II 428
Avatāra concept and, II 347
Brahmanical attitude towards, II 51-2
confused with Brahmanism, I 372
driven out of India by Brahmans, III 458
ethics of, same as Christian, I 437
Indian religion and, II 52
Nirmāṇakāya as used in, III 386
no Individuality in, II 375
Prayāg letter on Esoteric, II 54-5
Pure Land teaching of, I 86-8, 438
a pure religion, III 174
Rājanya race and, I 429
seems pessimistic to Westerners, II 429
superstition of exoteric, II 430
T.S., Brahmanism and, II 57-8, 428
T.S. does not favor, I 361-4, 424-5
Theosophy draws from, III 174

Buddhist(s)
Amita Buddha is Savior of, II 157
asceticism & middle path, I 92-3
attempt to restore Buddha-Gayā, I 363; II 427
belief in Karma, III 39
countries influence West, II 372
ethics, III 168
Hindus call, Nāstika, I 475
honor purity of heart above intellect, II 394
Masters not Brahmans or, II 54-5
newspapers call Theosophists, II 428
Olcott a, I 68; II 51
schools in Ceylon, III 117-8
sects in Japan, I 85-8, 438, 439
story of flying machine, I 447
teachings, I 91-2, 281, 438-9
T.S. does not promote, I 361-4, 424-5

The Buddhist (Colombo)
"Madame Blavatsky" biography in, III 204
Budhists
Mahātmas as Esoteric, or "pre-Vedic," I 475-6
Buffalo Express (New York)
described *The Path* office, III 115
Builders
of global system, II 227
project Humanity, II 227
Bulwer-Lytton, Lord. *See* Lytton, Edward G. Lord Bulwer-
Burgoyne, T. H.
and the "H.B. of L.," II 192-3
——— *The Light of Egypt*
an impudent fraud, II 193
Burnouf, Émile (1821-1907)
on T.S., III 6
on T.S. & religious development, I 149
on T.S. as one of 3 great religious movements of the age, I 174; III 165, 200
Burrows, Herbert (1845-1922)
spoke at T.S. convention, III 100
Butler, Hiram
as Editor of the *Esoteric*, I 112
wealth scheme exposed, I 113

C

Cabalists. *See* Kabbalists
Cables, Josephine W.
ed. of *The Occult Word*, III 125
Cagliostro, Count Alessandro di (1743?-1795?)
a messenger, II 366
no charlatan, II 366
no imposter, I 170; II 301
on Talleyrand and, I 170-1
working for humanity, I 170
Calamities
banquets of evil daemons, I 122
The Canadian Theosophist
bio. of D. N. Dunlop in, II 3
Smythe on Mr. Judge memorial, I xxiv-xxv
Capital Punishment
See also Criminals
different than death by lawful war, II 376
greater evil than crime itself, II 285, 369
as legal murder, II 303
morally wrong, I 488-90
murder not diminished by, II 285
practice deplored, II 369
premature separation of real man in, I 488-9
versus moral laws, II 285
Cariyāpiṭaka
mentions Buddhist perfections, III 305n
Carnegie, Andrew (1835-1919)
Karma of success and, II 162
Caste(s)
abuse not sanctioned by Vedas, II 113
in ancient times, I 428-9
Brahmanical system of, II 113; III 164
in Europe, II 262
four Hindu, listed, II 262
origin of, idea, I 277
system abused in India, II 113, 250, 262
Cataclysms
on American continent, II 25, 345-6
Black Magic &, II 345-6
dying races and, I 206-7
geological, III 66-7
Karma and, I 336
not obscurations of the globe, II 425
Catastrophe
not always evil karma, II 256
Catherine di Medici (1519-1589)
a perfect devil, III 169
Catholic. *See* Roman Catholic Church
Cause(s)
danger in repressing, of disease, II 292
of disease from mental plane, II 291-2
of Masters' defined, II 10

moral, as well as physical, III 71
of perfection & Brotherhood, II 12
Caves
Ajanta, I 451
of Ellora & Elephanta, I 451
Kailās, carvings, pagoda & courts, I 451
Celibacy
no necessity for, II 389
not required in E.S., III 302
violates law of nature, II 389
Cell(s)
atoms group to form, III 348
brain, in sleep, II 431
conscious potentiality of the, III 351
a conscious unit, III 348
constructive vs. destructive, I 482
diagram of organic, III 349
each man is, in body of Manu, I 117
Esoteric Doctrine on, II 36
governed by psychic not noetic action, III 351
hierarchies of, I 215
liver & spleen, III 349
in occult science, I 213-14
polarity of, altered, II 37
recollections of, II 33-4
seven differentiations & 8 states, III 349-50
wall cp. to man's body, III 349
Censorship
Mohammedans accused of, I 373
none in the T.S., I 371
Center(s)
astral and physical, I 296
each man a, of force, II 435
of force confused with action, III 406
radiate from one Center, III 417
sun symbol of true, I 137
Century Path (Point Loma)
on Karma & Reincarnation, III 245
Ceylon [Sri Lanka]
Col. Olcott's work in, I 68
T.S. & Buddhist schools of, III 117-18
Ceylon Catholic Messenger
on T.S. backing of Buddhist schools, III 117
Ceylon Diocesan Gazette
Bishop of Colombo on Buddhist school, III 117-18
Chain(s)
See also Earth(s); Earth-Chain; Globe(s)
are evolutionary developments, I 369
each globe of, has 7 principles, II 286
Evolutionary, II 228, 230-1, 286
Evolutionary, & globes, I 330-2
Evolutionary plan for, II 233
septenary stages, I 369
Chakra [Cakra] (Skt)
cross a symbol of, I 14-15
weapon of Nārāyaṇa, I 15
Chakravarti, G. N. (1863-1936)
Annie Besant and, I xliv-xlv
biographical sketch, II 487-9
claims Mahātma letter false, I 476
as delegate of T.S., II 133
on materialism in the East, II 150
represented Brahmanism at World's Fair, II 122, 124, 489
Chāndogya-Upanishad
on lotus of the heart, I 61
on man's identity with Universal Soul, I 34
on sacred syllable OṂ, I 5-6, 6-7
Character
on building, II 466-7
low, degrades atomic lives, III 318
low, pollutes astral of Earth, III 317
true, preserved, III 448
Charcot, Dr. Jean M. (1825-1893)
on danger of hysteria from hypnotism, III 213
experiments in hypnotism, I 145
on Hypnotism, II 281
pleads for legislation on hypnotism, I 145, 417
revival of hypnotism by, III 212
Charity
among zealous Theosophists, II 253n

beyond material, I 156
helps one rise above Karma, III 248, 429
Karmic investment in, I 316-17
law of, I 46, 505
motives for, II 462-3
need for, on all levels, I 504
in not presuming to be a "Karmic Agent," II 327
palliative effect of, II 315; III 38-9, 248, 429
rich must show, to poor, III 194
Saint Paul on, I 315q
seeing one's own weakness fosters, III 436, 438
of wish to relieve suffering, II 462

Chatterjee, Mohini M. (1858-1936)
Hodgson report and, III 124-5
——— *Man: Fragments of Forgotten History*
authority of, questioned, II 456 &n

Chāyā(s) (Skt)
See also Disciple(s)
Chāyā Race and, III 465
gave physical aspect in our evolutionary scheme, III 294-5
as primordial prototype cp. with astral light, III 317

Chela(s) [Celā] (Hindi)
above all, must serve others, III 277
Adept alone knows his, II 440
Adepts help, transfer to new body, II 450
fan spiritual flame of T.S., III 91
and grades of discipleship, I 366
Karmic conflict of, II 262
know stage within, II 440
Mahātmas and, II 91
as Masters compared to us, I 365-6
Masters do not criticize, after their passing, I 367
as medium of his Master, I 53
occult maxim for, III 282
real tests in everyday life, III 276, 282
secret work of, II 440
unexpended karma of, III 275, 280
will reach goal in 7 births, II 263

Chelaship
concealed, II 440
desire for, II 416
on false claims about, I 367
not the object of T.S., II 416
steady desire for, precipitates Karma, II 262

Chew-Yew-Tsâng
inspired by Adept?, II 430
nom-de-plume of E.T. Hargrove, II 430

Chicago Daily News
summarized Judge's talk, III 115

Chicago Evening Journal
Judge defends H.P.B. in, III 152

Chicago Evening Post
summarized Judge lecture, III 115

Chicago World's Fair
Parliament of Religions at, II 119

Child
astral body of, made at conception, II 302
Ego of, connects about age seven, II 302, 362
Karma brings, to mother, II 302, 434-5
Karmic relations with parents far-reaching, II 435
mother's influence on body of, II 302
parents and wicked, II 434-5
parents should expose, to Theosophy, II 453-4
psychic powers in a, II 366-7
suffering of, II 362
Sunday school dogmas and, II 453
taught dogmatically, II 453

Chinese
Ancient, knew sidereal cycle, II 164
discovered precession of equinoxes, I 447
nation dying out, I 206

Chirognomy. *See* Palmistry

"Chohans of Darkness"
as Planetaries who impersonate gods, I 475
preside at Pralayas, I 475

Choice
between Good or Evil made in 5th Round, II 321
"moment" of, II 224, 418; III 65-6
power of, for race, II 259-60
Cholera
yellow fever &, curable, III 192
Chosen
few are, II 10-11, 255
Christ
ethics of, & T.S., II 155
no, Jesus, II 266
not represented in Churches, II 155
purpose of Theosophy &, I 46
Christian(s)
advice to, healers, I 283-4
danger awaits, nations, I 35
did not originate idea of Brotherhood, II 143
era & other great cycles, II 265-6
hymn on heathens, II 156
images borrowed, III 109
nations have unclear clues to Path, I 35
prophecy on end of the world, II 436
reincarnation taught for 500 years, II 142
should we partake in, festivals?, II 285-6
Theosophists as, III 104
view of the Ego, II 365
The Christian (London)
called *The Path* office pagan, III 142
Christian College Magazine
published forged letters, I xxiii
Christianity
altered since early times, III 105-6
Āryan & Jewish roots of, III 108
Buddhism, Hinduism and, I 437-8
on capital punishment, I 488
Churchianity vs., III 175
cp. with Theosophy, II 452-3
cycle of, II 167
doctrinal intolerance of, III 104
doctrines found in East, III 108-9
dogmas of, being replaced by Indian philosophy, I 184
on formalism in, III 104
heathen origins of, I 275
hypocrisy in Church, III 105, 175
of Jesus cp. to Judaism, I 437
lost chord of, I 417ff
not alone in claiming a Savior, II 157
Reincarnation & Karma found in, II 142; III 110-11
spirit of, vs. letter of, III 175
Theosophy not opposed to, III 104-6, 109-10, 174-5
true spirit of, is Theosophy, I 468
Christian Science
See also Metaphysical Healing
causes diseases to retreat to inner planes, III 398-9, 410
dangers of, to free will, I 227-9, 295, 297
on denial of disease, I 295
on denial of pain, I 238
H.P.B.'s warning about, III 410
hypnotism and, III 409-10
logic ignored by, I 282
Mānasic insanity often result of, III 410
Mind-cure and, I 227, 238-41, 283; III 398-9, 409-10
Theosophy &, contrasted, II 405
Christos (Gk)
as Inner God, III 337
-Sophia, III 358
Church(es)
do not represent Christ, II 155, 452
hypocrisy of, & theology, III 105
impracticality of, III 69
no answer to poverty, III 98-9, 105
rituals of, borrowed, III 108-9
society not regenerated by, III 69
threat of Science to, III 106
too materialistic to join T.S., I 246
Cities
buried, rediscovered, I 300
destined to be built, I 109, 301-2
pictured in astral light, I 109, 301
Civilization(s)
causes of extinction, III 66-7
elementals swarm over future, I 109
fountainhead of, in India, I 186
glitter of, not true progress, I 372

Hindu cp. to our, II 261-2
Karma of race and, II 447
not-spirit regarded as Spirit by, I 44
past and present, I 450-1
periodically rolls around globe, I 132
progress of, is superficial, I 44
rebirth of, II 166-7, 414
soul's progress more important than, III 102
unequal development of, III 67
Western, must uplift Eastern, I 479

Clairaudience
according to Spiritualists, I 52
inner senses and, I 75
known for ages, I 352

Clairaudient(s)
perceptions reversed on Astral planes, III 408
what is heard by, I 52

Clairvoyance
according to Spiritualists, I 52
an affliction, III 38
animals have, I 177
Astral Light's use in, III 45, 408
of distant events, I 449
etheric fluids in, I 178
explanation for, I 329
imagination and, II 300
inner senses and, I 75, 177-8, 255
known for ages, I 352
mediumship &, III 145
nervous derangement often results in, I 177
not at all profitable, I 4
question on, in blind, II 288
thoughts become objective in, I 177
warnings on, I 176-9

Clairvoyant
easily deluded, I 74, 177-8, 255-6
medium not reliable, III 145
seeing the future by, II 300
sees astral records, I 52
sees your thoughts, II 95
true, must rise above plane of Astral Light, III 408

Classification
system cp. with Esoteric Buddhism, II 104
ternary, believed best for Kali-Yuga, II 105

Cobra
experiments with poison of, III 192

Cohesion
force of, in phenomena, I 401

Coin
experiment with Indian, II 83-5

Coleman, W. Emmette (1843-?)
enemy to Blavatsky, II 182-4
Kiddle incident and, III 122-3

Collins, Mabel (1851-1927)
conspired with Coues against H.P.B., III 150-1
and Coues libel suit, II 188n
H.P.B.'s associate ed. of *Lucifer*, II 180; III 141
retracts claim of Adept inspiration, II 254; III 151

——— *Idyll of the White Lotus*
temptation of Kamen Baka in, II 450
on work of Adept, I 42

——— *Light on the Path*
alludes to Vāch, III 337
on attitude to life, I 19
on authorship of, II 254
on chelaship, II 440
devotional reading of, II 464
on energy of motive, II 445
influence on reader of, III 134
inspired by Adept in writing, II 188n, 254
on man's Karmic struggles, II 443
origin of name, III 375
on source of, II 447
true Occultism in, I 4

——— *Through the Gates of Gold*
Buddha and, I 42
commentary on *Light on the Path*, I 36
meaning of "Golden Gates," I 37-44
quoted, I 36ff
reviewed, I 36-44
wide appeal to Westerners, I 37

Colmache, Édouard
——— *Reminiscences of Prince Talleyrand*

on Cagliostro, I 170 &n
Color(s)
abstract, II 296
meditation on some, cautioned, III 456-7
related to wave-lengths of sound, III 309-10
seven, & OṂ meditation, I 8
table of vibrations, III 309
thoughts and, III 379
yellow as, of Buddhi, III 456-7
Comets
astronomers & Adepts on, I 481
defy laws applying to other celestial bodies, I 481
function of, II 234
worlds begin as, I 482
Common-sense
E.S. members urged to use, III 284, 288
Communism
cannot bring true reform, III 160
Compassion
Absolute, as Occult commandment, III 326
Adepts', for mankind, II 259-60, 272, 349-50
of Nirmāṇakāya, II 410
as true sympathy, II 330
of Yudhishṭhira, I 341-2
Complaints
keep crying &, within, I 20-1
outgrowth of heresy of separateness, III 316
prohibited in E.S., III 316
Concentration
awakens inner organs, I 75
a constant practice, I 78; II 8
culture of, Rāja-Yoga, I 73
exercise in, III 147
first step towards knowledge, I 73
memory in conflict with, II 8
mental tendencies and, III 147, 261
needed for astral travel, I 73
objects for, should not be petty, III 455
perfecting, II 8-9, 167-8
poor, among Occidentals, II 416-17
practice in daily life, III 399, 452, 455
and practice of virtue, I 76
purpose of, III 399, 454
as road to philosophy, III 374
and Self-Culture, I 70
Soul as spectator during, III 261
subjects for, I 82
superficial reading vs., III 147
Union with Supreme Being, I 72
value of, on spiritual, I 81, 82
as Yoga, I 72
Conditioned Existence
rising above, II 394
Confession
cannot wipe out Karma, II 441
no, in Theosophy, II 441
Conger, Margaret (d. 1945)
——— *Combined Chronology*
I 318n, 327n
Conscience
divine, II 349
elementals devoid of, I 288, 289
"voice" of, II 364
What is source of?, II 343, 364
Consciousness
See also Self-Consciousness
actuality of objects &, I 159
is cosmic, III 167, 263, 368
Cosmic, cp. to human, II 248-9; III 263
eternal?, II 449
functions on different planes, II 317
Life and, as aspects of Absolute, III 368
One, as Witness, III 260
plants & animals have, I 213
Principles relating to, III 416-18
raindrop simile, II 449
root of Unconditioned, II 296
self-perceptive cognition of, II 317
seven states of Cosmic, II 248-9; III 263
seven states of human, III 263, 367-8, 405-6
States & Planes of, II 233
Unity seen by higher, I 181-2
Conservation of Energy
law of Karma and, II 182

Conservatism
human nature and, III 160
Constitution
See also Principle(s); Sevenfold Division
of man a working hypothesis, III 62-3
Man's sevenfold, related to cosmic differentiation, II 310
sevenfold, & phenomena, I 351-2, 357
Constitution of T.S.
members on, II 202-4
organic law of, II 204
Constitution of U.S.
Adepts oversaw, II 77
great American experiment and, III 157
term "God" left out of, III 157
T.S. frees soul, frees body, III 153
Continent(s)
dwellers of sixth, II 25
first Imperishable Sacred Land, II 24
prediction on fifth, I 150
remains of, today, II 24
S.D. on "five great," II 24-6
Convictions
argument changes no, but absorption of truth does, III 244
assertion of, is proper, II 46-7
dogmatism and, I 384-5
Conway, Moncure D. (1832-1907)
on Adyar phenomena, III 199-202
on coin trick by fakirs, III 198
HPB's prediction about, III 196
on inaccurate report of, III 195-6
met H.P.B. twice, III 195
on "myth" of Koothoomi, III 200
rehashes old charges against H.P.B., III 195, 200-1
Cooper-Oakley, Isabel (1854-1914)
biographical sketch, II 509-13
delegate to World's Fair, II 133
H.P.B.'s last message for T.S. given to, II 510
interested in Woman's Suffrage, II 509
nursed H.P.B. in India, II 510
Copts
not descendants of Egyptians, I 518
only remnants of ancient Egyptians, II 166
Cordilleras
lost tribe in, mountains, III 228
Corey, Dr.
experiments in thought transference, II 96
1 Corinthians
on charity, I 315q
on spiritual gifts, I 103
Correspondence Class
course of study, II 202-4
system of study for, II 64-6
Correspondences, Law of
all occult systems built on, I 369; III 312-13
definition & analogy, III 312
Earth-Chain, man and, I 369
examples of, III 313, 378
importance of, III 312
not cause and effect, II 276
shows likeness not identity, III 378
Coryn, Dr. Herbert A. W. (1863-1927)
bio. of, in *Collected Writings*, II 487
photo with A. Keightley, II 484
Cosmic
Ākāśa as, Principle, II 224
Consciousness cp. to human, II 248-9
Ideation, Substance, & Energy, III 368
matter & comets, II 234
planes of, Consciousness and man, III 263
seven, planes, II 233, 248-9
system cp. to human, II 321
Will as formless radiations, III 351
Cosmic Blood
currents from sun correspond to human circulation, III 313
Cosmopolitan (New York)
story illustrating abject fear of public opinion, I 508
story on reincarnation in, I 496
Cosmos
circulation of the, cp. with human, III 313

and Cosmic Ideation, III 333
higher planes in, II 233
man a copy in minature of, I 214; II 321
no spot in, lacks consciousness, III 167
sound as expressed in, III 336-8
Coues, Prof. Elliott (1842-1899)
attack on Theosophy & H.P.B., II 183-4; III 150-1
confused about Theosophy, III 128
conspiracy with Mabel Collins, III 150-1
glamorized Gopal Joshee, III 127-8
libel by, in *New York Sun*, I xl
on libel suits against, II 188, 200-1; III 163
T.S. presidency ambition of, II 188n; III 150
Coulomb Conspiracy
alterations at Adyar &, I 264-7
caused H.P.B. to go to Europe, I 298
Cooper-Oakley on, II 510
Judge investigates, III 123-5
Missionary report and, III 124, 201-2
money paid for, III 202
predicted, II 102
predicted in a Nāḍīgrantham, I 11
shrine alterations &, III 123-4, 201-2
Tukaram's view of, II 506
Council of Constantinople
rejected doctrine of rebirth, I 307, 422; II 142
Cow
symbolism & esoteric meaning, III 335-6
Vāch as melodious, III 335-6
Crawford, F. Marion (1854-1909)
——— *Mr. Isaacs*
Oriental view of, III 130
a theosophical novel, II 81
——— *Zoroaster*
Oriental themes of, III 130
Creation
See also Evolution
cosmic law controls, III 34-5
evolution of worlds, II 234-5
evolution vs., I 159-60
Light, Sound & Number as factors of, III 337-8
no, of new souls, II 419
term evolution preferred to, III 35
Creed(s)
era of wild unbelief replaces, III 161
no dogmas or, in Theosophy, II 151-2, 380
Cremation
helps astral to quickly dissipate, II 358
new to Western lands, II 194
preservation of mummies vs., II 348
sanitary benefits of, II 358
Criminal(s)
denouncing of, I 500-2, 503; II 309
execution of, II 285, 303
how to reduce number of, I 5
problems for, justice, I 94-5
revenge of executed, on living, I 489; II 303, 369
Crinkle, Nym. *See* Wheeler, Andrew C.
Criticism
of ourselves prevents unkind, of others, III 373, 378
of own views helpful, III 87
a waste of time & energy, II 282-3
Crookes, Sir William (1832-1919)
laid basis for Meta-chemistry, I 209
London Lodge member, II 373
Cross
Egyptian, I 249-53
symbolism of Gnostic, I 14
Crux Ansata (Lat)
meaning of, I 15-16, 252-3
in T.S. seal, I 249
very ancient symbol, I 253
Crystal
experiment with Ceylon, II 89
Cultured Classes
acme of selfishness, II 11
Cures
metaphysical, II 289

Current Literature (New York)
sonnet on Nirvāṇa in, I 185n
Curses
do "come home to roost," III 61-2
Cycle(s)
Adepts can know true, II 234, 266, 346
Adepts can only modify minor, II 259; III 17, 283-4
approaching end of T.S., III 284
ascending & descending, III 59-60
of civilizations and nature, I 523-5; II 166-7, 414
coincidence of, II 266
cosmic, seem slow, II 414
Dawn of New, I 36, 304
Doctrine of, I 57, 121-30, 514-27; III 59-60
Elder Brothers subject to, I 520
of Eternity or Manvantara, I 250
evolution another word for, II 168
evolution fulfilled by effort not, II 259-60
expiring, of 1897, II 9-10, 433
Gods issue forth in, I 122
govern all worlds, II 234, 414
of great beings in World history, II 346
Hindus on Great, II 164
idea accepted by science, II 164
Jñānis descend in, III 60
Kalpas & Yugas or ages, I 124, 459-60, 514-18; III 58
Karmic impressions return in, I 519
of last quarter century effort, I 461-2; II 9-10, 301, 409-10; III 283-4
man is the authority in this, I 36
of Masters aid to West, II 9-10, 433
minor, now converging, I 130
must run their rounds, II 259q, 414
Nature's, affect man's, I 518-19
overlap each other, II 413; III 59
psychological, I 522-3
of rebirth, I 339; II 166
ref. to Higgins' *Anacalypsis* on, I 518
revolutionary, I 527
Saros & Naros among ancient, I 515
secret law of, II 234
seventy-five+ years, & *S.D.*, II 10
sidereal, & cyclic law, III 12, 17
sidereal, and sub-races, II 25
sidereal, known by ancients, II 164, 234
sidereal, related to Yugas, I 460
of Spiritual regeneration from Masters, I 461-3
of thought & feeling, II 167-8
thoughts conform to, I 44
unrest of this, I 293-4
vary among nations, I 129, 459-60
Cyclic
depression may be overcome, II 167
effort of Adepts to help humanity, II 9-11, 301, 346
law, II 164, 234, 259, 346
law of Nature, II 167
laws are just, II 414
return of impressions, II 167

D

Daily Life
temptations, II 418, 451
Daily Surf (Santa Cruz)
reviewed Judge talks, III 115
Daivīprakṛiti (Skt)
abstract ideal matter, III 358-9
as Fohat Cosmically, III 358-9
Light of the Logos, III 358
Padmapāṇi or, III 356
Daksha (Skt)
separation of sexes allegorized by, III 357
typifies early 3rd Race, III 357
Vāch is daughter of, III 360
Damascus
"Eye of the East," III 249
Dāmodar. *See* Māvalankar, Dāmodar
Daniel
alludes to cycles, I 525
Dante Alighieri (1265-1321)
——— *Inferno*
quoted on hope, II 262
Darwin, Charles (1809-1882)
evolutionary pattern of, I 173-4
"missing link" of, I 214

Davis, Andrew Jackson (1826-1910)
as a medium, I 350
Day
events of, and occult meaning, I 22
Dayānanda Sarasvatī (1825-1888)
sent T.S. ceremonial degrees based on Āryan Masonry, II 476
Death
See also Capital Punishment
accidental, & Kāma-Loka, II 303
of brain & Devachanic state, III 43
causes for infant, II 307-8
consciousness of Real Ego at, III 263
consequences of violent, I 488-9
cult, I 108
destructive cells given upper hand in, I 482
doctrine of hell-fire and, III 34
doctrine of purgatory and, III 220
executed criminals' state after, II 303
fear of, I 424
fire conquers, I 115
force emitted by being at, III 33, 189
hypnotism shortens life, I 417
karma and sudden, II 280
as King of Terrors, III 219
on moment of, II 449
no escape from responsibility in, III 221
no such thing as, I 120; III 189
penalty not right, II 285
preliminary, in suicide, III 219-20
séances & state after, II 404
state after, II 139
states after, before reincarnation, I 81
sudden, & higher principles, II 303
as transformation of energy, I 9
untimely, III 219, 236
violent, & Kāma-rūpa, II 280
vision reveals soul's purpose, II 384, 449
of warrior & criminal cp., II 276-7
Degrees
attained in T.S. by moral and mental state, II 440-1
higher T.S., held by Adepts, II 258
in the T.S., II 439-41
Deity
is one whole, III 55
there is no fall for the Ineffable, II 401
Delusion
of Astral World, II 357, 359
hypnotism fosters, II 42
of Nature is powerful, I 49-50
Democracy
demagogues in, III 160
inflated sense of power in, III 163
universal suffrage wasted in, III 160
Demophilus (Pythagorean)
on intellect, I 211
Depression
ending cycles of, I 522-3; II 167
The Desātīr
teaches transmigration, I 567-8; II 421 &n
Desbarolles, Adrien A. (1801-1886)
gave respectability to palmistry, II 97
——— *Les Mystères de la Main*
on Chirognomy, II 97 &n
Desire
See also Kāma
basis of action or karma, I 25-6
ceases to attract when overcome, II 337
deserve before we can, powers, II 417
Eros as Divine, III 333
on how to conquer passions and, III 262-3, 438
killing out, I 37
for occult development, II 415-17
and passions are not abstract qualities, II 339
rebirth and, II 339-40
satiation of, a dreadful doctrine, I 495
self-analysis destroys, III 262, 437-8
subtle, of lower manas, III 437-8
transmutation of, I 28
for truth, II 9
and will power, II 8-9, 289-90
worldly ambition and, II 352

Destiny
of good & evil occultists, I 45-6
and Karma, II 271
man's, and altruism, II 235
self-ordained, I 41; III 71-2
Theosophy on origin and, of man, III 62-6
turning point in, of race, II 224; III 65-6
Detachment
from results, II 464-5
needed to be free of Karma, I 31
Detroit Review of Medicine
Dr. Corey's experiment, II 96
Deuteronomy
on necromancy, I 288
Deva(s) (Skt)
Adept's fate as a, II 375-6; III 66
compared to fairies, I 231
conflict with Asuras, I 15
consequences of becoming a, III 38, 385
Hindu belief in, III 38, 126
illusions of, may take one against will, I 148
Karma of, III 38, 126
man may become a, III 38
project future cities to men, I 301
a so-called god, III 385-6
state of temporary bliss, III 126
Devachan [bDe-ba-can] (Tib)
Adepts can enter, of others, II 382
Adepts not subject to, II 381-2, 450
animals have no, I 428
aspirations of soul fulfilled in, III 42, 252
and Avīchi, I 439
Bhagavad-Gītā on, III 252
cell has its, & rebirth, I 118
compared to heaven, II 139, 308
compensation in, I 114, 168
cp. to heaven, III 63
a delusive state, II 312, 381
as delusory as earth-life, II 308
domain of spiritual effects, III 41
Ego extracts goodness in, III 252
energies exhausted in, III 42, 43, 45, 191-2, 252
illusionary nature of, I 167
Indra's heaven among Hindus, III 245
Jīvanmuktas do not experience, II 272
Kāma-Mānasic forms and, II 248
Kāma-rūpa separates from higher triad before, II 281
Karma draws us out of, III 245
length of time in, I 167, 169, 336-9, 384, 428; II 294
length of time in, longer than earth-life, II 311
life in, rooted in joy, III 42
locality of, II 318-19
loved ones are with us in, I 84
mediumship can make one in, twinge, I 108
necessity of, explained, I 167-9
not dreaming, II 302
period of rest, I 168-9; II 139, 311, 381, 396; III 62-3, 252
post-mortem division in, III 41, 42
prevents total degradation, III 252
as reflection on past life, III 192
on refusal of, III 449-50
release from body, III 42
reminiscence in, II 281
for rest, not action, II 381
seeds of rebirth, II 330
shapes there resemble our real characters, II 359
skipping, rare & seldom helpful, II 450
soul of infant and, II 359
state of being, III 236
thought and, II 311
threshold of life, III 41
unmerited suffering &, II 332, 336
and victims of violent death, II 280
Devil(s)
egotism is personal, I 40
never announces his coming, II 451
obsession by, I 288
shells of the dead are, I 356
as Typhos in Egypt, I 126
Devotion
leads to unseen help, I 341
leads to work for humanity, I 135
meditation on OṂ needs, I 9, 163

more valuable than money, II 205-7
path of, leads to knowledge, I 162
a single thread of, can unite a group, III 422
study with, is best, III 379-80
through action, III 39
to H.P.B. & Masters, II 58-63
true, needed to unveil nature, I 155

Dharmapala, David H. [Anagarika] (1864-1933)
biographical sketch, II 492
Buddhist at Parliament of Religions, II 129, 171-2, 492
Parliament of Religions &, I xliv
represents Ceylon T.S. at Parliament, II 172, 492
resuscitator of Buddhism in Asia, I xliv
secretary of Mahā Bodhi Society, II 428, 492
tries to restore Buddha-Gayā, II 492

Dhyānis (Skt)
incarnation of, II 268

Dhyāni-Buddhas (Skt)
emanate from 2nd Logos, III 362-3

Dhyāni-Chohans
Absolute unknown even to, II 225
Adepts can communicate with, III 15
as "Builders" preside at every Manvantara, I 475
direct evolutionary movement, III 14, 16
elementals and, II 235
evolution of, II 232-3, 235
guardians of cardinal points, III 14
men become gods, III 16, 64, 358
no hand in physical creation, III 294-5
not "personifications" of powers of nature, II 225
Padmapāṇi as synthesis of, III 357-8
Rounds each have their own, II 225
six Hierarchies of, III 358
subject to immutable laws, III 15, 16
symbolism in hosts of, II 226
true center and, I 140

Diamond
atomic vibration rate in, I 466
Mountain & Adepts, I 545-8, 571-2
as radiance of Eternal Truth, I 546

Dick, Fred J. (1856-1927)
initiated by Judge in 1888, II 6
tribute to Judge as martyr, II 6

Dictionaries
Judge defined terms for major, III 233 &n

Diet
See also Vegetarianism
in itself, not enough, I 20
true "Theosophic," I 101-2
of vegetarians, I 99-102, 468; II 384

Diplomas
higher degrees of chelaship require no, II 440

Discernment
how to acquire, I 73

Disciple(s)
See also Chela(s)
Adepts guide human thought through, III 27-8
forbidden to boast, III 30
gain only by merit, III 30
ineffaceable marks on person of, III 28
lifted only by own efforts, I 21
on loneliness of, III 30
rules of ancient schools for, I 155
training is a pilgrimage, III 29-30
true sun is goal of, I 137

Discipleship
not conferred by fees or passwords, III 28
on true, III 30, 65

Discipline
See also Self-Discipline
daily life, II 451
in Path of Eastern Occultism, III 393
self-, II 429; III 64, 442
sure foundation for, I 155
union with divine needs, II 306

Disease(s)
See also Healing; Metaphysical Healing

causes of, on mental planes, I 295-7; II 291-2
cure of, helps evolution, II 436
cure of, of more interest to some than cause, I 282-3
cyclic recurrence of, II 167
healing of, II 436
magnetic cure of, II 288
"mind healers" throw back, I 284, 294-5
much attention to, I 281
physical Karma & imagination as causes of, II 290-1, 294
protecting children from, II 293
purify man, I 284
replanted to mental plane, I 284
repression of, II 292
seeds for future, fostered by mind cures, III 257
sin of separateness and, I 213, 215
use of will power in cure of, II 289-92

Divine
act on, impulses at once, I 105
Brothers almoners of the, I 210
"Descent," II 401
flames of Archetypal Worlds, III 333
goodness from, within, I 104
Life, within, II 270-1, 386, 398-9
Radiance & OṂ, I 8
on realizing, Love, I 105
self-discipline needed to reach, III 64
Sophia of Jacob Boehme, II 110
union with, Will, II 451
virtues needed for union with, II 306
will, II 392-3

Divine Monad
immortal Ego or Holy Ghost, III 66
as Īśvara or divine spark, III 65
moment of choice and, III 65

Divine Resonance
Divine Light is not, I 8
or Nāda-Brahmā, I 7-9

Divine Science
ancient Indian term, I 236
as Theosophy, I 236

Divine Wisdom
not limited by environment, II 386
object of search rather than study, II 398
seek, in all directions, II 400

Divinity
how to approach, III 452
in ourselves, II 270-1, 386, 398-9

Doctors
among Theosophists, II 471, 478, 485
help evolution, II 436

Doctrine(s)
ancient, revived by H.P.B., II 135
dreadful, of Satiation, I 495
few Theosophical, new, I 467; II 62
of highest importance, III 8
Masters want more Heart-, I 318
only, with power to save, I 46
purpose of Theosophical, II 20
of Theosophy from the East, I 179
universal, I 440-1
universal application of theosophical, I 114-20

Dods, Dr. J. B. (1795-1872)
Electrical Psychology lecture to U.S. Senate, I 145
gave mesmerism lecture to Senators, II 32
warns about hypnotism, I 145

Dogmatism
avoided in T.S., I 436
convictions and fear of, I 384-5
crumbling, I 176
none in Theosophy, I 221-2; II 379-80
T.S. has no, II 46, 130-1, 151-2

Dolgorukov, Princess Helena. *See* Fadeyev, Helena Pavlovna

Dolma [sGrol-ma] (Tib)
Tārā in Sanskrit, III 360
two Virgins, as dual Manas, III 318, 360

Donations
large, not encouraged, II 206-7

Doubleday, Maj.-Gen. Abner (1819-1893)
biographical sketch, II 474-6

Civil War books of, II 474 &nn
donated Āryan Branch library, II 476
left in charge of New York City T.S., I xxii
as President *pro tem*, II 210
Doubt(s)
Karma of, allegory, I 551-2
Dragon's Teeth
analogy, II 315
Draper, John W. (1811-1882)
——— *History of the Conflict between Religion and Science*
science of soul has own rules, II 90-1
Dream(s)
Astral Light &, II 263, 391
causes of, unclear, II 263, 431
consciousness during, III 37, 176, 405-6
dreaming and, I 80-3, 448-9
forms seen in, II 248
guidance from, II 260-1
on high, and visions, III 406
influence waking state, I 81
inspiration not only in, II 263
Lytton on initiation in, II 260
perceptions unclear in, II 391
prove man's inner self, III 176
reason for not remembering, I 152
reversion of images in, II 264
Sushupti state beyond, II 261
Svapna state cp. with Devachan, II 302
visions and astral senses, II 431
Druids
magic stones of, I 572
Seer of the, I 572
Drunkard
karma of, II 280
Du Potet, Baron (1796-1881)
feats of mesmerism by, II 32
Duality
rules universally in Nature, II 344-5
Dublin Lodge, T.S.
focus for Irish Literary Renaissance, II 3
founded by Charles Johnston, II 3
Judge a "spiritual Hero" to, II 3
prominent members of, II 3
Dumas, Alexander (1802-1870)
novels influenced by Cagliostro, II 366
Dunlop, D. N. (1868-1935)
editor of *Irish Theosophist*, II 3
Duration
ever-present, & man, I 215
Duty(ies)
allegory on, I 543-4
of another, II 326-7, 371
of another, dangerous, I 205
battle of life and, II 353
done leads to wisdom, III 374
each Vedic caste had own, II 376
Higher life only through, I 105
kindness a, II 405
of Kshatriya caste, II 376
man's, to own atoms, II 421
man's true, I 181
Masters' advice on, II 245
personal desires versus, III 442-3
sense of, not ambition, II 352-3
spiritual culture and, III 64-5, 430
Theosophical, I 205; II 260, 285; III 203-4
to family & E.S., III 405, 422
to humanity and family, III 422
universal, of humanity, II 148
Upanishads on, II 463
Dvivedi, Manilal N. (1858-1898)
publisher of old edition of Patañjali, I 411
surname means "two Vedas," III 165
T.S member cited by Judge, III 165
Dweller of the Threshold
all evil done by man is, I 155
in astral light, I 155
constant menace until conquered, I 97
dwelling place of, I 97-8
as an entity, I 97-8
evil genius for next incarnation, III 330-1, 353
exaggerated idea of, in *Zanoni*, I 537
extraneous to student, I 98
human elemental, III 382

Kāma-rūpa haunts new ego, III 353
Māyāvi-rūpa haunts new ego, III 330-1
need not be feared, I 98-9
no fiction, II 264
not a "lost" soul, III 382
not product of brain, I 98
Parent Ego's new personality attacked by, III 353
sum total of general wickedness, I 97; III 382
in *Zanoni*, I 96-9

E

Eagle (Brooklyn)
Judge talk in, III 192-4
Earth(s)
See also Evolution; Mars; Mercury; Venus
always life on, II 238
astral light of, polluted, III 317
a condensation of seven primordial principles, II 110
corresponds to physical body, III 335
early stages of, II 238
enters new points in space, II 165-6; III 11-12
formation cp. to man's, II 231
a fourth-plane planet, I 369
geological development, III 188
Hell is on, III 33
humanity cycles around, II 165
man causes, changes, III 18
Mars, Mercury and, I 383-4, 513; II 228
monads do not arrive on an empty, II 229-30
moon is parent of, I 434; II 427
moon's spiritual principles transferred to, II 228
one of seven globes in earth-chain, II 422; III 58-9, 335
seven, not 7 globes of chain, II 286
has seven principles, II 286
shifting of, axis, II 317-18
stars & planets within astral of, II 391
stars fix destiny of, II 16
sun's Zodiacal cycle affects, I 517
will be a satellite in next Chain, III 387
Earth-Chain
archetypal Man on Globe A of, II 228, 233
Besant changes mind about, I 498
cp. with other globe chains, I 513q
Devachan within, II 318-19
in *Esoteric Buddhism*, I 323-4, 368-70
evolutionary periods not confined to our, III 16-17
evolutionary process on, II 228
kingdoms evolving on, II 230-1
Life-Wave evolves through, I 323-4; II 424-7; III 58-9
Mars & Mercury not of, I 368-70, 498
seven "fellow-globes" of, II 233, 286, 422, 424
and seven orifices in man's head, III 335
states of consciousness and, III 263-4
in *The Secret Doctrine*, I 324-6, 368-70, 513
Earthquakes
See also Cataclysms
foretold by astrologers, I 422
East
"craze" for, in T.S., I 476; III 459
includes more than India, III 459
needs energy of West, II 107
not focus of 19th century occult effort, III 458-9
The Path relies on teachings of, I 57
source of Theosophy, I 179, 275
as storehouse for ancient literature, III 458
Easter Island
statues, III 9
Eastern
literature often allegorical, II 87, 89
religions older than Western, II 155

T.S. revival of, literature, etc., II 89, 189
Eastern School of Theosophy
See also Esoteric Section
called Esoteric Section first, III 273
on changes after H.P.B.'s death, III 343-4
formed to vivify T.S., III 369
heart of the T.S., III 340, 343
name change from Esoteric Section, III 370
Pledge & its occult effects, III 274-7
vision for, III 284-5, 344-5
Eckstein, Friedrich (1861-1939)
prominent Theosophist, III 142
The Eclectic Theosophist (San Diego)
on *Ānandamaya Kośa* document, II 122
Edison, Thomas (1847-1931)
phonograph ridiculed at first, I 216
Education
limits conscience, II 343
not crucial to study of Theosophy, II 373
T.S. views on, II 152
Eek, Dr. Sven (1900-1966)
See also Māvalankar, Dāmodar K.
——— *William Quan Judge: His Life and Work*
Judge biographical sketch, I xvii-lxviii
Effects
overconcern with, of our actions, II 444
Efflux
current of, II 228
Effort(s)
only own, will uplift one, I 21; II 236-7
only steady, leads to wisdom, I 18
Egg
universe in form of, II 35, 225
Ego(s)
See also Higher Ego; I; Individuality; Personality
Adepts know prenatal & postmortem state of, III 10
after age 7, entangled in body, II 302, 362
apparent suffering understood by, II 362
is Ātma, Buddhi, & Manas, II 330
chooses its own earthly habitation, I 276-7, 484-5
conscious on some plane always, I 216, 449-50
consciousness of, during hypnotism, III 214-15
continuous identity of inner, I 449-50
at death, III 263
desire deludes, II 339
in Devachan, II 312
as eternal pilgrim, I 212-14
God and, II 365
groups of, leave races, I 206-7
Higher Self cp. with, III 296
Higher Self or, must triumph, II 433
immortality of, III 10
karma and, III 63
language of, in sleep, I 152
law of ripening Karma, III 65
of lower kingdoms become men, II 361-2
and "Māyā," I 213
mother cannot touch, of child, II 302
Nature an aspect of, II 365
no strangers among, II 314
overshadows body, II 301
on punishment of, in 8th sphere, III 65
is responsible if lower self rules, II 312-13
on reward & punishment of, III 33
seeds of rebirth in, II 330
sex evolves from tendencies of, II 299
stars source of, I 250-1
subordination of passions by, III 74
sub-races express varied stages of, II 425-6
throws out energy at death, III 33
unborn, changeless, & all-knowing, II 365

use matter of previous, and other, I 119; II 320
Egotism
examples from daily life, III 83-4
of lower self, II 433-4; III 84, 296
as sense of separateness, I 39-40
Egypt
ancient glory of, & Adept kings, III 17
ancient learning of, I 58
electricity in ancient, I 447
gradual decay of, II 414
rapid rise of ancient, I 523
as silent on Āryan philosophy, II 371
united science & religion, III 176
Egyptian(s)
advanced civilization of, I 58, 447, 523-4
ancient, returning to America, II 166
ancient, taught reincarnation, III 178
civilization & its decay, II 414
Copts are only remains of original, II 414
descendants of, not Copts of today, I 518
gods of, & their shapes, I 536
knew cycles of atoms, II 320
knew hidden laws, II 72, 164
longed for the Gods, II 377
measured sidereal cycle, II 164-5
mummies, II 348
mummies enchain souls, II 376-7
mummification beliefs, I 517-18
mummified ibis psychometrized, III 121
mysteries & rites, II 450
Recorder is astral light, III 47
and Semitic race, I 524
a small-handed race, II 99-100
we are the ancient, I 524
wiped out as a material race, II 166, 414
Eidōlons
or spooks can assume bestial appearance, II 420
Eighth Sphere
separation from divine spark in, III 65
Ekaterinoslav (Russia)
birthplace of H.P.B., III 204
Electricity
an entity, II 226
Fohat and, II 227
known to ancients, I 447
lower fires and, II 399
sun's, influences earth, II 279
Element(s)
Esoteric order of, II 237
seven cosmical, II 224
Elemental(s)
adepts can use, II 312
of "airy" kingdom, II 93-4
all, are harmful, II 353
astral remains and, III 45
atoms and, as future men, III 400
automatic obedience of, I 560
compacts with humans, II 94
control of, not profitable, I 4
copy only what exists, I 512
danger of opening door to, II 340-1, 353, 403-4
Egyptian papyrus and, I 535-6
exist everywhere, II 432
exist in astral light, II 72
exist in astral plane, II 353
in forces of nature, II 228
foretell spots to be civilized, I 109, 301-2
generated by other beings, II 228
hallucinations of, I 22
H.P.B. not controlled by, I 512
incorporating *reliquiae* of dead, II 404
lack conscience, I 289; III 61
means for Karma, II 72, 297
mediumship attracts, I 453, 455
men are mediums for, I 52
motions & shapes of, I 535-6
movements of, I 109
nature-spirits as, II 237, 404
as nerves of nature, I 353
not all, reach man's state in this Manvantara, III 400
obey laws peculiar to, II 432

precipitation and, III 61
protection from, II 392
Saptaṛishis are advanced, II 250
scavengers of astral record, I 555-7
at séances, I 200
seemingly "intelligent beings," II 340-1
skin of Earth and, I 559-60
some friendly some not, I 289
subject to Karma, II 235
as a Succubus, II 94
symbols for classes of, II 413
thoughts coalesce with, III 61
transformation of, II 297
transport objects, I 356
vices attract hordes of, I 76-7
water, dangerous, II 237
what are, II 235
Elemental World
applies to nature spirits & lower lives, III 335
corresponds with Prāṇa in man, III 335
Elementary
beings in man's lower nature, II 297
obsession by, I 288
Elias
came back as John, II 141, 158, 453
Elixir of Life
Devachan and, II 396
Ellis, Dr. W. Ashton (?-1919)
London associate of H.P.B., III 141
Elohīm (Heb)
cp. with Lunar Ancestors, III 295
Embryo(s)
earlier ages took years to gestate, II 423
passes through former evolutionary changes, II 423
Emerson, Ralph W. (1803-1882)
essay on "The Oversoul," III 248
Emotions
control of, not extirpation of, I 219
Encyclopedia Britannica
precepts of Islam in, I 374
Energy
conservation of, II 182
of human heart in T.S., II 159
transmutation of, & spiritual dynamics, I 380
Enghien (France)
H.P.B., W.Q.J., and others at, II 21
phenomena at, II 22-4
England
H.P.B. impetus to T.S. in, I 192
Ireland &, gateways for new race in America, II 27
London headquarters and Besant, I 190
palmistry once prohibited in, II 97
on Theosophical Society in, I 149, 175, 192-3
English
influence in America, II 26-7
poverty of, language, II 105, 324
Sanskrit &, terms combined, II 385
Entity(ies)
Fohat not an, II 228
hosts of, in man's totality, II 227
T.S. is an, I 58
Environment
entity chooses birth, I 26-7, 31-3
Envy
influences ethereal body, I 77
Ephesians
ref. to verse 32, I 21
on spiritual evil, III 328
Epidemics
moral, as well as physical, III 192-4
Theosophy has cure for, III 194
Equinoxes
on precession of the, I 516-17
Eros (Gk)
definitions, III 333
and deities born of Venus Aphrodite, III 319
as One Ray, "sets fire" to Absolute, III 333
sexless life-giving principle, III 333
Esdaile, Dr. James (1808-1859)
surgical use of Magnetism, III 212-15
——— *Mesmerism in India*
used magnetism in operations, III 212-13 &n
Esoteric
degrees not conferred, II 439-40

elements & elementals, II 237
rule on metaphysics, II 229
teachings can't be sold, II 193
teachings same in all major religions, II 430
work done by Adepts & their chelas, II 440-1
The Esoteric
"College" a conspiracy, I 113
false claims of editor of, I 113
secret organ for Christian sect, I 113
Esoteric Buddhism
See also Sinnett, A. P.
Brahmanism and, from same source, III 250-1
driven out of India, III 250-1
found in *Bhagavad-Gītā*, III 251
secret teachings of Jesus cp. to, II 430
term as used in T.S., III 250-1
true philosophy, I 475
Esoteric Doctrine
Brahmanism and Buddhism from same, III 250-1
Brahmans kept key to, for themselves, III 251
of Correspondences learned via diagram, III 415-17
of Correspondences must be learned, III 312, 404
H.P.B. guarded against betrayal of, III 432
on intellectual study of, III 460-1
on Macrocosm & Microcosm, III 416-18
method of teaching, III 285-6, 430-1, 432
study & devotion required to grasp, III 379
in study of Kosmos & ourselves, III 437
on universal evolution, III 252, 294-5
well known in India, III 251
Esoteric Section
accord between Heads of, III 375, 392, 414, 428-9, 441
in America & H.P.B., II 409
authority over Exoteric members not claimed, III 392-3, 421
avoids astral messages, psychism, etc., III 288, 423-4
Besant Inner Group Recorder of Teachings, III 340, 441
care of Instructions, III 300, 324-5, 415, 428-9, 432-3
correction of E.S. diagrams in, III 380
Correspondence Course in, III 278-9, 376, 377
Council for Eastern Division of, members announced, III 453
dangers to, III 457
Dark Powers seek destruction of, III 433
different lines for, in each country, III 412
dismisses transgressions, III 316, 421, 429
drawing help from Masters for Humanity through, III 330
drawing help from Masters for Occult training, III 393
drawing help from Masters for T.S., III 343
electioneering prohibited in, III 307
Examination Papers of, III 287, 341, 355, 361-9, 402-10, 415
fault finding and, III 457
gossip & careless speech prohibited in, III 324, 457
group study in, III 300-1, 311, 331-2, 354-5, 371-2, 384, 388-9, 422-3
H.P.B. still Head of, after her passing, III 441
H.P.B.'s appointment of Judge to, I xxx, xxxii n
hoped to be life & core of Theosophical Movement, III 284, 340
hoped to be life & core of T.S., III 433
inaction of one member can deter whole, III 356, 378
on induction into, III 300

Instructions & Diagrams, III 406, 416-18, 433-5
on interdependence after departure of Teacher, III 344-5, 429
Judge's role in the, I xxx-xxxii
known about in 1875, II 409
lack of altruism prevents new teachings for, III 457
later called Eastern School of Theosophy, III 273, 370
life of Theosophical Movement, III 441
marriage not prohibited in, III 302
Masters &, after H.P.B.'s death, III 411, 439, 441
meditation in, III 373-4, 453-7
mediumship prohibited in, III 331
model for meetings, III 311-12, 331-2, 371-2
money in, III 372
on motive for entering, III 421-3
no "Index Expurgatorius" for, III 315
no irrelevant talk, a rule in, III 301
not deserted by Masters, III 411-12
not disciplinary body, III 421, 429
not for personal power, III 421
not for practicing magic, III 305
number placement in E.S. diagrams, III 406
obstructions to progress in, III 301-2, 315, 343, 354-6, 378-9, 384, 391, 457
papers revealed, II 183-4
pledge to Higher Self in, III 316, 421, 422
poor concentration in, III 371
prime object of, III 284, 330, 421, 433
probation extended, III 307
recall & revision of Instructions, III 428-9, 439, 441
relation between T.S. and, III 284, 345, 376, 378, 391-2, 414-15, 421-3, 429, 433, 439, 440-1
on secrecy in, III 371
secrecy violated, III 428-9, 441
Secret Doctrine study in, III 312, 322
on study of Instructions, III 285-6, 322, 406, 460-1
T.S. saved from danger by, III 429
topical study advised for, III 300-1, 331-2
on training and testing of, III 293, 432-3
on training for occult development, III 404
use of passwords in, III 324
W.Q.J. as only channel for, in America, III 273, 288, 339, 414, 439-40
Esotericism
of Kabbalah, Gnosticism, etc., II 430
opening of, in last 25 years of each century, II 410
two objects of, III 433-5
Essence
primordial, II 239
Eternal
Boundless Principle, II 323
Cause is beyond speculation, II 323
Nature or Brahm, II 108
Eternity
cycle of, I 250
Ether
elementals move in currents of, II 432
fifth cosmical element, II 224, 237
gross body of Ākāśa, II 237
imponderable & star-like, III 46
of Kabbalists not Ākāśa, III 60
lower form of Ākāśa, II 224
luminiferous, of science, III 46
radiant matter and, III 46
semi-material, II 224
thoughts produce sound, color and motion in, I 178
warp & woof of the Imperishable, I 115
Ethereal Body. *See* Astral Body
Ethics
atomic exchange and, II 146-7
of Buddha and Jesus cp., II 378, 396, 430
codes of, III 168-9
definition, III 168

disease and, I 297
high, will purge nations, I 297
law of Karma and, I 502-5; III 63, 70-1, 162, 168-9
logical basis for, in Āryan thought, I 245
Masters on T.S. and, I 155
modern, behind science, I 210
needs right basis, I 280
nothing new in, of Theosophy, II 63
occultism requires, I 155; III 465-6
practical exposition needed, I 281
preserves knowledge, III 448
right, has reasonable basis in Theosophy, II 139
same in all religions, I 441; III 105
Theosophic code of, III 168-9
Theosophy gives basis for, III 237
Europe
Eastern philosophy and, I 275
poisoned by emanations of its former peoples, I 524
European(s)
in America, II 25-6
Atlanteans once, III 19
continent and 5th sub-race, II 25
Fifth Root-Race includes, III 200
European Section of T.S.
appoints Committee to revise First Object, I 501
Evening Express (Los Angeles)
on West Coast tour of Judge, III 116
Events
molding of, by Adepts, II 259-60
Evidence
of Masters in testimonies, II 328
Evil
absence of soul as, III 329
activity & fate of, soul, III 353
astral light is, III 9, 45-9
compensation of, II 70-2, 182
dreamless state can check, I 81
dreams can be, influences, I 81
fate of dabbler in, I 45-6
on, "genius" of man, III 330
good and, as illusions, II 410-11
and Good as relative, I 14, 19
is good gone astray, I 19
in heart of disciple as well as man of desire, II 447
inevitableness of, II 109
as intellect without love, III 329
legislation can cure no, II 182
punishment of, II 253-4, 285
reflected in astral light, II 231-2
remedy for, II 285
remedy to avoid, II 293
spiritual, defined by H.P.B., III 328-9
Theosophy explains, II 70-3; III 70
thought causes sorrow, II 293-4
Evolution
See also Earth-Chain; Race(s); Round(s)
aim of, I 179; III 56, 75-6, 158, 161, 234, 388
aim of, acc. to science, I 380
compels rebirth, II 308
creation theory vs., I 160-1
crest wave of, in West, I 479
cyclic impressions and, I 522-7
cyclic law governs, I 519
cyclic law of, II 168, 259-60
each period on higher plane, II 224
each period unique, II 223
of Earth-Chain, I 519-20; III 58-9, 389
on Earth-Chain of globes, I 330-2
of elementals by man, III 318
failures in, III 388
global, II 229-30, 233, 422-3
impulse to, II 230-1, 360
laggards in, II 230
law of correspondences seen in, III 313
of life-waves & forms, III 58-9, 75, 318, 389
line of higher, I 215
Mahātmas and human, II 250
of man, II 136-9, 229-31, 321-2, 360-2, 425-7
of man in "fiery dust," II 231
man should assist, I 15
of matter from subjective plane, III 35, 55-6, 161, 388
meaning of, I 157-61; II 136-8

moment of choice in, III 65
of Monad, II 229-30, 233
of monads, II 321-2
Natural Law and, III 328
no apes in man's, III 21
not a sudden transition, III 75
perfection of, at 7th Round, II 233
plan of, impressed on matter, III 161, 186, 294-5
Pralaya and, III 55
purges & ennobles man, III 76, 318
purpose of, II 136-7, 233, 360-1
requires "all experience," II 360-1, 380-1
requires repeated experience, II 139
of Rounds & Races, II 422-3
on seven planes, III 186-8
in theology, science, and Theosophy, I 159-61
theosophical scheme of, II 168; III 31, 75-6, 234-5
Theosophy sounds note of, II 170
through reimbodiment, II 138-9, 160-1, 360-2
transferred from Moon Chain, III 389
triple scheme of, III 294
turning point of, II 259
universal and simultaneous with Spirit, III 56
universal, outlined, III 56-7
vast periods of, & man's age, III 31, 55

Exaltation
cycles of, II 167

Execution
"legal," cp. to murder, II 303

Exodus
on killing a witch, III 191
numerical values of phrase in, III 107-8
on witches, I 288

Exorcism
in ancient India, I 288

Exoteric
first degree of T.S. was, II 440
Indian philosophies on Universe, III 252
Max Müller limited his scope to, III 251
superstitions of Buddhism & Brahmanism, II 430
work involves chelas and laymen, II 440

Experience
all types of, needed in Manvantara, II 380-1

Extraterrestrial Beings
do exist, III 66-7

Eye(s)
See also Third Eye
"Cyclopean," & its resurrection, III 381
evil, and astral light, II 72
Humanity will have three, when spiritually awake, III 381
may see only part of spiritual being, I 108-9
retina of, and astral light, I 116

Ezekiel
wheels of, I 15; II 72

F

Fadeyev, Helena Andreyevna (1814-1842)
H.P.B.'s mother, III 205

Fadeyev, Helena Pavlovna [Dolgorukov] (1789-1860)
maternal grandmother of H.P.B., III 205

Failure
of fault-finders to correct others, II 282

Fairies
Irish belief in, I 230-1
of lake, I 544
mysterious haunts of, I 551
once ruled by men, I 551
stem from Hindu "devas," I 231

Fakirs
feats cp. to those of Adepts, II 306-7
feats of, I 402
Hindu jugglers, yogis and, III 170-2
marvels of, explained, III 170-1

Mohammedan, in India, III 170
on path of error, I 475
solitary mountain dwellers, III 225
training of imagination by, II 300, 306-7
Fall
for Deity there is no, II 401-2, 406-7
of man into generation, II 232, 268
for man's inner Deity there is no, II 136-7
man's, into ignorance, II 401-2
not abnormal, II 268
two-fold, in Theology, II 268
Fame
desire neither notice nor, I 19
Family Duties
Esoteric duties and, III 422
T.S. and, III 405
Family(ies)
causes of birth in, of sages, II 43
die out like races, I 207
Fanaticism
to be avoided, I 23
Fasting
balanced view towards, and life, I 20
Fatalism
neither Kismet nor Karma is, III 40
Fate
Karma is not, II 271, 273
as Saṃsāra, II 444
Faults
constant watch over, I 220
daily effort to remove our, II 417
not failures but lessons, III 397-8
our, influence others to crime, III 258
repair our, not others', II 282-3
seeing our own, as others see us, III 395
Fear
Brotherhood and, III 103
effect on ethereal body of, I 77
major cause of disease, II 291
T.S. members abandon, III 101
Felt, George H.
lectured when T.S. proposed, I xviii
W.Q.J. experiments with, I 322
Female
characteristics & karmic bias, II 299
no alternation from, to male, II 298-9
Finger(s)
characteristics of, in palmistry, II 98-9
fashion of raised, II 99
related to intellectual life, II 98
Fire
conquers death, I 115
electric, and Mahātma's body, III 419
and "fire body," III 464-5
high aspiration as spiritual, III 447
the invisible Deity or Aether, III 358
Lords of, III 464-5
manifested, is Sun, III 358, 447
most mystic of elements, III 358
in preceding Rounds, II 237
principle pervades Masters' bodies, III 446
on Spiritual, III 447
as symbol of duty & virtue, I 543-4
two sorts of, II 226
Fire Dhyānis
or Lords, progenitors of etheric body, III 464-5
many classes of, III 465
Fire Lords. *See* Fire Dhyānis; Solar Pitṛis
Fish
a single scale shows identity, II 98
Five Years of Theosophy
"Elixir of Life" on fire principle, III 446
ref. to article on Morya Dynasty, I 430
on Tattvas, II 270
on transmigration of Life-atoms, II 319 &n
value of, III 95
Flammarion, N. Camille (1841-1925)
member of T.S., III 46
——— *Uranie*
on astral light, III 46q

Floods
as karma for nature & man, II 255
Flower Ornament Scripture
chapters on Buddhist perfections, 305n
Fohat(s)
Archetypal World is noumenon of, III 333
catches image in Logos to impress on cosmic matter, III 333, 359
comprised of entities, II 228
conscious energy of Logos, III 336, 358-9
electricity a form of, II 227
as many, as there are worlds, II 228
Mūlaprakṛiti, Logos and, III 358-9
Sound and, III 336
universal prototype of Buddhi, III 333
Force(s)
blind, of cyclic law, II 259
Masters on transmutation of, I 147-8
Occultist directs, with knowledge, I 147
seven, of Brahm, II 108
study of lower, leads to black magic, III 436
Forgiveness
mercy and Karma, II 245-6, 326-7
rights and Karma, II 253-4
Form(s)
astral & kāma-manasic, differ, II 248
exudes from medium's body, II 458
infinite in variety, II 367-8
primordial, of everything is like an egg, II 225
Fossils
of antediluvian animals & age of man, III 31-2
astral man could leave no, III 31-2
Foulke, Henry B.
claimed to succeed H.P.B., II 28-30
not a T.S. member, II 28-30
Franck, Adolphe (1809-1893)
——— *La Kabbale*
on Origen & metempsychosis, I 431
Fraternity, The. *See* The Brotherhood
Freedom
individual, defined, I 508
of thought in America, II 86, 169
Freemasonry
See also Masonry
Adepts and, III 15
Dayānanda sent degrees based on Āryan, II 476
Founders of U.S. knew symbolic degrees of, II 78
interlaced triangle symbolism in, I 252
speaks of "lost word," II 225
T.S. and degrees of, I 321-2
T.S. government cp. to, I 486
Theosophy as branch of, II 35, 225
U.S. seal inspired by, II 79 &n
vows of, broken daily, I 553
Friends
on future, or enemies, I 316-17
Fujiyama, Mt.
sacred legend about, III 229
Fullerton, Alexander (1841-1913)
acting editor of *The Path*, II 47
handled *Forum* with Judge, II 253
summary of T.S. history, II 354 &n-57
Funds
tempts cupidity of man, II 205
T.S. has no corporate, II 205
Future
man shapes own, I 40

G

Galatians
on fruits of the spirit, I 104
on karma, III 111
on reaping justice, III 99 &n
on sowing & reaping, II 139
Galaxy
Sun's orbit around, II 165n
Galileo, G. (1564-1642)
recants theory about Earth, III 106
Gandharvas (Skt)
or celestial musicians, III 45

Gandiva
  Arjuna's bow, as gift of the Gods, I 163
Ganson, Joseph W.
  received bogus Mahātma message, I 469
Garfield, James A. (1831-1881)
  astrology and death of, II 75
Garrett, John
  ——— *The Classical Dictionary of India*
  on Kuthumi, III 200
Gautama. *See* Buddha
Gāyatrī
  an aid to self-culture, II 464
  appeal to duty, I 313
  composed by a Kshatriya, I 429
  quoted, I 311 &n
  sacred verse of Hindus, I 311
  translation of, II 464
Gebhard, Gustav (1828-1900)
  astral bells at home of, III 142
  leading German Theosophist, III 142
Gebhard, Mme. Mary (1832-1892)
  pupil of Éliphas Lévi, III 142
Gem
  tale of one who found a, III 267-9
Generation
  evolutionary cause of, II 268
  "Fall" into, II 232, 268
  one principle involved in, II 274
Genesis
  alludes to rebirth, I 413q
  on Elohīm, III 295
  on living soul, II 401
Genii (or djin)
  elemental spirits which Solomon cast in Red Sea, II 93
  released from iron pot, II 93-4
Genius
  Blavatsky on, II 263
Geometrical Figure(s)
  cube within the sphere, III 417
  of Microcosm & Macrocosm, III 416-17
  sphere represents Auric Egg, III 417
  square within circle, III 416-17
Gestation
  time will be less in future, II 423-4
al-Ghazālī (1059-1111)
  nature of soul &, II 91
Ghizeh [Giza], Pyramid of
  modern architecture comp. to, I 450
Ghost(s)
  "ghost hunter" and, III 330-1
  as Kāma-rūpa, III 330-1
  or spooks of the séances, II 420
Gichtel, Johann Georg (1638-1710)
  vision of stray thought, II 301
Gifts
  from higher to lower nature, I 104
  spiritual, a misnomer, I 103-4
Gilgūlīm (Heb)
  as reincarnation in Talmud, I 419
Gladstone, Wm. Ewart (1809-1898)
  Jerusalem Societies and, I 185-6
Glamour
  a degraded art in America, I 358
  its place in magic, I 359
  as psychological fraud, III 198
  a science in occultism, I 358-60
  use in phenomena, III 198
Globe(s)
  See also Planet(s)
  Archetypal Man on, II 228
  are phases of consciousness, I 325-9, 513q
  in co-adunation with Earth, I 513q
  is creation of monad, II 230
  development of original plan on, II 233
  each, in chain is septenary, II 286, 422-3
  Esoteric Buddhism on Earth-Chain, I 323-4
  first and 7th, are archetypal, II 233
  humanity passes through seven, III 59
  Mars a sleeping, II 427
  not separated, I 324-9, 368
  S.D. about, I 323-9
  seven, in each chain, III 58
  seven races traverse 7 rounds on seven, II 422

six companion, of Earth-Chain invisible, I 368, 498, 513q
stars and planets within astral of this, II 391
on superior planes to earth, I 513q

Gnomes
astral beings, III 45

Gnostic Cross
svastika or, I 14
symbolism of the, I 14

Gnosticism
secret teachings of Jesus, II 430

God
aim of man to become, I 103
alleged appearances of, II 266
calling upon, at death, II 449
Ego and, II 365
faith in, barrier to Brothers, I 475
first teachers of man as, II 239
gave religion in beginning, I 436-7
Higher Self is, II 35; III 255
idea of "loving," repels many, II 349-50
inconsistency with religious precepts about, I 41
infinite, only if man included, II 310
Infinite is, I 41
Islam and, I 374-5
Jehovah a personal, III 16
just and merciful, II 158
justice and, III 98-9
love is, I 103
man is, incarnate, II 12, 361; III 210
Man, Universe and, one whole, II 360
as means of salvation, II 157
no Fall for, or Deity, II 401-2
no personal, in Theosophy, II 239; III 14, 16
Occultists' task more than longing after, I 147
personal, is imaginary, III 17
realizing, via human perfectibility, II 12
search for, II 395
subjugation to will of, II 400-1
true Will is, II 393
universal belief in, explained, II 239
we are, II 361
Who and What is, I 61
why, not in U.S. Constitution, III 157
within each man, I 41; II 270-1

Gods
The Brotherhood a colony from the, I 122, 127
dark forces impersonate, I 475
descend according to cycles, I 122
employment of the, I 122, 126
faith in, barrier to Brothers, I 475
man can be as the, I 212, 214; II 147, 161-2
monads & atoms potential, I 212
perfected men in former Manvantaras, III 16
robbing the, II 275

Gold
wealth cp. to knowledge, I 139

The Golden Gate (San Francisco)
on concentration, III 147
on Coues-Collins' attack, III 150-1
dangers of mind cure, III 256-7

Good
all, comes from Divine within, I 104
cannot force, but plant seeds of, II 443
consorting with, people, II 291
Evil and, both illusory, II 410-11
Evil and, relative terms, I 14, 19; III 328-9
fades from astral light, III 9
impulses should be acted on at once, I 105
Karma defined, II 249, 295
mankind must choose, or Evil in 5th Round, II 321
obtained by being, I 105
occult path brings out, & evil Karma, II 264-5
razor's edge between bad &, I 54
some men inherently, II 264
as working with Nature's Laws, III 328

Gospels
on reincarnation, II 141-2

Grant, Ulysses S. (1822-1885)
Adepts inspired, III 23-4
Gravitation
Occult viewpoint on, I 356, 401
Gravity
changed in apportation, II 313
Great Breath
or "breath of Brahmā," III 55
cause of manifestation, III 55
Space and Germ, III 15
Great Lodge. *See* Lodge
Great Orphan. *See* Humanity
Great Work
of returning all to source, I 14
Greaves, E. T.
describes Algerian rope trick, III 172
N.Y. *World* correspondent, III 172
Gribble, Mr. James D. B. (?-1906)
in Coulomb conspiracy, III 124
Griffiths, Allen (1853-?)
biographical sketch, II 479-80
Griscom, C. A.
first T.S. office described by, I xxvi
initiated into T.S. by Judge, I xxvii
on Judge using a borrowed body, I xxxiii-xxxiv
Guiteau, Charles J. (1840?-1882)
state of, after hanging, III 191
on trial & death of, I 490
Gupta-Vidyā (Skt)
imperishable Occult Schools of, III 327
occult knowledge, III 298, 325
Twentieth Century will give proof of, I 303
Vedāntins echo the, III 327
Guru(s) (Skt)
obedience & loyalty to, III 393
only the adjuster, III 373
require no confession from chelas, II 441
woe for one who belittles, I 514

H

Haeckel, Ernst (1834-1919)
——— *The Pedigree of Man*
praises Darwin, I 173-4
Hahn, von Rottenstern Family
paternal lineage of Blavatsky, III 204-5
Hall of Learning
or Astral Light, III 408
cave of illusion outside of, I 55
Hand(s)
astral, I 75
astral, in apportation, II 313
description of, in palmistry, II 99-100
destiny of man in lines of, II 100
small, built civilizations, II 99-100
Hanuman
antedates "missing link," I 214
Harbottle, Mr.
astral form of Hindu seen by, I 261
Harding, Burcham
lecturer for Theosophy, II 218
Hardinge-Britten, Mrs. Emma (1823-1899)
misguided spiritist who denied reincarnation, II 451
——— *Ghost Land* . . . [ed.]
medium for writer of, II 451-2 &n
Hargrove, Ernest Temple (1870-1939)
biographical sketch, II 514-15
Chew-Yew-Tsâng revealed as, II 430
treasurer of Blavatsky Lodge, II 515
Harper's Monthly (New York)
editorial on Karma in, II 180-2
Harris, Thomas Lake (1823-1906)
alleged community of, II 192
Butler plagiarized book of, I 113
power over reporter L. Oliphant, II 192
Harrison, Frederic (1831-1923)
on choice of books, I 506n
Harrison, Vernon (1912-2001)
——— *H. P. Blavatsky and the SPR*
criticizes SPR report, III 125n
Harte, Richard
in error about Judge, I xx, xl-xli
Hartmann, Franz (1838-1912)
hears Christian admit bribing Coulomb, III 202

more a mystic than Theosophist, III 142
shrine joke on Hodgson, III 123

Hate
Buddha on, II 254
can bring souls together, I 84

Haṭha-Yoga (Skt)
breathing experiment in, III 327
dangers of, I 186-7; II 246-7, 416
discouraged by E.S., III 308, 327
Hindus of today bring only, II 371
must be followed completely if at all, III 308
no benefit without a guide, II 416; III 327
purely physical, I 72
Rāja-Yoga cp. with, III 308

Healer(s)
changes in astral currents of, II 292-3
have hit upon a law, II 304-5
metaphysical, in danger of Black Magic, II 290
spiritual, and money, II 275

Healing
See also Diseases; Metaphysical Healing
affirmations, denials and, I 238-41
dangers of mental, I 227-30
money and, II 275
not condemned by Theosophists, II 436

Health
and healing, I 228-9
moral aspects, II 290-1
restoring, naturally, II 292

Heart
See also Heart Doctrine
allegory of the, I 539-41
anatomy of the, I 387-9
arteries & astral nerve leading from, II 458
better tool than intellect, II 400
a blind for pineal gland, III 349
Buddhists honor, above intellect, II 394
chief organ of Higher Ego, III 349
ether in the, I 61
"eye-knowledge" not of the, I 78
is focus of Spirit, I 40
Intellect and, useless beyond a certain point, II 395-6, 400
"knot" of the, I 39-40, 61-2
medical views on, I 387-8
mystic has a joyful, I 18
plexus of the, I 388-9
poverty of, subdues vanity, I 77
pulsation of, and tides, II 226
soul's seat in, II 458
of T.S. is work, not money, II 150
untying knot of the, I 31
Way lies through, I 51
way to open, II 395
yoga practice dangerous to, I 187

Heart Doctrine
See also Heart
Masters want more, in T.S., I 318-19
poem about, I 51

Heat
two sorts of, II 226

Heaven
"ambient," in ancient astrology, II 15
Devachan cp. with, III 42, 63
diet & kingdom of, II 371
Eastern teaching of, II 154
hell &, in Christianity, II 154
hell &, in Christianity, Buddhism & Brahmanism, I 439
hell and, relative to man's thoughts, II 363
kingdom of, & diet, I 248
kingdom of, taken by violence, I 79
monotony would stagnate soul, III 42
not desirable, III 181
propitiated by Christians, III 42
virtue leads only to, II 283

Heber, Bishop Reginald (1783-1826)
hymn on heathens composed by, II 156q

Hebrews
on cloud of witnesses, III 444

Hell
Buddhist teaching on, II 154, 363
Christian teaching of, I 439; II 154
on "descent" into, of matter, I 312

earth as, II 363
Kāma-Loka as, II 363
mental suffering and, II 363
Naraka or Avīchi, of Orientals, I 439
not a mythical after-death place, III 33
sins punished on Earth, not in, III 33
Yudhishṭhira stays in, for friends, I 101
Herald (New York)
use of term Mahātma in, I 496
Heredity
Adepts' influence and, I 273
cannot account for variations in man, I 203
cannot explain musical genius, II 160
character not explained by, III 183
as discipline & reward, II 161
diseases and, I 282
justice of, I 94-6
Karma and reincarnation cp. to, I 93-6; II 180-2
karmic tendencies and, I 26, 276-7
not a cause, I 95
reincarnation and, II 160; III 183
remote ancestral traits reproduced by, I 94
Hermes (Paris)
T.S. journal, III 143
Hermetic Axiom
philosophy of, I 118-19
séance phenomena and, II 331-2
self-knowledge through study of, III 134, 326, 404
Vedāntin axiom &, cp., III 326-7
Hermetic Brotherhood of Luxor
a spurious occult society, II 193
Hierarchy(ies)
of caste, II 262
celestial, II 235
doctrine of, III 363
doctrine of, ancient, III 14
of early Church Fathers, III 14
on elect germ of, III 357
of Elementals, II 235
Lipikas, Adepts, & men progress in, II 227
man composed of various, III 363
of progressed souls, II 231
in T.S., II 258
Hieroglyphs
See also Symbolism
Path reference to Theosophical, II 435 &n
symbolism of Egyptian, I 12
Higgins, Godfrey (1773-1833)
——— *Anacalypsis*
includes study of cycles, I 518
Higher Ego
See also Buddhi
cannot act directly on body, III 348
crucified by Lower Ego, III 382
in Devachan, II 248
as Individual Self, III 366
not Absolute, III 326
as reincarnating entity, III 352, 364
relation of "Dweller" to Parent, III 353
Higher Manas
See also Lower Manas; Manas
Antaḥkaraṇa links, to Lower Manas, III 365, 374
cannot act directly on body, III 364
as creator of Lower Manas, III 367
on Devachanic state of, III 365
incarnates through Lower Manas, III 365
not fully developed, III 364
responds to Lower Manas' efflux, III 375
separates from Kāma-rūpa, II 281
Higher Self
See also Lower Self; Self
aid from, via dreams, II 260-1
Ātma-Buddhi is, III 322
AUM or upper triad, III 367
body medium of, I 53
is conscience, II 343, 364
continual war between lower and, II 433-4
defined, III 366-7
in Devachan, II 281-2
difference from lower self, III 296-7

Emerson's Over-Soul is, II 460
extended life and, I 42
free & unconditioned, III 304
is God in man, II 35, 310; III 255
Higher Ego not to be confused with, III 296-7, 322, 366
inner man far from, II 34
internal sun, I 312
Karma and, II 295, 342-3, 351
and Law, Action & Karma, I 562
lower nature must open to, III 57
Lower Self versus, III 82-4
meditate on, III 277
Mesmerism and the, I 254-6
must conquer Lower Self, II 433-4
not in man but above, III 57
not swayed by mesmerizer, II 33, 35
obscured by descent into matter, II 325
One Consciousness, III 260
only road to Masters, III 431
pilgrimage of the already Divine, II 359-61
prayer to, III 404
qualities of, III 57
reason for dwelling on, III 430-1
reliance on, II 349, 433-4
rule by, develops spiritual will, III 442
source of religions, III 217
as spark or ray of Ātma, III 296, 367
as Witness or Spectator, III 260
Hijo, G. (pseud.). *See* Griscom, C. A.
Hindu(s)
abhor spiritualistic obsession, I 288
basket trick of, etc., III 170-1
becoming materialistic, I 478
belief in Mahātmas unshaken, III 130-1
characteristics & beliefs of, III 39, 153-4, 178-9
characteristics balance Anglo-Saxon, III 155
civilization declining, II 261-2
class of agnostics, III 131-2
confused with Buddhists, II 52
Devachanic system of, III 41-2
feared T.S. partial to Buddhism, I 361-2, 442
on great cycle of Universe, II 164
healers on dangers of yoga, II 292-3
high metaphysical faculty, III 155
idea of cycles derived from, I 518
intellectually too active, II 112
Judge urged, to translate Āryan philosophy, II 106
on mastering vital centers, II 457
members of T.S., II 53
metaphysical acumen of, II 371
more evolved spiritually, II 261
not idolators, III 154
T.S. promoted, revival, I 442-4
Theosophists and needed reforms, II 114
Hinduism
See also Brahmanism
Buddhism and, in Prayāg letter, II 54-8
cp. to Buddhism & Christianity, I 437-8
mistaken ideas on, II 52
reverence for animals, II 420
serpent worship in, II 267
Hindustan
cradle of the Āryan race, I 518
Hiraṇyagarbha (Skt)
or Brahmā's Egg, III 403
corresponds with Auric Egg, III 403
History
profane and religious, has tradition of Masters, II 328
Hodgson, Richard (1855-1905)
accuses Blavatsky of fraud, II 408
investigates letters from Adepts, II 408
misrepresents Judge, III 123-4
poor investigator of Coulomb case, III 123-5
and unfair S.P.R. investigation, II 510
Hollis-Billing, Mary J. (1837-?). *See* Billing, Mrs. M. J. Hollis-
Holy Ghost
female, is ākāśa, III 60n
real sin against, III 66

Home, John (1722-1808)
——— *Douglas*, I 130
Homeopathic Medicine
cures by Count Matte with, I 283
Dr. J. D. Buck practiced, II 472
Hope
for gratification must end, I 23-4
Hsien-Chan (Chinese)
illusive form of universe, III 359
Hübbe-Schleiden, Dr. W. (1846-1916)
on certificate from Masters re. *S.D.*, I 343-4
editor of *Sphinx*, III 142
K.H. letter sent to Judge about, I 344q
letters from M. & K.H., I 319 &n, 343, 345-6, 347
Huc, Abbé E. R. (1813-1860)
on Tibetan travels of, III 225-6
visit to Tartary, II 155
——— *Travels in Tartary* . . .
book burned by Clergy, I 438
on similarity between Buddhist & Christian ceremonials, I 438
Human(s)
condemnation re-generates fault, III 61
consciousness, II 248-9
destiny & altruism, II 235
Dweller is, elementals, III 382
elementals partake of, thoughts, III 61
evolution circles globe chain, III 59
great goal for, soul, III 16
Jñānis as ordinary, II 235-6
Kingdom closed to any new Monads, II 314
laws and Karma, II 285
life-wave traverses globe chain, II 424
matter of, shared over lifetimes, II 319-20
Monad, II 226, 229-31, 314
nature unchanged, I 378
not confined to this Globe, II 226, 235
races evolved in 4th Round, III 59
Humanity
See also Man; Mankind
Adepts protect, from true sun, I 141
all actions for sake of, II 9
Atlanteans reborn as present, I 128-9; II 224, 352; III 362
cannot force development of, III 203
desire for reward in, I 155
on desire to help, II 395
Devachan and work for, II 396
efforts of Adepts for, II 259-60, 272, 329-30, 410
in era of wild unbelief, III 161
the Great Orphan, II 21, 272, 349-50
greatest truth of all is, III 203
Masters' love for poor orphan, I 70; III 330
meditation on true sun aids, I 137
natural devotees work for, I 135
progress of, and law of cycles, III 387
rebirth acquaints us with whole of, II 314
self-produced, II 349
service of Self hidden in, II 5
Theosophy on subject of, III 62-6
work for, is sure path to Supreme, I 105
Humbleness
Beatitude about, III 256
importance of, II 451
practice of, II 429
in wearing the "yellow robe" internally, II 454
Humboldt, F. H. Baron von (1769-1859)
tried to find lost Cordilleran tribe, III 228
Hume, Allan Octavian (1829-1912)
an exception as to correspondence with Adepts, I 475
K.H. letter to, quoted, I 327
——— "Fragments of Occult Truth" I 67 &n
Hunton, Wm. Lee (1864-1930)
Favorite Hymns compiler, II 156n
Huxley, Prof. Thomas (1825-1895)

essence of matter unknown to, I 353
on reforms & criminal classes, III 162
on superior beings, II 329
Hyderabad
visited by Judge in 1884, II 84
Hyperborean
remains in North Asia, II 24
Hypnotism
See also Mesmerism
Adepts do not use, III 25
astral light a, machine, III 8
compulsion is, III 25
contraction of cells in, III 214-15
contraction of molecules in, I 417
crime committed under, III 213
dangers of, I 297, 357-60, 414-17; III 213-15
delusion fostered by, II 42
Dr. Charcot & revival of, III 212
dreams and, III 176
dual personification in, III 48-9
experiments in, I 414-15; III 212-15
glamour employed in, III 198
imagination in, I 359, 399-400
leads to earlier death, I 417
magnetism is not, III 212
makes one a puppet, II 399
of man by astral light, III 47-9
Mesmerism and, II 31-9
Mesmerism as term for, I 144
normal functions abated in, I 412
proofs of a Hidden Self in, I 145-6
self-, compared with operator-induced, I 415-16
should be law against, I 417; II 280-1; III 214
should be restricted even by doctors, I 145
and spiritualists, I 52
split personality and, III 214-15
spread of moral epidemics and, III 194
suggestion used in, I 414-17
Theosophical explanation, III 214-15
use of will and imagination in, II 307
Hypnotist(s)
Charcot favored legislation for a, I 145, 417
controls subject's will, I 159, 416
imposes his mind to inhibit his subject, II 385
a medium, I 52
should be competent physicians says Charcot, II 281

I

I
See also Ego; Individuality; Personality
illusory, I 31-2
illusory sense of, II 419
manifestation of a continuous entity, II 390
separate, basis of world illusion, I 31-2
Ibn Gebirol (1021?-1070?)
——— *Kether Malkhuth*
on the soul, I 419
Iḍā (Skt)
See also Nāḍī
piṅgalā &, as "sharp & flat," III 314
sushumṇā and, III 314
Idea(s)
common, point to truth, I 35
of cycles, I 518
gradual effect of new, III 95-6
on Hinduism, II 52
innate, and evolution, I 161
man sees only, II 385
personal, fosters envy, I 77
response to, determined by Karma and Reincarnation, I 13
thoughts of mesmerist color subjects', I 255-6
three great, of Movement, II 12
Universe is Will &, I 400
as "voluntary visitors," II 78
Ideal
intuition fostered by, I 183
thought must be on highest, I 28-31
Idiocy
Karma of, II 71-2

shown in palmistry, II 100
Idolatry
not necessary, II 249
Ikshvāku
last of Rājanya sages, I 428
Illness
bearing, patiently better than Mind-Cures, III 399
remedy for, II 291-2
Illumination
direct way to, or Theosophia, II 391
Illusion(s)
Adept on escaping, I 400
Devas can make powerful, I 148
"I" is an, I 31; II 419
and imagination, II 300-1
material world an, II 407
separate "I" basis of world, I 31-2
vanity as, of nature, I 77
Western concept of old Hindu doctrine of, II 411
Image(s)
in Astral Light, I 154; II 23
in dreams, II 263-4
-making power, II 269-70, 300, 307
Imagination
a cause of diseases, II 290-1
in conception of Cosmos, III 333
cultivation of, and will, II 269-70
fakir's feats performed through, II 300, 306-7
important & noble faculty, I 307
in Occult phenomena, I 397-8
in phenomena by "controls," I 308
plastic power of the soul, III 333
in precipitation, I 308-10, 354-5, 359, 397; II 300
What is?, II 300
Immortality
Adepts achieve conscious, III 430
for individual consciousness, II 449
of man & Supreme Being, I 35
of man's soul, I 432; III 10, 14, 29, 155, 167, 178
must win our own, III 260, 430-1
as nothing in Universe is dead, III 167
taught in every religion, II 159
unending struggle to achieve, II 267
Walt Whitman on, III 178
Immutable Principle
the Rootless Root, II 323
Imperishable Sacred Land
at North Pole, II 24
Impersonality
self-discipline of, II 429; III 256
Impulse(s)
evolutionary, II 230-1, 360
for mental life beyond Astral, II 397
passions and, II 339
to the living from executed criminals, II 369
Inaction
in deed of mercy, II 284; III 356q
student retrogresses through, III 356
Incarnation(s)
Ātma never in, II 274-5
balance-sheet of Karma and, II 295-6
in both sexes needed by Ego, II 298-9
considered a misfortune, II 295
many, for man, III 62
moment of grand, II 255
not possible to skip, II 449-50
as types of experiences, II 466
Independent (Stockton)
characterization of Judge in, III 173
Judge lecture reported in, III 173
India
ancient storehouse of Āryan philosophy, II 371-2
Brahmans of, re T.S. as engine of Buddhism, II 51
Buddhism does not prevail in, I 361
Buddhism driven from, III 458
caste system in, II 113
cause of decadence of, II 112-13
conserver of Wisdom-Religion, I 150
cradle of civilization, I 186
danger of orthodox Brahminism, III 459
degraded & materialized, I 478; III 458-9

destiny of, II 80-2, 88-9, 91
East is more than, I 477
feats of fakirs in, III 170-2
gods & sages appear to some in, I 358
H.P.B.'s & Olcott's mission to, II 209-10
knowledge needed on social life in, II 190
"Land of Mysteries," II 86
literature of, will infiltrate West, I 184
Masters & Brahmans in, II 50-1
Masters despair for, I 478
Mogul invaders of, I 183
need not go to, to learn Occultism, III 444, 458-9
on pilgrimages to sacred shrines of, III 29
spiritualism in, I 287-8
spiritually degraded, II 56, 372
T.S. activity in, II 429, 432
T.S. branches in, I 149, 175
Theosophy as a lamp in, III 132
true religion in books of, II 50
truths of, brought by H.P.B., I 361ff
West can help reform, III 459
Western discovery of treasures of, II 50, 87-9
a world center of T.S. work, I 193
Indian(s)
American, beliefs & Hindu cosmogony, II 25
ancient, astrologers, II 103
disciples of Bradlaugh, II 90
on dying of American, I 206-7
"Guardians of the Gods," II 267
influence on West, II 50-1
our debt to, sages, II 106
Individualism
in America, III 8
in America & Black Magic, II 257-8
in variety of occupations, II 380
Individuality
achieved by evolution of Divine Spark, II 380
in Buddhism, II 375
compared with personality, II 334, 390
on loss of, II 449
is manifestation of an entity, II 390
raindrop simile, II 449
Infallibility
belief in own, not a mark of saintship, II 402
Infancy
causes for death in, II 307-8
does not pertain to soul, II 359
immediate rebirth after death in, II 359
in "world of spirits" delusive, II 359
Infinite
Eternal Cause and, II 323
has no attributes, II 310, 323q
Ingersoll, Robert (1833-1899)
an iconoclast, III 102-3
misses spirit of Bible, III 175
Ingratitude
Adepts incapable of, I 511
basest of vices, II 60
Initiate(s)
aspiring, prepares well & hopes, I 21-2
behind the Theosophical Movement, III 444
bound by evolution, II 135
don't proclaim themselves, II 193
don't sell Esoteric teachings, II 193
many obscured, I 127-8
married in some life, I 20
preserve Wisdom-Religion, II 135
Initiation(s)
Adepts only in higher degrees of T.S., II 258
basic virtues for, II 451
can be forgotten, I 128
daily, prepares one for higher, II 417-18, 451
Judge opposes ritual in, I 321
keys in striving for, I 21-2
seeking, causes more trials, I 22
self-denial needed for, I 180; III 64
story shows one preliminary, I 89
trials of, II 450
Innisfallen (Ireland)
Destiny of, I 542-4
gem at Mount of, I 543, 545

Innovations
Adept influence on, II 259-60
dark shadow follows all, II 10
Insanity
and hypnotism, I 416-17
inability to correlate soul and body, II 287
obsession a form of, II 287
Inscriptions
modern & ancient, I 450-1
Insects
karma of tormenting, II 70-1
Inspiration
through dreams, II 263
Instinct
is recollection, II 161
Intellect
cultivate both, & heart, II 395-6
must serve the heart, II 394
Theosophic truth and, III 65
use, to affect hearts of men, III 102
wide, & Occultism, II 277
Introduction to Theosophy (1855)
printed before T.S. founded, I 274 &n
Intuition(s)
how cultivated, II 369-70
how illumination or, cultivated, II 391, 395
ideal side of life, I 183
more important than mere intellect, III 461
not a sense, II 370
reason and, II 435-6
in recognizing a true teacher, I 43-4, 394-6
should be acted upon without delay, I 105
Invisibility
on power of, I 410-12
Invocation
T.S. has no ceremonial, II 148
Ireland
abode of Atlanteans, I 231
Adepts in ancient, I 544-5
Dublin Lodge, II 3
influence on America, II 27
Isle of Destiny, I 231, 542-4, 545-6
Literary Renaissance movement, II 3 &n
on people of, I 230-1
remnant of ancient Atlantis, II 27
tales in, of magical appearances, I 358
Irish
belief in supernatural, I 230-1
Irish Literary Renaissance
Theosophists part of, II 3
The Irish Theosophist (Dublin)
aim as a magazine, II 3
founder of, and Irish Literary Renaissance, II 3
Īśa-Upanishad
all beings same in kind, not degree, I 435q
invokes true sun, I 140q, 168q
on Self as all things, I 431q
on unity of beings, I 168, 435
Islamism
See also Mohammedan(s)
conversion of F.T.S. to, I 372
five main precepts of, I 374
and polygamy, I 373
Sufis preserve inner doctrines of, I 373
Īśvara (Skt)
determines experiences to be karmically met, I 196-7
karma and, II 407-8
not affected by karma, III 37
spirit in man, I 70-1; III 37
is the Supreme, I 35

J

Jacob's Ladder
symbol of cycles, III 302-3
Jacolliot, Louis (1837-1890)
on magical feats empowered from high mountains, III 226
Jāgrat (waking state) (Skt)
contrasted to dreaming & deep sleep, I 81-3
salvation only in, I 80
Jains
reverence for animals, II 420

James
on self reflection, III 82
on source of "perfect gifts," I 104
on Spirit, II 167
on works, III 110
James, Dr. William (1842-1910)
experiments with hypnotism, III 214-15
——— "Hidden Self," I 144
experiments with hypnotism prove inner self in man, I 145, 414
Japan
Shin Buddhism one of 12 sects in, I 85
Jehovah
no power in pronouncing, I 61
a tribal god, I 288-9
Jenness Miller Illus. Monthly (N.Y.)
article on Hypnotism in, III 212-15
Judge piece in, III 212
Jeremiah
alludes to rebirth, I 419-20
Jerome (347-420)
Origen &, I 431
Jesus (ca. 100 BCE)
Buddha and, cp., II 378, 430; III 106, 109
Christianity of, I 437
on concentration, III 399
crucifixion of, I 526
descends into hell, I 312-13
divine incarnation dogma about, III 105
doctrines of, preached but not practiced, I 32
educated by Essenes, II 378
ethics of, & Theosophy, I 155
forgiveness taught by, II 253
great renunciation seen in crucifixion of, I 526
healing power of, I 283-4
high mountain trials of, III 227-8
H.P.B. on ethics of, III 436
humility taught by, III 256
impostors of, I 493-4
instructed from Egypt, II 396
on justice, III 99, 155
on Karma, III 110-11
and Kṛishṇa as Saviors, I 439-40
mission of, I 304
Mosaic Law and, III 107
the Mysteries taught to disciples, I 440
Name obtained by, I 286
no, with a divine mission, II 266
order of, enemy of Cagliostro, I 169-70
on perfectibility of man, II 12; III 109
on poor in spirit, III 256
on poverty, III 98
on prayer, III 404
reincarnation and, I 304-7, 419-22; II 141-2; III 109-10, 155
on self-examination & repentance, III 436q
Sermon on the Mount and, III 256
taught same ethics as Theosophy, II 452; III 105, 436
on temptation, II 442
temptation of, III 255
on thought & deed, II 378
Jews
believed in reincarnation, I 413, 417-22; II 141
books of, filled with cyphers, III 107-8
bull horns sacred to, III 336
Jesus' only mission to, I 304
learned magic from Egyptians, I 287, 288
Zohar an authority among, I 419
"Jim Nolan"
described astral Light, III 136-7
explains materialization, I 198-200, 354, 406-8
mediumistic spirit, III 136-7
no elemental or spook, I 200
a person not a spook, I 408
prophecies of, I 404-5
a published séance with, III 136 &n
spiritualistic control, I 198-200
Jinarājadāsa, C. (1875-1953), compiler
——— *Letters from the Masters of the Wisdom*, 1st Series
on purpose of T.S., I 69-70 &n, 318-19
T.S. not for occult arts, II 415&n-16

to A. P. Sinnett on main T.S. Objective, I 318-19
——— *Letters from the Masters of the Wisdom*, 2nd Series
on true philanthropy, I 319-20
Jīva(s) (Skt)
as atomic and monadic lives, III 335
confusion of term, II 407
energizes man from great pranic ocean, III 235, 335
individual lives, I 158
Karma and, II 407-8
as "life-energy," III 234
as "life-principle," II 407
potential vitality of, III 350
Prāṇa recombines with, after death, III 335, 368
Jīvanmukta(s) (Skt)
helps Humanity through T.S., II 272
liberated state of, II 272, 408
at new day of Brahmā, II 257, 415
not destroyed at night of Brahmā, II 415
or White Adepts, II 257
Jīvātman (Skt)
Karma causes connection of, with matter, II 407
plan for, during manifestation, I 158
so-called soul spirit, II 407
Jñāna(m) (Skt)
complete knowledge, III 364
definition, I 11n
Jñāna-Yoga (Skt)
Bhagavad-Gītā &, I 54
Jñāni(s) (Skt)
attracted to earth from higher regions, I 127; II 236
H.P.B. a, II 236
not Mahātmas or Adepts, III 60
progressed Beings who aid Earth, I 127; III 60
work as ordinary humans, II 235-6
Job
alludes to rebirth, I 420
an altered form of Egyptian *Book of the Dead*, I 252
on brotherhood with all life, II 70q
on deep sleep, II 260
on dreams, I 81
mentions palmistry, II 97-8
on mystic path, II 107
John
blind man and rebirth, III 110
on rebirth, III 76
on the Word as Logos, I 7
John the Baptist
Elias reborn as, I 306; II 141, 158, 453
Johnston, Charles (1867-1931)
article on races quoted, I 428
on ethnology of Rājputs, I 428-9
founder of Dublin Lodge, II 3
sends Judge quotation by Synesius, I 121
Johnstown Flood
and karma, II 255
Judaism
secret teaching in its Kabbalah, II 430
Judge
not any man, I 55, 502-4; II 254
Judge, Frederick H.
astrology and death of, II 75-6
father of W.Q.J., I xvii
Judge, John H. (W.Q.J.'s brother)
helps H.P.B. prepare *Isis Unveiled* for printer, I xix
Judge, Mary Quan
mother of W.Q.J., I xvii
Judge, William Q. (1851-1896)
See also The Path
accused of creating discord in T.S., I 476-80
advice to Hyderabad branch, II 85
Adyar visited briefly by, I xxiii-xxiv
Æ's regard for, II 3-4, 5-6
American section formed with, as General Secretary, I xxv
Antaḥkaraṇa between East & West, I xxxix; III 414, 439-40
astral hand of, writes death-bed message, III 222-4
astrology experience of, II 74-6
attacks upon, & struggle with illness, III 460
believes in Vedas, I 362
bibliography of, I lvi-lviii

blended with Nirmāṇakāya, I xxxiv
born of Christian parents, II 80
borrowed body of, I xxxiii-xxxvi
chaired European T.S. Convention, II 44-5; III 51
chela of thirteen years standing, III 339, 440
on concealing Masters' names, II 45
cremation of, I lxi
Dāmodar corresponded with, I xxiii
on death of, I liii, lix-lxv
described by journalists, III 116
editor of *The Path*, II 198-9
E.S. *Book of Rules* by, I xxx
E.S. representative in America, I xxx, xxxii (facsimile reproduction)
family and early years, I xvii-xviii
favors ternary division for this age, II 105
a Founder of T.S., I xix-xxii
and George H. Felt, I 322
"greatest of the exiles," II 502-3 &n
H.P.B. asks, to suggest T.S. founding to Olcott, I xviii n
H.P.B. occultly writes in book of, I 398
H.P.B. on ancient tie with, I xxxvi-xxxix
H.P.B. showed, precipitation process, I 310
H.P.B. strongly defended, I xxxvi-xli
H.P.B. taught, reincarnation, II 334
helped H.P.B. in Paris, I xxiii
helped H.P.B. with *Isis Unveiled*, I xviii-xix
hoped for world disarmament, II 81
independence of American T.S. and, I li-lii
on India and British rule, II 81
as initiated Hindu disciple, I xxxv-xxxvi
initiation ritual and, I 321
investigates Coulomb conspiracy, III 123-5
last moments described, III 222
Last Will of, I lxv-lxvii
lectures in India, II 80-9
letter to 2nd annual convention, II 44-5
literary heritage of, I xxviii-xxix
on London visit in 1884, I 533
Master's letters to, I liv-lvi
meets H.P.B., I xviii; II 16
meets Smythe, I xxiv
modesty & power of, II 439
never depressed, I 523
nominated Olcott as T.S. chairman, III 216
nominated Olcott for T.S. presidency, I 64, 67
not Jasper Niemand, II 47-8
offices of, described, I xxvi-xxvii
official election as Vice President in 1890, I xxxiii
Olcott's contemplated resignation and, I xlii-xliv
one of T.S. Founders, II 86
as pamphleteer, III 51
praised by P. Iyaloo Naidu, II 85
Prayāg letter and, I 470-6; II 54-8, 215-17
president of Āryan Lodge, II 439
press coverage of, III 115-16
pseudonyms of, I xxvi
recalls bird migration seen as youth, I 519-20
on replacing term "principles," I 143-4
represented H.P.B. in America, III 273, 288, 339, 414, 439-40
represented T.S. at World's Fair, II 121
on *S.D.* authorship, I 342-4
S.D., *Isis Unveiled* and, II 21
sailed for London after H.P.B.'s death, II 47
says charges are false, I xlvii
served eternal Self, II 5
sole channel in America, III 339
South American adventures, I 531-3
a "spiritual Hero," II 3
as "successor" to Olcott, II 114n
tested by loneliness, I xix, xxii-xxiii
T.S. first object and, II 81-2
travels to India, II 69, 80

tributes for, II 3-6
valued men by their work, II 5
vegetarianism injurious to, II 384
Vice-President of T.S., I xxi-xxii
on writing of *S.D.*, III 238-41
——— *Epitome of Theosophy*
on Adepts who become Devas, II 375-6
distribution of, III 68
on spiritual training, II 336-7
——— *Letters That Have Helped Me*
first step in magic, III 134
recommended for study, III 277
on resignation, II 411 &n
suggested by H.P.B., II 502
——— *Ocean of Theosophy*
apparent contradiction in, II 361-2
corrected on rebirth, II 353
on egoic stature in Manvantara, II 361-2
on evolution of earth-chain, II 422 &n
teaching as a whole therein, II 362
written in very few days, II 354
——— *Reply by William Q. Judge to Charges . . .*
Masters taught Judge from early days, I 1q
——— *Yoga Aphorisms . . .*
cited, II 7n

Justice
criminal, system is karma, II 285
in doctrine of karma, II 70-1, 139; III 33-4, 71
Karma is mercy and, I 335; II 158, 342
Revelation on, III 100
self-styled Karmic agents &, II 325-6
sensitives to evil and, II 231-2
universal law of, III 98-9

K

Kabbalah [Qabbālāh] (Heb)
Great Light and, II 107
Hebrew, on Word, II 225
hidden key to Jewish scriptures, III 107-8
holds key to occult numbers, II 229
on interlaced triangles, I 251-2
reveals *Exodus*, III 107-8
secret religion of Jews, II 430
on Sephīrōth as 7 sacred planets, III 338

Kabbalists
hunger for power by, I 60
refuse to divulge psychic experiences, II 69

Kāla-Haṃsa (Skt)
as universal resonance, III 359

Kali-Yuga (Skt)
See also Yuga(s)
age of decadence & obscuration, I 292-3; III 387
astral images during, III 62
Atlantis in its, when destroyed, I 459
black adepts come later in, II 257, 415
close of present cycle &, III 390
cycle of, I 124, 459-61
cycle of materialism, I 292-3
digits of, I 124, 125-6
efforts for good quickened in, I 461
length of, II 257
prediction about, I 102
reason called "dark age," I 293, 461
seeds of black magic in, II 257
ternary division of principles and, II 105
what can be done in, III 58, 390
White Adepts preceded black in, II 257, 415

Kalpa(s) (Skt)
divided into ages by ancient Hindus, I 518; III 58
Mahā-Kalpa and, I 124
Manas begun in 4th Race, III 357
minor, & lotus symbol, III 356-7
period of manifestation, I 518
as Race as well as Age, III 357
Sanskrit term for cycle, I 514

Kāma (Skt)
See also Desire; Kāma-Rūpa

blends with astral body after death, II 338
blood as aspect of, I 313
cause for Ego's embodiment, II 302
control of, I 219
on "desire-form" of, after death, III 320-1
furthest descent of spirit into matter, III 296
integral part of man, I 219
many gradations of, III 385
no, -rūpa during life, III 295-6, 320-1
relative to 4th Round & 4th Globe, III 296
sympathy and, II 330

Kāma-Loka (Skt)
after-death state, III 42, 236
on dissipation of Kāma-rūpa in, III 352
fate of suicide in, III 220
Hell is a stage of, II 363
Kāma-rūpa is formed in, III 236, 295-6
last conscious state for evil man, III 236
many different states of, II 333
Purgatory, III 220
purgatory?, II 281
recognition of friends in, II 305, 333
some unaware of death in, II 333
state is still quite physical, II 308, 333
suffering in, II 281, 305
suicides stay longer in, II 280
victims of violence in, II 303

Kāma-Manas (Skt)
See also Lower Manas
animal soul & root of separateness, III 296, 406-7
battleground of this stage of earth-life, III 297
finite aspect of Manas, III 408
as lower self or personal Ego, III 296-7, 322, 364
personal self, III 367
psychic action of cells and, III 351
relates to passional organs, III 348
Sanskrit for lower manas, II 385

Kāma-Mānasic Entity
black magician as, III 407
as control in séance, III 407
as lost soul, III 406-7
more real than dreams, II 247-8
obsesses next personality, III 407

Kāma-Rūpa(s) (Skt)
of Adept, refined & harmless, III 385
in animals as well as man, III 295
astral soul, III 44
confusion about, in Sinnett's classification, III 296
degraded, attracted to séances, II 280, 353; III 330-1
desire body, III 44, 236
dissipates after death, I 278-9; II 280, 420; III 320-1, 352-3, 365
dissipates into Tanhic elementals, III 352, 365
as Dweller on Threshold, III 330
fate of long-lasting, III 330, 352-3
fate of long-lasting, questioned, III 321
formed & released after death, III 191, 236, 295-6, 320-1, 330, 383
formed by Astral Body with Kāma, III 385
gravitates to animal kingdom, II 420-1
how formed, II 337-8
how Manas separates from, II 281-2
Karmic record of, forms model for new foetus, III 321
lower mode of consciousness, III 374-5
only an aspect or temporary form, III 319
in séance imitates dead, III 44, 295-6, 330-1
separation of higher triad from, II 281
spirit "bride or groom" as demons, III 331
suffering of the, II 281
of suicides and violent deaths, II 280
as vehicles for mediumistic séances, II 280

Kamma. *See* Karma
Kansa [Kaṃsa] (Skt)
tried to destroy Kṛishṇa, I 126, 440
Kant, Immanuel (1724-1804)
and "equal freedom" theory, I 220
on galactic rotation, I 516n
not a materialist, III 14
——— *Träume eines Geistersehers* . . .
on belief in human soul, III 14
Kardec, Allan (pseud. of Rivail, Hippolyte L.D., 1803-1869)
H.P.B. denied personal reincarnation as taught by, II 334
Karma (Skt)
as action, II 295-6, 407, 412, 443-4, 445, 462-3
acts on all planes, III 36, 37-8, 71, 126, 169, 245, 247
Adepts themselves are, II 284
on agents of, I 492-3, 500-1; II 226
of all manifestation, II 255
all share common, II 245
Aphorisms on, I 333-6
applies to all beings & worlds, I 117; III 125, 126, 246
astral light vehicle for, III 62
of atoms & human lives, III 36, 246
balance sheet of, II 295-6, 332, 342, 351, 448
of beggary, II 70-1
Bhagavad-Gītā on, III 36, 39q, 245
Biblical ref. to, II 139, 162-3, 444; III 33, 34, 99-100, 110-11, 169, 247
brings true reform, III 162
the Brothers do not interfere with, II 455
Buddhist morality on, I 120
cannot be avoided or mislaid, II 442, 446
cannot be deposited like money in a bank, II 351
cannot interfere with, II 245
cannot judge another's, I 335
capital punishment and, I 488-90, 492; III 35
cellular, I 118
Christianity taught, I 441
is continuance of the nature of the act, I 24-6
conversion of energy of, II 447
as cosmic law, II 343
Cosmos has, as well as man, I 117
deeds of sentient beings, III 33, 71, 99-100, 155, 245
definition, III 245
desire for Truth governs, III 275
destiny?, II 447-8
as destiny not immutable, II 271
determines sex, II 299
Devachan and, I 167-8; III 245
different types of, I 335-6, 504; III 37-8, 63-4, 247
of diseases from past life, II 291-2
as Divine Law, II 446
doctrine of reincarnation needed to explain, III 155
"dragon's teeth" of future, II 315
draws us out of Svarga, II 408
on entering occult path, II 264-5
environment and, I 31-3, 483-5
equilibrium restored by, I 334, 502-3; III 35, 162, 246
as ethical causation, II 139, 162, 447-8; III 63, 71, 162, 168-9, 235
exhausted more quickly in case of chela, III 275
explains class differences, II 162
"failures" of, compensated, I 114
family, racial, national, etc., II 435, 443, 461
and fear of retaliation, II 341-2
field of, not just body, II 407, 442
forgiveness and, II 245-6, 326-7
of friends & relatives, III 40
friends & relatives bound by, III 246
good & bad cp., I 483-5; II 295-6, 314, 342, 351, 447-8
good, of working for Humanity, II 417
governs astrology, II 273
governs material existence, III 37, 63, 100
as great benefactor, III 246-7
heredity and, I 93-6, 276
immutable & implacable, III 17, 40, 71, 99-100, 110-11

includes altruistic acts, II 245, 350-1, 405
of inflicting pain, II 71-2, 315
of judging others, I 502-4; II 326-7, 405; III 110-11, 247q
as justice with mercy, II 158, 246, 342
Kamma is term for, in Ceylon, III 33
kinds and fields of, I 335-6, 504
latent during Pralaya, II 408
Law of cause & effect, III 161-2, 167, 169
Law of Compensation, II 70, 139, 412, 448
Law of Ethical Causation, I 502
Lipikas and, II 227
Master's words on, III 345-6
of material world, II 256
meaning of, I 24-31, 195-7, 275-9, 333-6, 483-5
mental & moral defects are, I 138
"mental deposits" of, I 278-9
mitigated, I 334-6
moral & spiritual, II 180-2, 350-1, 412, 447-8
motivation governs, I 139, 157; II 343, 351, 407, 462-3; III 89, 345
national, I 26, 118; III 162
of nations, races, planets, etc., III 236
natural law of, II 70-1
no, beyond the mind, I 25, 31
not cause of incarnation, II 295
not exhausted in one life, III 63, 71, 246
not fatalism, I 24-5, 28; III 40
not interfering with, II 237, 284, 404-5, 442
not just reward and punishment, II 255, 412, 448
not retaliation, II 341-2
not subject to time, I 334ff
not vicarious atonement, III 33, 70-1, 110
nullification of, III 38, 63-4, 247
of one is, of all, I 504-5
opportunity as, III 40, 176-7
Oriental doctrine of, III 33, 35-6, 39, 110
of past affinities and enmities, II 314-15, 447-8
perfect justice, III 33-34, 35, 39-40, 63, 71, 94, 98-100, 110, 176, 246
planes of causation, I 25, 27, 502
"pledge fever" and, III 275
postponement of, via mind cure, III 256-7
power of a vow upon, I 335
problems explained by, III 66-7, 94, 98-9, 162, 176-7, 235
produced thro' ignorance, II 407-8
as punishment or reward, I 137-8, 196-7, 276, 502-4; III 397
rebirth and, I 26-8, 156, 316-17
recorded in astral light, III 47-8, 62
reincarnation part of Law of, I 33
repentance and, I 31
as responsibility, I 276-7, 316-17, 502-5; III 71, 162, 169, 345-6
restores harmony, I 334, 502-5; III 35, 162, 246
ripening of, III 63-5
rules entire universe, II 227, 273, 407
salvation & freedom from, I 93
salvation by works as, III 110-11
simile for, II 70
spiritual plane not affected by, III 37, 247
stored up from past, I 88, 276-9, 295-6; II 442, 446-7
on swaying power of, III 63
three aspects, I 562
three principal kinds of, II 255-6, 463; III 36-7
"Topics in," II 325n
transmutation of energies and, I 28, 504
twin doctrines of, and reincarnation, I 156-7; III 6, 19, 35, 94, 99, 245-7, 252
on unexhausted, I 278-9
on unexpended, I 334-5
of unmerited suffering, II 332, 335-6
of world, II 412, 443

Karma-Yoga (Skt)
  true renunciation is, III 39
Karmic
  all are, "agents," II 325-7
  balancing of, causes, II 271
  bloom and fruit, II 444-5, 447-8
  effects, II 271, 444-5
  propensities, II 447-8
  real, agents need training, II 326-7
  retaliation from enmity, II 313-15
  reward, II 342, 445
  reward in Devachan, II 336
  stamina, II 444
Kāśyapa. *See* Mahā-Kāśyapa
Kate Field's Washington
  chose Judge's pen-name and series title, III 3
Katie King
  Crookes saw her materialize, I 290-1
Keely, John W. (1837-1898)
  competitive science and, I 210
  liberated atomic force, III 351
Keightley, Archibald (1859-1930)
  biographical sketch, II 485-7
  E.S. Instructions and, III 290-1
  married Julia Ver Planck, II 487
Keightley, Bertram (1860-1945)
  astrological correspondences and, III 290-1
  biographical sketch, II 481-5
  corrected on Auric Egg & colors, III 288
  General Secretary T.S., II 432
  on H.P.B.'s method of instruction, III 285
Keightley, Julia (1855?-1915)
  biographical sketch, II 499-503
  as compiler Jasper Niemand, I xxix
  H.P.B. asked Judge to send *Letters That Have Helped Me* to, II 502
  as Jasper Niemand, not W. Q. Judge, II 47-8
  nom-de-plumes of, II 500, 502
  receives Master's message, II 48
  tribute to Judge, II 5
  wrote poetry & plays, II 500
Kerning. *See* Krebs, Johann Baptiste
Kether Malkhuth. *See* Ibn Gebirol
Khandalavala, Navroji D.
  President of Poona Lodge, II 83
  reports Judge's lecture, II 82-3
Khunrath, Heinrich (1560-1605)
——— *Amphitheatrum* . . .
  on Kabbalah of the Hebrews, I 535
Kiddle, Henry
  claims K.H. plagiarized him, III 121
Killarney, Lakes of
  dream recollections at, I 541ff
Kingdom(s)
  man responsible for salvation of lower, I 117
  mineral, vegetable, animal and human, II 228, 230, 322
  monads encased in lower, II 230, 231
  regular progression from lowest to highest, II 322
Kings
  Adept, of Egypt and mummification, II 348
Kingsford, Dr. Anna (1846-1888)
  H.P.B. warns, I 500
  violently opposed to vivisection, I 500
——— *The Perfect Way*
  graduating thesis for *Royal Microscopical Society*, III 350
  on states, death & rebirth of a cell, III 350
Kirchberger, Nicolas A. (Baron de Liebestorf) (1739-1799)
  agent of Adepts, II 301
Knife
  analogy in occult feats, II 307
Knot
  of heart, II 457
  "philosophical," in palmistry, II 99
Knower
  and the Known, II 317
Knowledge
  aspiring to, not enough, I 147
  compared to virtue, II 283
  discernment leads to full, I 73
  of good and evil, II 402
  intellectual, regarding men, I 73
  meditation on OṂ leads to, of Secret Doctrine, I 8

must be seized, I 79
occult, leads to altruism, I 19
occult phenomena and, I 397
path of devotion leads to, I 162
power and, needed to avoid illusions of Devas, I 148
scientific, of minerals, I 73
of Self must come first, I 50
of soul evolves slowly, III 74
true Will speeds one to, II 391
virtue needed for, I 155
Knowles, James S. (1784-1862)
——— *William Tell*
play quoted, III 228
Koot Hoomi
alternate spelling of, III 200
Conway's assertion about, III 200
defended by Judge, III 121-3
on fellow countrymen, III 458
inspired T.S. inaugural address, III 122
Judge regretted, name being revealed, III 200
picture of, in Adyar shrine, III 196
Koran [*Al-Qur'an*] (Arabic)
compared to *Ṛig-Veda*, I 374
compelled by the sword, I 373
quoted on polygamy, I 373
Kośas (Skt)
sheaths or environment of the Self or Supreme Soul, I 33
Kosmos (Gk)
See also Cosmos
Verbum of manifested, III 337
Krebs, Johann Baptiste (1774-1831) [pseud. J. B. Kerning]
recognized mantric power, I 89
ref. to German mystic's story, I 89
——— *Der Freimaurer*
practical examples of power of mantras, I 90-1 &n
Kṛishṇa (d. 3102 BCE)
appeared in days of Kansa, II 345-6
as Avatāra, I 439
both good and evil, I 13; II 109
calling upon, at death, II 448-9
as Logos incarnated, III 357
is Purusha and Prakṛiti, I 13
on real man, I 17
as shepherd, I 101
a son of God, I 439-40
threatened by evil Kansa, I 126, 440
white adept, I 126
Kshatriya(s) (Skt)
Buddha & Kṛishṇa were, I 429
descendants of solar race, I 429
duty of, II 376
once above Brahmans in mystical knowledge, I 428
Kumāra(s) (Skt)
compelled to complete divine Man, III 360
Elect, as germ of Hierarchy, III 357, 402
Four, as progenitors of 4 Races, III 357
Mānasa-Putras & Lunar Pitṛis and, III 361-2
Planetary Spirits as highest, III 402-3
on Sacrifice of four, III 357
"Virgin Youths" or "Sons of Mind," III 294, 360
who refused to create, III 360
Wondrous Being and, III 357
Kunte, Mahadev Moreshvar (1835-1888)
translated some of Patañjali, II 83
on youth of India, II 83
Kurukshetra
sacred plain of, I 27n
Kwan-Shi-Yin (Chinese)
as Avalokiteśvara, III 359
as mystic Fire, III 358
Kwan-Yin (Chinese)
female aspect of Padmapāṇi, III 358
Kāla-Haṃsa symbolic bird of, III 359
and Kwan-Shi-Yin, III 358
as potency of occult sound, III 359
as Śakti, unified by Light of Logos, III 358
as Trinity, III 358
as Water, III 358
Kwan-Yin-Tien (Chinese)
melodious heaven of sound, III 359

L

Laheri, Rai B. K.
appeals to T.S. for impartiality, I 361
leader of Hindu Revival, I 442-3
letter to the Brahmans and, I 425, 443
on society for Hindu revival, I 443
on yogi meeting Mahātma, III 418-20
Lakshaṇa (Skt)
distinctive mark of, on T.S. work, I 273
Lamas
rebirth of high, II 450
Lamasery
retreat to, form of selfishness, II 454
The Lamp
reprint of Judge article in, III 218
Language
coeval with reason, III 336, 360
development of, in early races, III 336
on, of Ego, I 152-3
origin of, as Vāch, III 336, 360
poverty of English, II 105, 324
on Universal, I 456-8
Law(s)
Adepts follow White, II 257
all comes to us by, II 335-6
all is under, not chance, II 138
ancient Egyptians knew hidden, II 72
of attraction & repulsion, I 356, 401
of causation, II 158
of Compensation explains inequities, II 70-3
of Correspondences, I 369; III 312-13
criminal, & heredity, I 94
of cycles, I 158, 515, 519; II 164-5, 259
eternal, obeyed by Adepts, III 15
of impressions & their cyclic return, I 514-25
justice as, governing man, III 98-9
of Karma & rebirth, I 33
Lodge helps in search for, II 304-5
natural, of karma, II 70-1
of Nature, II 158
of Nature & Brotherhood, II 87
Nature's, & their abuse by man, III 328-9
no miracles, only, I 403
One Fundamental, of Occult Science, II 226
people not developed by, III 203
punitive, and Karma, II 285
reincarnation & Karma &, I 95
as restoration of harmony, II 71
submission to Higher, II 182
theologians vs. Theosophists on, III 99-100
T.S. does not make, II 152-3
universal, I 114, 115
universal, needs no authority, III 62
of universal unity, I 42
Laws of Manu
on benefit of pronouncing OṂ, I 6
Lawyers
prominent, in early T.S., I 64
Laya Center(s) (Skt)
energy propelled into, from dying globe, I 483
in evolutionary scheme, III 389
life impulses from Moon to Earth produced a, III 389
origin of evolving comets, I 481-2
primordial substance in, II 234
sidereal principles pass through, II 234
Lead
sacred to Saturn, II 446
used as a talisman, II 446
Lebaudy, Max
millionaire martyred by public, I 507-8
Left-Hand Path
See also Black Magic
fate of dabbler in, I 45-6
Legislation
ethical reform needed not, I 527; III 203
T.S. has nothing to do with, II 153
truth cannot be known by, II 152

Leibniz, Gottfried W. (1646-1716)
on Monads of, III 337
Lemuria
as 3rd Great Continent, II 24
Lester, Leonard (1870-1952)
on W.Q.J. as teacher, II 439
Leucippus (5th century BCE)
on lateral motion of atoms, II 223
Lévi, Éliphas (pseud. of Alphonse Louis Constant) (1810-1875)
on plastic medium of astral light, III 136
as sham occultist, I 79-80
——— *Dogme et Rituel*
on astral apparitions, III 47
on astral phantom, III 48
on evil influence of astral light, III 47q
Levitation
of Christian Saints, etc., I 399
of Hanuman in the *Rāmāyaṇa*, I 399
how achieved, I 355-6
Liberalism
cannot legislate human nature, III 160
Life
Absolute, as "dark" flame, III 337
all Adepts married in some, I 20
aspect of Absolute, III 368
consciousness and, compared, III 368-9
daily, our real initiation, II 417-18, 451
death vs., III 189
doing good in, a duty, I 138
every, has a moment of choice, II 418
in every point of space, III 189
evolution of conscious, I 380
lacking traditional virtues is vain, III 448-9
on living a theosophical, I 17-24; II 395, 417, 466
meditation throughout entire, II 7-8
no void of, in universe, III 363
object of each, governs soul's environment, I 278-9
only ONE, & One Consciousness in all forms, III 260
pervades universe, II 297
principle of, III 189
reverence for animals, II 420
seek meaning of each event in, I 22
T.S. belief in Unity of, II 203
Theosophy in daily, I 280-1
as universal principle, I 208
yielding to small vexations of, II 451
Life-Atoms. *See* Atoms
Life-Wave(s)
evolve through Earth-Chain, I 323-4; II 424-7; III 58-9
sleep and, III 13
sustain body in waking state, III 13
Light
"gracious," of Boehme, II 111
Great, leaves traces, II 107
how one, becomes the many, III 337-8
man ensouled by Pillars of, III 363
Nature set in motion by, & sound, III 359
as Sun or Fire manifest, III 358
Light on the Path. *See* Collins, Mabel
Like
produces like maxim, II 331
Lilly, William (1602-1681)
predicted plague and great fire of London, II 74
——— *Introduction to Astrology*
on Horary Astrology, II 74
Lincoln, Abraham (1809-1865)
premonition of his destiny, III 24
Liṅga-Śarīra (Skt)
See also Astral Body
Adept may use, of another body, III 382, 446
aspect of Auric Egg, III 367
astral body or, model for physical, III 44, 189-90, 235, 334, 446
essence derived from Violet Hierarchy, III 405
of our globe is Astral Light, III 317, 334
pollution of Earth's, III 317
subtler than body, III 44

- transformed by radiant fire principle, III 446

Link
- "Keep the, unbroken," III 340q

Lipika(s) (Skt)
- compared with Builders, II 227
- highest Adepts know little about, II 227
- of "middle wheel" of Space, III 14-15
- as recorders in book of fate, III 18

Lives
- interchanging, II 146-7
- plan for, within, I 158
- why we don't remember past, II 161

Lodge
- almoners of the divine, I 210
- a call from the, I 245
- communication with, II 10
- cyclic help for man, II 9-10
- door to, closed in 1897, II 9-10
- familiar with "pledge fever," III 279
- Great, helps good people, II 304-5
- highest in, and Dhyāni-Chohans, III 15
- Master's, & cyclic help for man, II 301
- meditation subject, III 454
- teaching on change, I 460
- White, opposed to psychic development, II 11

Lodge of Mizraim
- Masonry signifies nothing, III 129

Logarithms
- taught in ancient mysteries, I 313

Logic
- affirmation, denial, & rules of, I 241
- a foundation of occult path, I 155
- metaphysical healers ignore, I 282

Logos (Gk)
- Avalokiteśvara is, III 358
- awakener of the Universe, I 7
- conscious energy of, is Fohat, III 336-7, 358-9
- and Cosmic Ideation, III 333
- Kṛishṇa as incarnation of, III 358
- male & female divisions of, III 359
- manifested, or Creative Word, III 333, 359
- noumenon of Fohat, III 359
- as reason & speech, III 336
- and sexless power Eros, III 333
- symbols for, III 336
- Third, as Mind of Universe, III 298
- unmanifested, in upper triangle of Absolute World, III 332-3
- Vāch and, III 335-8
- Vāch, Virāj and, III 359

Loka(s) (Skt)
- Rūpa and Arūpa, II 394

London
- fire, forecast by stars, II 15, 74
- plague predicted by Lilly, II 74

London Times
- Sinnett seeks phenomenal production of the, I 377-8

Longfellow, Henry W. (1807-1882)

——— *A Psalm of Life*
- quoted, I 195 &n

——— *The Song of Hiawatha*
- quoted, I 191-2

Lotus
- of the heart, I 61

Le Lotus (Paris)
- French T.S. periodical, I 56; III 143

Love
- Adepts embody spirit, unity and, II 257
- on attaining Divine, I 105
- brotherhood is not so-called, but true compassion, III 356
- God is, I 103
- Harmony and, duty of man, I 181
- Infinite, annihilates evil, I 47
- Karma and, II 315
- Masters moved by universal, III 329-30
- Path of, essential, III 438
- patriotism and, II 374
- for soul vs. personality, I 83-4
- Theosophists must express, I 316-17

Lower Manas
- *See also* Kāma-Manas; Higher-Manas; Manas
- Antaḥkaraṇa links Higher Manas to, III 365, 374-5
- desires & delusions of, III 437

does not exist in Devachan, III 365
"green" when not absorbed in Kāma, III 367
Higher Ego and, II 297; III 296-7
Kāma is negative cp. to, III 416
must be freed from desire, III 367
must be subjected to Higher, II 297
must win immortality, III 408, 409
physical memory of, II 281-2
rules man at present, III 364, 437

Lower Nature
on control by Higher Ego, II 297
must open up to spirit, III 57

Lower Self
See also Higher Self; Lower Manas; Personality; Self
Auric Egg is not, III 297
distinct from Higher Ego, III 296-7, 366-7
Higher Self must triumph over, II 433-4
must permit soul to act, III 447-8
as personal Ego, III 296-7
as personal self not the body, III 367
versus Higher Self, III 82-4

Loyalty
family & E.S., III 405, 422
to H.P.B., II 63
to ideals & Theosophy, III 429-30
to Masters, III 275-6, 391, 413, 419-20
to theosophical cause, II 44
to Theosophical Society, III 430

Lucifer
morning-star as, II 15
once a prince of light, I 47

Lucifer (London)
on "Auric fluid" as magnetic force, III 334
cited, I 56
constant labor of H.P.B. on, III 138
costly labor of, III 141
on disease & imagination, II 291q
on founding of, I 192; II 115 &n, 180
on Judge meeting Olcott in Oakland, I xxii
on Māyāvi-rūpa of Adept, III 334
Path magazine cp. to, I 386
ref. to early Church views on rebirth, I 430
on religious tolerance in T.S., I 361
stirred up Theosophy in Europe, III 209

Luke
on beam in eye, III 436
epitome of Theosophy in, III 70
on humbleness, II 452q
on pride, II 452
on will, III 443

Lully, Raymond (ca. 1232-1316)
obscured adept, I 128

Lunar Pitṛi(s) (Skt)
See also Pitṛis; Solar Pitṛis
absorbed in auric essence become ourselves, III 464
or Barhishad Pitṛis, III 294-5, 361
on being incarnated by Divine Egos, III 463
Chāyās of, gave man his body, III 294-5, 363, 463-5
earth chain and, III 306
and evolution of man, I 214
form animal man, III 409
function in first 3 rounds, III 295
lower Prajāpati as 7 creative Forces of Nature, III 294

Lytton, Edward George Lord Bulwer- (1803-1873)
foresaw the "Coming Race," I 42
——— *A Strange Story*
on black magician, III 329
on dreams, II 260
——— *Zanoni*
on Dweller, I 97
on dweller of threshold, II 264
elemental shapes in, I 535
man more than body in, II 105

M

Machell, Reginald W. (1845-1927)
designed H.P.B.'s urn, II 196n

Macrocosm
Microcosmic Principles & Planes of, III 298

six-pointed star represents, III 380
Macroprosopus (Gk)
definition, I 14
Madness
vanity can lead to, I 77
Magh Mela (Hindi)
"The Hindu Revival" sect founded at a, I 442
Magi
abuses perpetrated in name of, I 45
Magic
See also Black Magic; White Magic
distinction between Black & White, II 290
E.S. not for practical, III 305
motive decides black or white, I 45
not child's play, I 47
as occult science, I 44
practice of, needs Universal Brotherhood, I 5
true, devotion to others, III 134
Magic Bracelet
in palmistry, II 100
Magician(s)
See also Black Magician(s); White Magician(s)
Black & White cp., II 256-8, 414
metamorphosis by, II 94
Magnet
analogy, II 338
Magnetic Affinity
between elementals & man, II 404; III 61
Magnetism
See also Hypnotism; Mesmerism
on auric fluid used in, III 334
can remedy obsession, II 288
in cure of disease, II 289
of erroneous & sincere beliefs, I 475
India's, stifling to adepts, I 477-8
metal prevents, II 93
not Black Magic, III 290
opposite process to hypnotism, III 214
of sitters in séances, I 406-8
stifling, of modern world, II 115n
use should be limited to doctors, III 214
used as anaesthetic, III 212-14
Mahābhārata
conflict over vase of Amṛita, I 15
on human races, I 428
key to, allegory of Draupadī, III 251
written in allegories, II 89
Yudhishṭhira's dog at gate of Heaven, I 101
Mahā Bodhi Society
not a T.S. Section, II 428
tries to return Buddha-Gayā to Buddhists, II 427-8, 492
Mahā-Chohan
on purpose of T.S., I 69-70 &n
Mahā-Kāśyapa
knew meaning of golden flower, I 85
Mahā-manvantara(s) (Skt)
Auric Egg endures for a, III 403
Planetary Spirits and, III 402
Mahā-Parinibbana Sutta
Buddha's advice in, II 63 &n
on cremation of Buddha, I 429n
Mahā-Pralaya (Skt)
Universal Dissolution, I 9
Mahārāja (Skt)
family motto of the Benares, I 249
Maharloka (Skt)
confusion concerning, III 464
Fire Dhyānis reascend to, III 463-4
Mahat (Skt)
See also Universal Mind
Divine Radiations from, form Omniscient Mind, III 334
Mānasaputras as Sons of, III 362
Mind-Born Sons of, are 7 Hierarchies, III 294
Prakṛiti and, III 161
on root-differentiations of, III 298
as Third Logos, III 298
Universal Mind, III 161, 294, 334, 368
Mahātma(s) (Skt)
See also Adept(s); Master(s)
above all Philosophies, II 56
become Planetary Spirits, III 56
belief in existence of, III 5, 22, 130-1, 227, 275, 434

Brahmans' view of, III 131
or Brothers, III 22
compared to Saptaṛishis, II 250
conscious immortality of, III 430
contact T.S. after H.P.B.'s death, III 411, 418-20
definitions, III 5, 22-3, 53, 225-6
as dwellers on high mountains, III 227
effect of contact with, III 425-6
efflorescence of an age, III 24, 56
as Esoteric Buddhists, I 475
etymology of word, III 22
evolution demands existence of, I 339-40
fear of declaring belief in, I 339-40
few Theosophical doctrines original with, I 467
helpers of mankind, III 5
of Himalayan Circle which sent H.P.B., III 419-20
H.P.B. did not invent, I 365; III 130
as human as ourselves once, III 434
human evolution, II 250
as ideals & facts, I 464; III 425
Karma not interfered with by, III 25, 126, 425-6
living but highly refined men, III 425
meaning of, I 339
message to Indian Theosophists, I 470-5
messages from, have peculiar odor, I 469-70
messages often in handwriting of recipient, III 124
not criticizing words of, II 47
not produced by miracle, III 23
not vanquished by SPR report, III 130
overcome bad magnetism, I 475
power of, can be hindered, I 340
powers of, III 22-3, 53, 226, 419-20, 425-7
promise help to altruists, I 462-3
psychical powers of, II 88, 91
secluded records of, III 5
stand by H.P.B., I 511-12
Svamiji K.B.'s encounter with, III 419-20
term part of our language, I 496
on terms Adept, Initiate &, II 374
T.S. founding and, III 5-6
tradition records existence of, II 328
transcend own Karma, III 125-6
true ring of letter from, II 216
on writing of *S.D.*, I 343-4
The Mahatma Letters. *See* Sinnett, Alfred P.
Mahā-Yuga (Skt)
and four lesser yugas, I 124
Maitland, Edward (1824-1897)
——— *Anna Kingsford, Her Life . . .*
as anti-vivisectionist, I 500
Maji (1827-?)
great Indian yoginī, II 298
Man
See also Humanity; Mankind
Absolute Principle in, III 404, 433-4
Adepts on beliefs of, III 8
affects matter to be used by other egos, I 119
age of, III 9, 21, 29, 31-2
ancestor not an ape, III 21, 31-2
animals before, in 2nd Round, I 331
Archetypal, II 228
Āryāsaṅga on, III 435
astral form preceded physical, III 9, 31
becomes "one with the Gods," III 234, 434-5
before animals in 4th Round, I 331
began as "fiery dust," II 231
body derived from Moon, III 34
character seen in hand, II 97-100
character of, hard to know, I 73
and civilization of 19th century, I 36
classifications of, cp., II 104-6
constitution derived from Cosmos, II 310
constitution of, esoterically, III 367-8, 416-18, 430-1, 433-8
continuity unbroken, III 29
a continuous entity, II 390

copy of Universal Mind, III 161, 351, 362
creative powers of, III 434-6
crown of all evolution, II 161-2; III 36, 161, 178, 435
development on this & other planets, III 5, 7, 10, 361-3
distinct in having Manas, II 317
Divine, III 360, 366, 404, 408-9, 435
dual nature of, III 437
duty of, I 181
each, connected to one Adept, I 140
each, his own creator, III 34-5, 40, 72, 434-5
each, is part of Manu, I 117
ennobled by evolution, III 76, 161, 166, 178-80, 234, 434
fashions own destiny, I 41; III 40, 62-3, 71, 184, 187, 351, 388, 435
is final authority now, I 36
5th Round "Rubicon" for, II 321
first in 4th Round, II 231, 322
flower of evolution, II 136
future elevation of, III 72, 75-6, 161, 184, 434
future perfection of, III 388
in geometric symbolism, III 395, 416-18
gestation period of, shortening, II 423-4
God incarnate, I 41, 212; II 12, 136-7, 147, 310, 361; III 210
god of his little universe, I 119
great destiny, II 235
great work of, I 14
greater self of, religions' source, III 217
immortality, III 10, 167, 178, 260, 431, 435
incarnations, III 62-3, 73-7, 182-4
inherited tendencies, III 84-5, 183
inner or astral, not spiritual, II 36
"know thyself," II 386, 429
know thyself to know all men, II 398
knowledge of spiritual nature of, will save, I 5
latent psychic powers in, II 88
life a pilgrimage for, III 29-30, 184
lives at once in two worlds, I 45
lives on thought, I 415
made of millions of lives, II 36
is microcosm of macrocosm, I 61, 115, 118-19, 214
misfortunes explained by Theosophy, III 67, 180-2
mistaken view of transmigration, II 420-1
Monadic evolution and, I 211-14, 331-2
Nature and, III 18, 77, 430-1, 433-8
not "fallen," II 232, 268, 361
not mere atomic-molecular organism, III 351
not originally sinful, III 434
on occult path, II 264
once a, always a, II 419
is own savior, I 31
owns nothing, I 21
part of Supreme Being, I 35
perfect, is in union with all, I 13
as perfected spiritual being, III 5, 10, 76, 161, 234, 388, 434
planetary influences on, II 15-16
potency of each, in work for Theosophy, I 205
potentially a God, I 103; II 147, 163, 310; III 404, 433-4
as product of Aum, III 338
progress of inner, II 433
psychical line of descent, III 85
responsible for life atoms, II 146-7, 420-1
sevenfold nature of, II 137, 310; III 166-7, 186-92, 234-5, 367-8, 416, 430, 435q
a Soul, I 415; II 40, 90, 161; III 10
a spiritual entity, I 95
stars' composition identical with, III 334
temple built gradually, III 21-2, 75-6
ternary division of, II 104-5
the thinker, II 138; III 187
the thinker due to Mānasaputras, III 351, 362
troubles of every, partly our own, II 309

true aim of, I 139; II 355
ultimate reunion with Divine Spirit, III 62
unity of, II 143-8
universe in miniature, II 137, 403
unseen help from Adepts to, II 329-30, 433
why no remnants of antediluvian, III 31-2
Manas (Skt)
See also Higher Manas; Lower Manas
advent of, III 357, 363-4, 462-3
Ākāśa visible when, fully developed, III 365
Antaḥkaraṇa as link between Higher & Lower, III 366, 374-5
Aphrodite myth cp. with, III 318-19
attracts part of Kāma, III 296-7, 367, 408, 416, 437-8
Auric Egg and, III 364
as basis for speech, III 336, 357
conflict between higher and lower, II 298
connects Ego with the body, II 302
as container of causes, I 295
as cosmic & universal principle, I 214
Divine Consciousness when united to Buddhi, III 365, 408
the doer, the enjoyer, the sufferer, III 397
dual nature of, III 397
essential to the Self, II 317
Eternal & non-eternal, III 408
in 5th Round, fully evolved, II 224, 321
fully developed in 5th Race, II 368
guided by Ātma-Buddhi, II 364
Higher & Lower cp., III 364-5, 367, 408-9, 416
as Higher Ego, III 296, 322, 364, 408
Human Soul, III 44, 334
individualized thinker, III 191, 296
limited to one Mahā-manvantara, III 296
lower, attracts part of Kāma, III 320
in man's constitution, III 367
or mind, II 137; III 44, 168, 191
or mind as form of Vāch, III 336
not limited to one Manvantara, III 319
proceeds from Ākāśa, II 224
projects into lower Quaternary, III 318, 334
the real man, the thinker, III 397, 398
seat of real memory in Higher, II 282
seeds of thought in, II 347
stores "mental deposits," I 279
subtle delusions of, III 437
third principle in Microcosm, III 319
training of, in E.S., III 389, 438
union with Buddhi our true aim, II 355
and Universal Mind, III 367
Vaikharī Vāch and, III 336
Mānasa-Dhyānis (Skt)
as Solar Devas in Intellectual scheme of evolution, III 294, 361
Mānasaputra(s) (Skt)
connected with Venus & Mercury, III 362
higher part of man, III 362
man as Thinker due to incarnating, III 351, 361-2
or Mānasa-Dhyānis, Solar Devas & Agnishvātta Pitṛis, III 361
Monadic evolution and, I 214
now ourselves, III 409
our reincarnating Egos, III 294, 362-3
as "Pillars of Light," III 363
seven Hierarchies of, III 294
some are Nirmāṇakāyas from preceding Manvantaras, III 362
as sons of Mind or Mahat, III 294, 362
Mānasic Entity
Ākāśic records guide incarnation of, III 364
becomes Higher Self as perfect Triad, III 322
as Higher Ego, III 296, 322, 364

on incarnation of, & Lunar Pitṛis, III 463-5
Mānasic World
corresponds to Mahat, III 334
Manas-Taijasi (Skt)
Auric Egg ascends into Devachan via, III 403
Manifestation
Astral before physical, III 31-2
black magicians swallowed up at close of, II 257
cycles of, II 234, 345; III 31, 253
Eros as desire for, III 333
purpose of, in Matter, III 388
Mankind
Adepts help for, unseen, II 329-30, 410
age of, III 31-2
astral light's effects on, III 62
Atlanteans reborn in present, I 128-9, 131; II 224, 352; III 362
can only be lifted gradually, I 378; II 329
in era of wild unbelief, III 161
evolution of, not automatic, II 259-60
lover of, and Kali-Yuga, III 58
majority of, are bad, II 264
nature of, I 378
Nirmāṇakāyas' devotion to, II 410
Occultism for use of, I 381
pollutes astral of Earth, III 317
sacred heroes help, I 122
spiritual helpers of, III 5
Theosophy chiefly for masses of, III 101-2
Mantra(s) (Skt)
German mystics recognize power of, I 89
power of united endeavor and, I 90
restore self-control, I 90
Manu(s) (Skt)
See also Laws of Manu
aggregate of men, I 117; III 34
a Kshatriya, I 429
Seven, or Prajāpatis, III 338
Manuscript(s)
newly discovered, to come, II 223
some *S.D.* doctrines found on ancient palm leaves, II 223
Manvantara(s) (Skt)
See also Cycle(s); Pralaya(s); Yuga(s)
continuity of each succeeding, II 223, 267; III 388
definition, III 55
on dissolution of, III 253
divided into four Yugas, I 123
Divine Spark individualized in, II 380
each, an outgrowth of preceding, I 117; III 246
evolutionary period, III 31, 35
Hierarchy transferred in next, II 235
Karma of failure in, III 388
Karma of indifference, II 321
Mahātmas evolved out of, III 56
man a miniature of, II 321
many, needed for perfection, III 388
number of human years in, III 31
OṂ declares 3 periods of, I 311
perfection is goal of each, II 267, 380-1
Planetary Intelligences preside at, I 475
purpose of, III 56
the reign of one Manu, I 117
and serpent symbol, I 250
soul may live during entire, II 306
two eternal principles of, III 55
Mark
on gaining truths, III 134
Jesus queried about rebirth, II 141
on poverty, III 98
on sin against Holy Ghost, III 66
Marriage
celibacy and, compared, II 389
Divine Mystery of, I 20-1
fear of its hindrance to occult development, II 389
lessons of heart gained by, II 389
no hindrance to occult development, I 20-1
a question for family forum, II 246
in some life for all Adepts, I 20; II 389

T.S. views on, II 153
Mars
Boehme on formation of, II 111
cosmic influence to Earth, I 383-4
Earth-Chain does not include, I 368-9, 498, 513q
and Mercury controversy, I 498-9, 510-13
and Mercury in *S.D.*, II 228
no satellites of, II 229
in obscuration, I 369-70; II 427
spirit of rage &, I 384
Masonry
See also Freemasonry
Adept brotherhood cp. with, III 27-8
means nothing to Theosophists, III 129
relies on outward signs, III 27
Master(s)
See also Adept(s); Mahātma(s)
advice for Theosophists, I 157
appears when disciple ready, I 107
barriers to, I 475
bequeathal of Schmiechen portraits of, I lxvi
chelas used as mediums by, I 53
compassionate though aware of secret offenses, III 421
condemn thirst for phenomena, II 403
on contact with, after H.P.B., III 411, 418-20
copy nature, I 505
cyclic help by, I 462; II 9-10, 301; III 97, 283-5
danger of, physical appearance among men, III 426-7
on declaration of belief in, I 385-7; II 47; III 413
demand altruism for chelaship, III 277, 457
dictated *S.D.* to H.P.B., I 319 &n, 343, 345-6, 347; III 412
disciples of true Arhats, I 475
do not deal with personal concerns, III 412, 424-5
do not interfere with Karma, III 425-6
exemplify man's perfectibility, II 12, 60
exist as facts, II 46-7, 328-9
facsimiles of letters from, I liv-lv, 345-7
faith in, brings victory, III 275q
fidelity to, II 46
great function of, III 64
help not withdrawn after 1898, I 462
help the T.S., II 46
H.P.B. did not invent, I 365, 386
imitate charity of, I 505
incapable of ingratitude, I 64, 511
influence T.S. through E.S., III 344-6, 391-3
on Karma, I 503-4; II 245; III 345-6
Karma respected by, I 462
on knowledge & curiosity, I 368q
letters to Judge from, I liv-lvi
live for humanity, I 70
living men, II 12; III 425
Lodge and, as ideals & facts, III 413, 425
love for orphan Humanity, III 329-30
loyalty to, & magnetic rapport with, III 275-6, 391, 413, 419-20
Māyāvi-rūpa of, III 385, 426
meaning in evolutionary scheme, I 313-14
meditation subject, III 454
messages and H.P.B., II 215-17
on messages claimed to be from, II 445-6
messages have peculiar odor, I 469-70
messenger of, comments, I 107-9
Messengers periodically sent by, I 303, 462-3
misconceptions about, III 424-7
on moral worth of T.S., I 155
most perfectly organized body in world, I 505
necessities of evolution, I 201
neither exoteric Brahmans nor Buddhists, II 54-5
occult help from, I 341

on Olcott as head of T.S. until his death, II 201-2
on Olcott's visit from, III 426
plan for world at large, II 11
prayer to, I 62
precipitation method of H.P.B. and, I 308-10
pretence to messages from, proves contrary, III 411
as "pre-Vedic Budhists," I 476
privilege of obedience to, III 392
proclamations of belief in, II 47, 328
program of, and T.S., I 243, 244-5; II 19
on purpose of T.S., I 318-20
radiance surrounding, III 446
refuse to drop Brotherhood object, I 69
reluctant to display magic, I 59-60
on Schmiechen portraits of, I lxviii
seal, II 48
Serpent symbolizes, I 250-1
Sinnett said H.P.B. deserted by, I 510-11
stand by Olcott & H.P.B., I 63-4
T.S. destiny in India and, III 418-20, 458-9
T.S. founding ordered by, I 58
T.S. of, open to all, I 55-6
is Thyself, I 51
traditions abound in Europe and Asia about, II 328
Truth not divulged all at once by, I 107-8
unknown philanthropists, I 380
on unselfish work for, III 412
urge brotherliness to dark nations, I 69
views of Science and, I 376-81
warning about psychic powers, II 11
why T.S. founded by, in America, II 114
why West chosen for new effort by, III 458-9
work scientifically not sentimentally, I 479
work to uplift humanity, II 329-30; III 344

Materialism
baneful glitter of, I 35
curse of money as, I 111
downward tendency of, III 329
driving, out of heart, I 112
enervates body & character, I 483
growing among Hindus, I 478
in human nature, I 110
Karma of, an affliction, III 19, 38
in modern science, I 379-81
a passive condition, III 329
requires selfishness, I 484
Spiritualistic, I 350-1
Theosophy opposed to, III 173
way out of abyss of, I 180-1
Western cp. to Eastern, I 479-80

Materialization
Hermetic axiom not negated by, II 332
medium as agent for, II 331
not the only element of mediumship, I 52
process of, I 198-200
of "spirits of the dead," I 352-3

Mattei, Count Cesare (1809-1896)
Homeopathic system of, I 283

Matter
See also Prakṛiti
atomic structure of, II 146-7
of bodies used by later Egos, I 119-20; II 320
in constant change of state, III 11-12
"descent" into, II 345, 360, 401-2
during Pralaya, II 225, 345
essence of, invisible, I 352
evolution by use of, III 35, 56, 161, 166
factors needed for power over, I 397
as fire-mist, III 188
an illusion, III 12
man responsible for, I 119-20
man's cast-off, used by lower kingdoms, II 322
mesmerizer exudes subtle, II 33
mind co-existent with, III 166
no such thing as dead, III 12
on "organic" & "inorganic," I 208

permeable by 6th sense, II 237
permutations of, II 319-20
potentiality of, II 40, 232
primordial or original, I 159; III 12, 188
radiant, of science is astral, III 46
relativity of, III 37
reused by Soul in next life, II 43
Spirit and, co-eternal, I 119, 159; II 136, 232, 238; III 186, 328
Spirit needs experience in, II 232, 360, 401
three dimensions of, II 237
Matthew
on contentment, I 21q
on diet, II 390
Elias reborn, III 110
golden rule, II 163
Jesus queried about rebirth, II 141
on karma, III 155
karma in every word & act, III 33, 110
on karmic account, III 100
on karmic stamina, II 444
on kingdom of God, II 356
on perfection of man, II 365
reincarnation in, III 110, 183
on temptation of Jesus, III 255
Maugraby
a Black magician, II 94
Māvalankar, Dāmodar K. (1857-?)
Adyar room of, I 265-6
called to Tibet, I 67; III 459
gave up caste, marriage, etc., I 470
Hodgson report and, III 124
joins T.S. in India, I 67
prophecy on departure of, II 102
——— *Dāmodar and the Pioneers of the Theosophical Movement* (comp. Sven Eek)
letters to Judge in, I xxiii
Māyā (Skt)
causes of, III 417-18
of material world, II 407, 411
self-created, I 213
Māyāvi-Rūpa (Skt)
of Adept cp. with Astral Body, III 385, 444-5, 446, 449
Adepts use kāma principle to form, III 334
Master visits Olcott in, III 426
yogic use in disappearance, I 410
McClure's Magazine (New York)
Herbert Spencer on society, I 423q
Spencer on coming despotism, I 423
Mead, G. R. S. (1863-1933)
on Basic Principles of man & their Aspects, III 325-7
biographical sketch, II 493-4
E.S. Instructions and, III 290-1
on E.S. Instructions vs. "Eye Doctrine," III 325
on two paths to Nirvāṇa, II 327 &n
Vāhan's ed. statement by, II 243
views of early Church on rebirth, I 430
Meaning
seek, of each event, I 22
Mechanics
ancients knew, I 447
Meditation
aspiration to Higher Self, III 64, 374, 452, 454
Aum should be subject of constant, III 455-6
best Teacher for, is 7th principle, III 452
calms the mind, III 292
centering in Buddhi, III 452, 456
color yellow and Mantra use in, III 455-7
concentration and, III 455
control of vital currents &, II 269
counteracts dark powers, III 457
daily, suggested, II 417
exam questions on, III 369n
on fame, money, & power, II 7
on fixed time & place for, III 292, 373, 394, 454, 455
on Highest Self, II 9; III 277
leads to inner self-dependence, III 292
on London paper for, III 453-4
Master on lifetime, III 455
a must for E.S. progress, III 373-4
mysterious power & dreams, II 261

obstructions to, II 372
on OṂ, I 6-10, 163; III 457
in Patañjali's *Yoga Aphorisms*, II 7
petty objects not recommended for, III 453-4
practical details omitted for E.S. & T.S., III 456
purify desire in life-, II 8-9
reason for not eating before, III 454
self-examination during, III 373, 374
study &, refines mind, I 327
subjects for, III 454
thoughts for, III 394
on tone, I 8-9
on true sun aids humanity, I 137
two sorts of, II 7
Union with Supreme Being, I 72

Medium(s)
A. J. Davis, I 350
Adepts are conscious, I 355, 395
advice on stock market, I 291-2
all men are, I 52-3
astral light used by, III 46
astral of, attracts soulless phantoms, III 48
condensing focus for astral forces, I 454-5
on control "Jim Nolan," I 198ff, 404-6
control of entity through, spleen, II 458
criminals infuse, III 191
dangerous to seek, I 351
evils attracted to, II 279-80
find no consensus from "spirit" world, III 146
Greek vestals were, I 287
holds back the departed, II 394
ignorant of source of phenomena, I 308, 391, 395, 452; II 357-8
money paid to, I 108
nervous imbalance of, III 48, 145-6, 190, 334-5
O.T. prophets were inspirational, I 286
of old took no money, I 286-7
on parroting of facts by, III 145
revealed no laws, III 146
same spook appears to different, at same time, III 143-4
what is a, I 51-4, 353-6; III 334-5

Mediumship
accusations of irresponsible, II 215-16
astral light used in, III 45, 136, 143-6
can be a blessing instead of curse, I 90
can be inspiration from higher planes, I 53
dangers of premature, II 357-8
evil consequences of, II 279-80, 394, 403-4
exists despite prejudice, I 51
explanation by "controls" of, II 458
explanation of, I 405-10
on flimsy proofs of, III 144-5
a Frankenstein created by Spiritists, I 51
illumination is not, II 367
irresponsible, II 29, 357-8
no true creativity without, I 53
not a blessing, II 367
not concerned with real Man, I 108, 353-7
not wholly messages from dead, I 51
physical memory and, I 453
in slate-writing, I 355
as worship of dead, III 191

Medulla Oblongata
has sensory plane function, III 323

Memory(ies)
animals have, of pain inflicted, II 72
astral, I 453-4
brain, differs from soul, II 281
every organ has its own kind of, II 41-2; III 348
main obstacle to meditation, II 8, 372
in mediumship, I 453
Occultism and, II 277

Men
See also Man; Mankind
all, are mediums, I 52
majority inherently bad, II 264

Menasseh ben Israel, Rabbi (1604-1657)
——— *Nishmath Hayyīm*
on transmigration, I 419
Mental
overcoming, bias, III 85-8
plane cannot be ignored, I 92-3
positions & karma, II 254 ; III 37-8
Mental Healing
See also Metaphysical Healing
danger of Black Magic in, III 256
on dangers of, I 227-30, 294-7
forces sickness to inner planes, III 256-7
Mental Science. *See* Christian Science
Mercury
awakening from obscuration, I 370
fed by solar substance, II 111
governs intellect, I 9
Mars &, controversy, I 498-9, 510-13
Mars &, occultly related to Earth, I 383-4; II 228
no satellites for, II 229
not of Earth-Chain, I 368-9, 498, 513q
in planetary wheel of Jacob Boehme, II 111
spirit of wisdom &, I 384
Mesmer, Anton (1734-1815)
agent of brotherhoods, II 31
mesmerism antedates, II 31
Society of Harmony founded by, II 301
Mesmerism
See also Hypnotism
accepted under name of hypnotism, III 174, 212
Ben Franklin condemns, II 31-2
cures by, II 31, 289
deals with material forces, I 254-5
denied by science, III 174
Dods revived, in America, II 32
Du Potet's "secret" work on, II 32
Higher Self not influenced by, I 254-6; II 33, 35
Hypnotism and, I 144-5; II 31-40
ideation of subject of, altered by operator, I 255-6
as magnetic anaesthetic, III 212-13
Mesmer only rediscovered, II 31
not a superstition, I 144
opposition & investigations into, II 32
process differs from hypnotism, III 214
proves that soul exists, II 91
rechristened Hypnotism, I 144
Senate lectured on, I 145; II 32
Mesmerizer
aura of, II 33
cannot touch Higher Self, II 33
escaping control of, II 39
fluid thrown off by, II 33
grossness of, II 35
misled unless a trained seer, II 36
Message(s)
bogus, claimed to be from adepts, I 393-5, 469-70
claimed from dead exposed, I 454-6
"Master's seal" and, II 48
on Masters', to H.P.B., II 215-16
Master's, to J. Niemand, II 48
Messenger(s)
cyclic appearance of, II 10; III 283-4
disappearance of, III 285
H.P.B. as, of Masters, II 215-16
Master's, comments, I 107-9
on preparing for 20th century, I 244
recorded in each century, II 301
of 20th Century, I 303; III 97
Messiah
tradition of the, I 441
Metal(s)
breaks magnetic connection, II 93
lead, sacred to Saturn, II 446
Metaphysical Healing
See also Healing
black magic and, I 227, 229
criticism of Judge's views on, I 232-5
dangers of, I 227-30, 282, 283, 284, 294-7; II 290-3
heals by mind only, II 436
Judge's reply on his criticism of, I 236-7

strong in U.S., I 282
teachers of, responsible for effects of, I 297
Metaphysics
Adepts emphasize need for, II 229
Adepts urge science of, I 381
little errors in, cause great problems, II 323
needed to escape illusion, I 400
Metempsychosis
See also Reincarnation
reincarnation cp. with, I 430
Metonic Cycle
in ancient Egypt, I 517 &n
Microbes
as builders & destroyers, III 193
theory in epidemics, III 193-4
Microcosm
macrocosm and, III 298, 380
pentagon symbol for, III 380
Middle Classes
support Theosophy most, II 373
Migrations
bird, cp. to human life-wave, II 426-7
Milky Way
other systems like ours in, III 16-17
Mill, John S. (1806-1873)
constant self-analysis affects, III 262
Millennium
Christian expectations for, I 292
Millionaire
Karma of an altruistic, II 350-1
Mind
See also Manas; Thought(s)
action proceeds from, III 259-60, 397, 398
action proceeds from Cosmic, III 351
alone suffers or enjoys, II 336
basis of speech, III 360
can ignore personality in Devachan, I 169
concentration and Thought, III 261-3
constitution of our, is monadic, III 351, 409
as container of causes, I 295
cosmic potential, & basis of all law, I 214
an entity, II 338
factors for power over, I 396-7
is field of all experience, III 397
grossness of Western, I 327
knot of the heart and, I 31
magnetic & electric ties of body to, II 288
Mahat or, of Universe, III 294, 298
on modifications of the, III 260, 261-2
mystical vs. practical, III 87
no Karma beyond, I 25, 31
openness of, needed, III 85-8
overcoming habits of, III 85-8
plane cannot be ignored, I 92-3
principle is creator & basis of all law, I 214
reading, II 95-7
real life of the, II 162
seeds left in, by thoughts, II 347
tendencies of, III 85, 261, 408
Theosophical doctrines leaven, II 20
training of, III 85-8, 260, 262-4
Mind Cure
and Christian Science, II 405
dangers of, I 227-8, 282, 294-7
defects of, II 290-3, 410-11
misleading and dangerous, III 398-9, 409-10
Theosophy &, contrasted, II 436
Mines
not found by psychic senses, II 271
Missionaries
corruption of East by, II 150
Coulomb conspiracy and, III 124
Missionary
work in Ceylon, III 117-8
Moderation
path of, I 92
Moggallāna
Buddha's disciple, II 442
murder of, II 442
Moguls
plunder India's treasures, I 183
Mohammed (570-632)
did not advocate polygamy, I 373

had only one wife, I 373
and high mountains, III 228
on kismet, III 40
visions of, III 228
Mohammedan(s)
See also Islamism
accused of forcing the *Koran* on others, I 373
devotees on the soul, II 457
fakirs of India are, III 170
legend on time in Paradise, III 248
Orthodox beliefs of, I 374-5
Mohyus, Ericius (also Eryci Mohyi)
——— *Sympathetical Powder of*...
on mesmerism, II 31
Moksha (Skt)
means release from bondage, II 408
Molecule(s)
atoms and, inform the organs, III 351
how atoms become visible as, III 351
in hypnotism, I 417
Keely ruptured etheric, III 351
Molinas, Miguel (1640-1697)
——— *Golden Thoughts*...
on paradoxes, I 19
on way of peace, I 17-18
Monachesi, N. R.
not a member of T.S., III 135
——— *The Hidden Way Across the Threshold*
not endorsed by T.S. secretary, III 135
Monad(s) (Gk)
Agnishvātta Pitṛis complete the, III 409
animal, may rise to a higher, I 427
are globes in various stages, II 229-30
Auric Egg ideal body of, III 403
do not "land" on empty Earth, II 229-30
door into human kingdom closed for new, II 231, 314, 419
each, mirrors own universe, III 351
on earth chain become human, II 228
as eternal pilgrim, I 212-14
evolutionary course of, I 211-14; II 229-30; III 158, 294, 361-3, 388, 409
evolutionary plan alters in 3rd Round, II 322
evolving now as Ātma-Buddhi-Manas, I 212; III 409
human, defined, II 230-1
the immortal spark, III 158
individualizes mind, III 351
interstellar atoms and, III 351
of Leibniz an Atom, III 363
limited number in each Manvantara, II 230, 314, 419
loss of soul not, II 306
Lunar, "ooze out" astral doubles, III 361
One Flame but countless sparks, III 409
potential gods, I 212
of preceding chain become human on Globe A, II 228
same, in all kingdoms it traverses, II 315-16
triple evolutionary scheme and, III 294, 361, 409
united by Cosmic Will, III 351
why, descends into matter, III 388, 409
Money
altruistic expenditure of, II 350-1
curse upon, I 111
dangers of large corporate funds to T.S., II 205-6
dedicated to T.S. work, II 205-7
desire for, II 330
healing practice and, II 275
medium's, haunted by astral beings, I 108
Monsters
parentage of, II 379
Moon(s)
analogy between Earth and, III 306
Chain, Lunar Monads, & Pitṛis, III 306, 361-2, 409
in Church imagery, I 433
comets and, I 481-2
corpse of our old planetary chain, I 434-5, 519-20; II 228; III 445

cycles of man's migrations &, I 569
a deserted planet, II 228, 423
eclipses of, & folk beliefs, I 550-1
fate of, I 434-5, 519-20
feast days fixed acc. to, I 433
in final pralaya, II 427
fourteen-year cycle of, I 517
globe of a previous Manvantara, II 423
influence on men's bodies, II 111-12
Julian calendar and, I 433
in last stage of dissolution, III 389
monthly cycle of, II 165
noxious emanations from, I 434
of planetary bodies, I 481
planets having more than one, or "astral body," III 445
progenitor of our globe, I 434, 519-20; II 228, 427; III 14, 34, 389, 445
spiritual principles transferred to earth chain, II 228
sun produces, says Boehme, II 111-12
when life impulse left, III 389

Moral(s)
Adepts help, progress of man, I 202
Adepts value, results of science, I 380
basis of, life, I 181
character and cyclic impressions, I 522
condemnation is immoral, II 282
cowardice can kill, I 507-9
of curing vs. control of others, II 289
discord caused by inflicting pain, II 71-2
disorder of our cycle, I 294
epidemics, III 192-4
hypnotism leads to, death, I 417
law of compensation, III 70-1, 167
Masters relieve, suffering, I 320
nature-spirits have no, II 404
responsibility, III 71
sample of, defects, III 83-4
sense spurred by Theosophy, III 72

Morality
of capital punishment, I 488-90
high, needed to practice yoga safely, II 337
Karma accords, of so-called "rights," II 254
law of Karma and, I 502-5
needed not legislation, I 527
science's lack of, and Adepts, I 379-81
T.S. progress and, II 403

More, Thomas (1478-1535)
obscured adept, I 128

Morgan, Arthur E. (1878-1975)
——— *Edward Bellamy*
excerpt of Judge letter, II 152n

Mormonism
similar to Islam, I 375

The Morning Advertiser (New York)
announces Judge's commemoration, III 224
death bed message of W.Q.J. in, III 222-4

Morphine
more degrading than alcohol, II 377

Morya Dynasty
claim Buddha was of their caste, I 429
and Koothoomi, I 430

Moses (ca. 1200 BCE)
an Adept, II 441
against witchcraft, I 286; III 191
law of, is retaliatory, I 490, 492, 502; II 341
lineage of, acc. to Jesus, I 441
received Law on high mountain, III 227
warned against necromancy, I 197, 286, 288-90

Moses, Wm. Stainton (1839-1892)
precipitated messages and, I 308

Moslem
scholars represented at World's Fair, II 129

Mother(s)
influence and reincarnation, II 302
karma brings child to, II 302, 379
milk of, and body of child, II 302
use of will on children, II 289-90

Motion
eternal, III 358
"fire" on our plane, III 358
as magnetism, electricity, sensation, etc., III 358
Motive(s)
brotherly, need testing, III 92
can nullify good karma, III 89
determines black or white magic, I 47
developing true, exercises Will, II 395
on elevating, III 422
energy expended on high, same as on low, II 445
for entering E.S., III 421-3
Karma and, I 139
on methods and, of Adepts, I 202
most important factor, I 146
no personal, in Great Sages' help for world, I 218
psychic capacities and, II 393
pure, atones for errors, I 55
pure, helps progress, I 50, 148
right, protects against black magicians, II 415
is root of morality, III 72
for seeking truth, III 92
source of good, II 463-4
transmutes energy, I 380
try our best for others, II 349
trying for better, II 395, 441, 463, 466
work for Theosophy and, I 204
Motto of T.S.
no dogma more binding than, I 57
sums up practice & belief, I 36
Mountain(s)
free of lowland's coarse magnetism, III 226
Moses given Law on high, III 227
Peter the Hermit & William Tell drawn to, III 228
retreat of fakirs, hermits & sages, III 225-7
sacred & forbidden fastnesses, III 227
why Mahātmas dwell in, III 226
world tradition about revered, III 228-9
Mukerjee, J. *See* Mukhapadhaya, Pandit Jagneshwar
Mukherji, Kali Prasanna
on ascetic powers, I 410-11
on yogic powers to disappear, I 410-11
Mukhopadhaya, Pandit Jagneshwar
leader of Hindu Revival, I 442-3
Mūlaprakṛiti (Skt)
abstract ideal matter, III 358
and laya center of higher world, III 332
primordial matter, III 12
Müller, F. Max (1823-1900)
gave only exoteric significance of Āryan literature, II 87
Morya translation of, I 430
on Nirvāṇa, III 25
says "self" best expresses Īśvara & Ātma, I 71
——— *Gifford Lectures*
on Buddhist idea of Karma, I 120-1
on Buddhist morality, I 120-1
——— *India: What Can It Teach Us?*
on Sanskrit literature, I 184
Mumbai. *See* Bombay
Mummification
and cremation contrasted, II 348
Egyptian reason for, I 517
not to chain soul to body, II 376-7
Muṇḍaka-Upanishad
analogy of bow, arrow, & target, I 10, 163
meditation on OṂ in, I 10 &n, 163
on One Light, I 435
"shaves" away error, III 96
Murder
burdens all mankind, III 219
capital punishment and, I 488-9, 492
easily justified, III 218-9
Karma of, I 500
why, a sin, III 219
Music
Buddha and, II 324
Music of the Spheres
is light of the Logos, etc., III 336

Pythagorean numbers and, III 338
Myalba [dMyal-ba] (Tib)
kāmic soul in, III 353
Mystery(ies)
logarithms taught in the, I 313
of Occultism on finding the Way, II 400
of primordial substance, II 239
Mystic(s)
no idleness for the, I 18
power of self-ideation, II 274
is smiling & joyous, I 18, 19
Mysticism
first step in, I 4-5
veiled language of, I 43
Myth(s)
Devil or serpent, II 92
reverberations of ancient times, II 93

N

Nāda-Brahmā (Skt)
meaning of, I 7-9
Nāḍī(s) (Skt)
definition, III 314
location in brain, III 322-3
preparation of, II 103
Nāḍīgranthams (Skt)
on Coulomb scandal, I 11
definition, I 10
duration of T.S. predicted by, I 10-11
on future of U.S.A., I 17
Indian astrological prophecy, II 101-3
predict Olcott's time of death, I 11
Naidu, Iyalu
helped Olcott form Adyar Headquarters, I 67
notes on Judge's talk, II 83-5
Nāma-Karaṇa (Skt)
name ceremony to identify castes, III 165
Nanjio, Bunyīu (1849-1927)
on Japanese Buddhist Sects, I 85-8
Napoleon I (1769-1821)
defeat of, and Nirmāṇakāyas' influence, III 26
downfall seen in heavens, II 15
Red Man's red letter and, III 26
Nara
and Nārāyaṇa, I 15
Naraka (Skt)
and Avīchi, or hell, I 439
Nārāyaṇa
See also Vishṇu
destroys with chakra, I 15
and Nara, I 15
Nasmyth, James (1808-1890)
"willow leaves" of, I 136
Nāstikism [non-belief]
H.P.B. sent to destroy, III 419
Prayāg letter does not induce, II 55
Nation(s)
each, affects all, III 8
have gone out like torches, II 259q
karma of Egos and, III 236
psychical inheritance of, II 262
Nationalism
has no binding inward sanction, III 160
Nature
See also Prakṛiti
alchemy uses lower agents of, III 436
alone is blind, III 16
aspirant never deserted by, III 398
Boehme's scheme of, II 108
control over, not transferable, II 29
co-workers with, vs. misusers of, III 328
duality of, II 344-5; III 416, 436-7
ebb and flow in, II 167
has endless power to delude, I 49
forms in, change, II 368
goal of worker with, III 396
harmony with, II 71-2, 226
hierarchies guide, III 14
laws of, impartial, II 87
man's destiny and, III 72-3, 328-30, 398, 431
mercy in heart of, II 245
no favoritism in, III 40
no intentions in, only laws, II 268-9

object of, I 380
one vast machine, II 76
as relentless & destructive, II 350
triune aspect of man &, I 403; III 430-1
unaided fails, II 269
unity of, II 226
wisdom of, is Theosophy, II 380
Nebular Evolution
cp. to human evolution, II 231
Necessity
orbit of, II 72
Necromancy
ancient uses in time of Saul, I 285-6, 290
practices of, I 148, 285-7
as spiritualism, I 197, 285, 290
Nemesis
See also Karma; Law
Karma a stern, to the worldly, I 31
Neophyte. *See* Chela(s)
Neresheimer, Emil A. (1847-1937)
Āryan T.S. Treasurer, II 513
biographical sketch, II 513-14
at World's Fair, II 122
Nerve(s)
altering of, in mesmerism, II 38
astral body & astro-, II 38
Nervous Fluid
and astral senses, II 37
Nervous Plexuses
seven great, I 389
New Age
not far away, I 36
scientific revelations do not herald, I 107-8
The New Californian (San Francisco)
founded by Jerome Anderson, II 479
Judge Lectures reported in, III 178-92
Judge talk in, III 203-4
published by Louise A. Off, III 178
New Order of Ages
Thomas Paine and, II 78-9
U.S. Great Seal and, II 79 &n
New Race
forming in America, II 25-8
New Testament. *See* Bible
New York Evening Sun
on ancient technology, I 447q
New York Morning Journal
describes American T.S. office, I xxvii-xxviii
New York Sun. See *The Sun* (New York).
New York T.S.
emphasis on Spiritualism, II 69
New York Times
on Blavatsky, III 208 &n
Newton, Henry J. (d. 1896)
early treasurer of T.S., II 434
Nichi-Ren (1222-1282)
Buddhist sect's founder, I 85
Niemand, Jasper. *See* Keightley, Julia
Nigamāgama Dharma Sabhā
Hindu Revival Society, I 441-4
Nirmāṇakāya(s) (Skt)
act for good under Cosmic laws, III 25-6
Adept may become, III 66, 449-50
Adepts of prior Manvantaras, I 127
definition, III 386
Egyptian Gods cp. with, I 127
guide humble as well as great, III 450
guide men of destiny for good, III 25-6, 450
influences mankind from behind scenes, II 410
Judge blends with, I xxxiv
Karma not interfered with by, III 25
of left path as well as right, III 383, 386
Māyāvi-rūpa of, III 449
and Mystery of "Metaphysical Moon," III 450
no sex to, II 410
partial incarnation of some, III 450-1
of Path of Compassion, III 386
refuse Nirvāṇa, III 25, 66, 396, 449
reincarnate for good of world, II 227
Spiritualistic phenomena &, III 26
as surviving spiritual principles, II 227

two grades of, III 449-50
Nirvāṇa (Skt)
avoidance of Karma in, II 70
goal of Eastern School is not, III 395
longings end in, II 394
Nirmāṇakāyas &, III 25, 66
Nirmāṇakāyas give up, II 410
not annihilation, III 25
not permanent state, III 396
pralaya for globe chain, II 425
reached by Middle Way, I 92
refined selfishness in, II 327, 351
refusal of, III 25, 396, 449
as taught in Buddhism, I 85, 86
two paths to, II 327
in unmanifested world, III 332
will all reach?, II 375
Noetic (Gk)
acts from within out, III 348, 351
Force is spiritually dynamic, III 348, 351
Nucleoles
"dark," compared with "atoms" of the Secret Doctrine, I 212
Nucleolus
in organic cell, III 349
Nucleus
of cell has consciousness, I 213
Number(s)
developing inner senses and, II 105
Dhyāni-Chohans and, II 226
everyone has a, value, I 148
in mathematical ratios, III 314
ten called perfect, III 314

O

Oakland Times
Judge tour reviewed in, III 115
Obedience
and loyalty to Guru, III 393
Obelisk
Egyptian, in New York City, I 253
Obscuration(s)
cp. with sleep, II 425
Mars is now in, II 427
Rounds, rings and, of deserted planets, II 424-7
Obsession
Bible accounts of, I 285-6, 288
capital punishment one cause of, II 303, 369
includes insanity, II 287
magnetism can cure, II 288
mediums can stop, with elementals, etc., I 90
phenomena of, II 287-8
Occult
chemistry in phenomena, I 398, 402
Occult Arts. *See* Occultism
Occult Development
desire for, not commended, II 277, 415, 417
Occult Phenomena. *See* Phenomena
Occult Powers. *See* Occultism; Psychic Powers; Psychism
"Occult Room"
and shrine at Adyar, I 263-5
Occult Science
no missing links in, I 208, 212
One Fundamental Law of, II 226
has own methods of research, I 379q
philanthropy the basis of, I 377, 379-81
philosophy of, I 207-18
prerequisites for, II 307, 416-17
synthesis itself supports, I 208
The Occult Word (New York)
on self-study vs. reading, III 132-4
T.S. orientation of, III 125
Occultism
See also Practical Occultism
age limit in, III 461
arouses lower forces, III 435-6
brings out latent good & evil, II 264-5
on charity, duty, and discipline, III 257
and cultured classes, II 11
on dabblers in, I 45, 146
definitions, I 216; III 261, 298
demands will, intellect & memory, II 277

depressing influences in, II 395
difficult among Westerners, II 416-17
discrimination of left & right paths needed, III 258-9, 466
dreams & visions as one begins in, II 397
evil fate of some students of, I 45-6
exists in West as well as East, I 468
false claims of progress in, II 446
for the few, II 244, 416-17
first step(s) in, I 4-5, 155; III 264
gnostic science, I 208
on gossip & slander, III 257
hidden elements in, I 147, 217
on higher students of, III 54, 277
how to study, III 285-6, 379, 460-1, 465-6
how to study correspondences, III 404
H.P.B.'s method of teaching, III 285, 430-1, 432
imagination in, I 307-10
independent spirit can interfere with, III 393
as knowledge of Self within, III 260, 277
law of correspondences and, III 298, 312-13, 416-18
on life of, II 395
loneliness in study of, III 461-2
magic in, I 45
Masters know Laws of, II 415-16
on Mind & mental energy in, III 261-2
moral preparation for, III 282
Nature as an explanation of, III 264, 433-5, 437
not book-knowledge, I 78
not child's play, I 47
not easy, I 106, 217
not for the emotional, I 147
not Theosophists' goal, II 277, 416
obedience required on Path of, III 392-3
one Life of, I 208
plethora of books on pseudo-, I 146
powers of, I 106-7, 307-11
powers of, explained, I 391-2
precipitation and, I 391-8
preparation for, II 417
pursuit of, I 106-7, 217-18; II 264-5, 397, 415-16
pursuit of, and ethics, II 243-4
results from self-effort, I 21
right motive before delving into, I 148, 381
rules on patience & humility, III 258
selfishness in, will destroy aims, I 19
on silence, III 257
spurious, II 446
spurious, of false prophets, II 193
student of, not alone, I 45
study without ethics leads to black magic, III 465
teaching karma & reincarnation better than, I 157
T.S. not a school for, I 244, 319-20, 379; II 277, 415-17
tobacco use and, II 278
transmutation of forces in, I 147-8, 380
true, based on ethics & philosophy, II 244
truths of, for man's use, I 381
Universal Brotherhood and, I 379-81
Universal Brotherhood first step in, I 4-5; III 264
as vast as Cosmos, III 465
warnings on psychism, III 258, 435-6, 457
Will used in, II 391
Occultism, Western
on Adepts & Nirmāṇakāyas of, III 451-2
geared to new race, III 451
Great Lodge influences, III 452
pure Indian practices not for, III 451
suited to its peoples, III 451
on teachers of, III 444
Occultist(s)
belong to no one country, III 451
how, developed, III 373
immortality must be won by, III 260

makes himself, III 373
must elevate plane of consciousness, III 260
needed in coming ages, I 146
not urged to follow Yogis, III 451
use mediums to tell truth to Spiritualists, I 198
use power for others, III 256
uses force with knowledge, I 147
Ocean
raindrops &, simile, II 449
tides in great, of Nature, II 167
Ochorowicz, Julian (1850-1917)
——— *Mental Suggestion*
on Bouillard and phonograph, I 216
Off, Louise A.
publisher of *The New Californian*, III 178
Olcott, Henry S. (1832-1907)
at Adyar, I 142
biographical sketch, I 63-70
Brahmanical thread worn by, I 68
a Buddhist, I 67
a Buddhist & a Brahman, I 363
Buddhist campaign of, in Ceylon, III 117
cremation of Baron de Palm &, III 6
declares belief in Masters, I 386
devotion to Masters, I 69
devotion to T.S., I 176
disagrees with Judge's views on India, II 114n, 115n
envied H.P.B., II 215-17
grateful to Judge, I xxxiii
H.P.B. not understood by, II 320
H.P.B.'s first Western disciple, II 215
on Hindu revival, I 442
Hodgson and, III 123
Inaugural address warns against dogmatism, I 221-2
Indian members propose retirement of, I 63
on "Indian Sybilline Books," II 101
interviews Hindu astrologer, I 10
Isis Unveiled proofread by, I 192
Judge as successor to, II 114n
Judge defends reputation of, I 363
Judge nominates, for president, I 64, 67; II 208
on Judicial Committee results, I xlvii
on magnetic cures, II 289
Mahā Bodhi director, II 428
Masters stand by, I 63-4
a Master's tribute to, II 202
on Master's visit to, III 426
Nāḍīgranthams described by, II 101
not a yogi, III 419
a parent to T.S., II 44
as President & Founder, II 209-10
resignation revoked, II 44, 201
sacrificing worker, III 90
on Theosophical Congress, II 171-2
on T.S. split in America, II 431
time of death prediction, I 11
tried to unite Buddhists, I 363
work in Japan and India, III 142
World's Fair message, II 134
——— *Buddhist Catechism*
a great work, II 51
——— *Historical Retrospect . . .*
on Judge & H.P.B., I xix &n
——— *Old Diary Leaves*
claims Masonic degrees proposed for T.S., I 321-2
date started, I 386n
on formation of T.S., I xviii
on Judge, I xxv-xxvi
on Masters' portraits, I lxviii
——— *People from the Other World*
on Eddy's homestead, I xviii
Old Testament. *See* Bible
Old, Walter R. (1864-1927)
unsavory role of, in Judge case, I xlvi, li
wrong prediction of, I 422
——— *What Is Theosophy?*
geological theories discussed in, II 317-18
Oliphant, Laurence (1829-1888)
T. L. Harris and, II 192
Oliphant, Margaret (1828-1897)
——— *Memoir of the Life of Laurence Oliphant . . .*, II 192n

OṂ [or AUM] (Skt)
avoid use of, until purified, III 286
awakening pineal gland by use of, III 321
cautions on pronouncing, III 321
correct pronunciation of, II 406
intones 3 periods of Manvantara, I 311
meaning of letters in, I 7, 311
meditation on, I 6-10, 163; III 454-5, 455-7
misuse of, in anger, III 310-11
never used in anger, III 286
not used for psychic power, III 321
pronouncing, III 286-7
pronouncing, with sign in Group only, III 394
on resonance of, III 338
sacred Vedic syllable, I 6-7, 14
and seal of T.S., I 12, 249, 253-4
should begin all prayers, I 6
true prayer & use of, III 404
Vedic study should begin & end with, I 6
verbal repetition of, I 4
OṂ MAṆI PADME HŪṂ (Skt)
geometrical equivalent of, III 380
The Omaha Bee (Nebraska)
Hypnotism article in, III 212
on Theosophy in America, III 156-9
Omnipresent
Infinite principle, II 296, 323
One Life
is Consciousness, III 369
doctrine of, I 118
pervades all, I 212-13
Open Path
versus secret, II 327
Opportunity
Law judges us by, used, III 356
Oracles
claiming to be Jesus or Buddha, I 112
Grecian, never to be bribed, I 287
used Vestals as mediums, I 287
Organ(s)
are centers of action, III 351-2
are centers of force, III 347
Dugpas use only physical, III 347
ethereal centers of, II 34
every, and cell has a memory, III 348-9
inner, I 75, 76; II 33-4
Karma unites material & spiritual, III 352
lower self acts through lower, III 348-52
Mānasic & Kāmic type, III 349
physical, not the real, III 351-2
on relation of, to higher planes, III 347
Oriental
is no heathen, II 170
religions at World's Fair, II 129, 170
Oriental Department
purpose & its beginnings, II 189-91
taken over by European section, II 191
Oriental Library, Adyar
archives, I 142
and Oriental Department, II 190
T.S. archives of Indian Section, II 189-90
Origen (185?-254?)
believed in reincarnation, II 158
condemnation of, by priestcraft, I 431
taught pre-existence of souls, III 110
taught reincarnation, I 307, 417-18, 430-2
——— *Contra Celsum*
on incarnation, I 431
Original Sin
doctrine of, & perfectibility of man, I 439, 440
Orthodoxy
Masters & Ṛishis are beyond, II 56
Osiris
and Typhos in nature, I 126
Ozone
Masters healed H.P.B. by using, III 139-40

P

Pacific Ocean Continent
home of future peaceful Race, II 25
Padmapāṇi (Skt)
legend conceals cosmological history, III 360
as lotus symbol, III 356-8
mystery of Great Sacrifice or, III 357
spiritual progenitor of men, III 356
synonyms of, III 356
as Wondrous Being & Tree of Adepts, III 358
Padma-Purāṇa
on mystic OṂ, I 6
Pain
as a kind friend, I 296
ladder of, can aid soul, II 245-6
meaning of, I 40, 41
pleasure &, both needed, II 400-1
Paine, Thomas (1737-1809)
and Adept influence, I 274; II 77-9
America's future and, I 423
America's future envisioned by, I 149
revolt against tyranny, III 156-7
unjustly libeled, III 156-7
——— *The Age of Reason*
envisions America's future, II 78
——— *Common Sense*
American independence inflamed by, I 149; II 78
——— *Rights of Man*
quoted on new order of ages, II 79
Palestine
not cradle of civilization, I 186
Pall Mall Gazette (London)
Besant review of *S.D.* in, III 209
Pall Mall Magazine (London) [begun in 1893 as offshoot of *Pall Mall Gazette*]
Theosophical terms in, I 496
Palm, Baron Henry L. de (1809-1876)
cremation and funeral of, I 267, 322; II 80; III 6
Palmistry
in Chaldean *Book of Job*, II 98
Arpentigny & Desbarolles &, II 97-9
of Gypsies aided by clairvoyance, II 97
notes on, II 97-100
well known in India, II 98
Pantheists
Deists, Theists, and, welcome in T.S., II 86-7
Parabrahman (Skt)
See also Absolute; Paramātman
apex of Absolute World, III 332
first proposition of Theosophy, III 55
God of Moses cp. to, III 108
no more vague than scientific notions of force, I 174
Parā Vāch and, III 337-8
unknowable nature of, III 108
Paracelsus (1493?-1541)
astral light called sidereal by, III 46
on astral spirit as hidden sidereal force, III 334
on lead as talisman, II 446
obscured adept, I 128
on original cometary matter, III 334
original matter known to, III 12
on sidereal light or force, III 334
Paramātman (Skt)
See also Parabrahman; Supreme; Supreme Soul
self-existing, uncreated, I 159-60
Pāramitā(s) (Skt)
Buddhist scriptures on, III 305n
Perfections of Bodhisattva, III 305 &n
Parent(s)
duty to influence child, II 453-4
karma of, & wicked child, II 434-5
power to influence child, II 302, 435
Parliament of Religions
at Chicago World's Fair (Columbian Exposition), II 119, 122, 127-8
conception of, II 169
Judge represents T.S. at, I xliv, 435n
message from Olcott to T.S. Congress at, II 134

scientific aspects of T.S. not emphasized at, II 156-7
summary of events at, II 168-70
topics of lectures, II 127-8
a triumph for T.S., II 133
Past
knowing of, lives profitless, II 468
Patañjali (ca. 650 BCE)
See also Rāja-Yoga
——— *Yoga Sūtras*
altruism the condition for studying, II 416
conditions for practicing, II 416
describes Ego as Spectator, II 364-5
on eye of perceiver & luminosity, I 358-9
on favorable karmic apparatus, I 524
glamour and, I 358-9
"ideal" striving, III 64
Judge version cited, II 7n
on Karma, III 246
Kunte translated part of, II 83
meat-eating ignored in, I 101
on mental deposits, I 278; III 280, 292
moral life basis of yoga, II 337
morality of, I 57
on one mind directing several bodies, III 26 &n
on perfection, III 38 &n
rules for destroying mental obstructions in, III 292
rules for meditation in, II 7
on seeds of mind, I 295
on self-reproducing thoughts, III 292
on Soul as spectator, III 261
study of, needed, II 407, 416
on three kinds of karma, II 463
Will only inferred in, II 8
on Yoga Powers, III 58
on yogic feat of disappearance, I 411-12
Path(s)
of action, I 54
alcohol & drugs obstruct, II 278
altruism & virtue bases of, I 78, 79; II 441
cause for rebirth in family advanced on, I 79
of devotion leads to knowledge, I 162
direction of true, I 3
finding the, II 370-1, 400
first step on, II 337, 399
foundation of occult, I 155; II 244
left- & right-, I 45
of love, III 438
meaning of the, I 34
no boasting on, III 30
not for the lazy, I 18, 19, 79; III 379
obedience & loyalty needed on, III 393
of occultism, II 264-5, 398-9, 451
only for self-reliant, I 21
overanxiety about one's, II 370-1
postures & breathing, not the, I 4
practical occultism is incidental to, I 4
self-discipline on entire, III 64
self-reliance and, III 30, 64-5
teachers' advice for treading, II 278
Theosophists follow, to Truth, I 34
Theosophy teaches, III 64-5
true, is simple, I 50
of true Theosophist, I 17-24
two, to Nirvāṇa, II 327
of wisdom & virtue, II 278
The Path (New York)
aims & purpose of, I 3, 62
change of title, I 497, 505
Fullerton as acting publisher, II 47
humorous letters to, I 223-7
independence of, I 237-8
Jasper Niemand and, II 48
Judge on, I 34-6, 47, 56-7, 62, 109-10, 191, 237, 248, 332-3
Judge on its future, I 141
most subscribers not in T.S., II 199
not official organ of T.S., I 48, 62, 386
not rival to T.S. journals, I 3
once sole journal for T.S. in our hemisphere, I 56
predicts unrest in U.S.A., I 293

recognition of Masters in, III 413
ref. to H.P.B. article in, on reincarnation, II 334
staff headquarters of, I 248
a world influence by 2nd year, I 48
Patience
a step toward initiation, II 451
Patriotism
a high sentiment, II 374
no defence needed for, II 374
of Thomas Paine, II 78
universality of love and, II 374
Paul, St. (1st century CE)
accords with occultists, I 315-16
an Adept, I 103
concerning next incarnation of, II 383-4
on Karma, II 140, 162-3; III 111
once a persecutor, II 384
possessed woman helped by, I 289, 292
reincarnation and, I 307
says some become a law unto themselves, II 337
on spiritual gifts, I 103-4
on spiritual wickedness, III 328
threefold division of man by, III 43-4
war of natures in man, I 14
Peace
seeking good in all brings, I 22
way of, is conforming to Divine Will, I 17
Pelletier, Ernest (1947-)
——— *The Judge Case*
on T.S. & E.S. Correspondence, III 273
Perfected Men
Adepts or, & H.P.B., II 135-6
Perfection
Cause of Sublime, II 12
human, III 434
human, and Brotherhood, II 12
human, and immortality, II 267
of Initiates, II 136
of lower man, II 419
purpose of each Manvantara is, II 267
of Spirit, II 406
When will, be reached?, III 388
Periodicity
of evolutionary plan, II 223
manvantaric, II 345
Persecutions
religious, II 343
stain pages of history, II 144
Personality(ies)
See also Lower Self
alteration of, in obsession, II 287
belongs only to body, I 84
blind to Ego or true Self, II 365
no one, can express all Karmic Atoms, III 353
separate "I" or basis of illusion, I 31-2
work against principle not, I 500
Peru
subterranean passages leading to Venezuela, I 532
1 Peter
on charity, III 38-9 &n
2 Peter
on time, III 248
Peter the Hermit (1050?-1115)
Crusaders attack from high mountains, III 228
Phenomena
See also Precipitation(s); Psychic Powers
of accelerated growth in plants, I 401
astral music signals, II 23
astral, no proof of spirituality, I 49-50
dangerous, I 4, 377-8, 409
demand for, II 60
discarded in T.S., II 356
of disintegration, I 400-2
excluded from Parliament of Religions, II 125-6
explanation of spiritualistic, I 352-3
few converts to Theosophy via, III 93, 94
force of, & types of, II 329
H.P.B.'s, and Society for Psychical Research, III 93
H.P.B.'s bell, II 23

H.P.B.'s early control of, I 193; III 207
H.P.B.'s early, not mistakes, II 19
imagination and, I 308-10
Masters on, and T.S., I 155
not explained by hypnotism alone, I 402
not for the masses, I 4, 377-8
not proof to skeptic, I 60; II 403
of obsession, II 287-8
path of, and allegory of the Heart, I 539-41
perfume often part of, II 22
pretended messages or, II 446
proper investigation of, II 357-8, 402-3
requisites for occult, II 307
rose, at Enghien, II 22
rule against claims of, II 446
of seeing elementals, II 432
of transporting objects, I 400-2
true wisdom not found in, I 4
types of, and elementals, II 340
will not solve world's sorrows, III 94
will power needed for, I 402, 410

Philadelphia Press
described Judge, III 117

Philanthropy
altruism or, basis and goal of T.S., I 280, 319, 379; II 277, 416
basis of occult science, I 377
benefits of, II 351
Brotherhood is highest, I 380
for inner man, I 280
richest pleasure from, III 70

Philosophers
impudence of modern, I 220-1
who believed in soul, II 90

Philosophy
craze for Indian, II 371-2
Eastern, and the West, II 371
Eastern literature and, II 89
Eastern, needed by West, II 87
foundation of occult path, I 155; II 244
of Jacob Boehme, II 107-12
Masters on, and T.S., I 155
nothing new in modern, I 221
of occultism is synthesis, I 208
only true, on earth, I 475
road to, III 374
study, practice altruism, I 179
Theosophy is, I 214
West needs Āryan, I 245
wrong, leads to sorrow, I 280

Physicians
helping evolution of the race, II 436

Pictures
in astral light, II 263, 412; III 45-9, 60
precipitated, of H.P.B., II 29
and recollections before sleep, II 432

Pilgrimage(s)
shrines of India symbolize man's, III 29
solitary nature of inner, III 30
soul's, timeless, III 29-30
why Man's, if already divine, II 359-61

Pineal Gland
former and future use of, II 368
function as third eye, II 458; III 380
misuse in eye cure, III 305
on motive for awakening the, III 321
on passage from 3rd ventricle to, III 303
soul ganglia and the, III 303

Piṅgalā (Skt)
Iḍā &, tonal correspondences, III 314
sushumṇā and, III 322-3

Piśāchas (Skt)
worship of, in India, I 57

Pitṛi(s) (Skt)
See also Lunar Pitṛis; Solar Pitṛis
ancestors of Humanity, III 294
lunar, and lunar chain, III 306
two main classes of, III 294

Pituitary Gland
soul ganglia and the, III 303
use of Word and, III 333

Plane(s)
See also Worlds
confusion of states with, II 248-9

cosmical, correspond to 7 states of consciousness, II 233, 248-9
interpenetrate each other, III 186-7
law of progress on higher, I 210
macrocosmic, correspond to microcosmic principles, III 298
mental, cannot be ignored, I 92-3
principles &, compared, II 341
Sages two, beyond us, I 209
seven, of differentiation, II 136, 233
seven, of evolution, III 187
as states of consciousness, II 233; III 186
of waking, dreaming & dreamless sleep, I 80-3

Planet(s)
See also Globe(s); Mars *et al.*
"dead," as objective, II 225
develop under cyclic law, II 234
during minor & great pralaya, II 224-5
on eccentric movements of, II 268
as "foci" in astrology, II 15
Kaballah on seven sacred, III 338
moon not one of seven, II 423
musical intervals & harmonious motion of the seven, III 338
other, inhabited, III 66
other, within astral of this earth, II 391
sevenfold evolution on each, II 422-3
stars influence greater than, II 15-16

Planetary
chain & its pralaya, II 424-5
life-forms vary on other, chains, II 368
scheme of evolution, II 233-5, 422

Planetary Spirit(s)
Avalokiteśvara is all, III 359
each man & principle has its own, III 402
guide future planetary evolutions, III 56
Mahātmas evolve into, III 56
mission & appearance on Earth, III 402
Rulers of 7 Sacred Planets, III 402
seven Ṛishis as, III 338

Platte County Argus (Nebraska)
"A Woman's Noble Work" in, III 204

Pleasure(s)
Bhagavad-Gītā on three kinds of, II 379
richest, is in giving, III 70
turn to poison in the end, II 378-9

Pledge of Esoteric School
alterations of 1891, III 340-1
as appeal to Higher Self, III 277, 345, 421-2
brings real character to surface, III 274-7, 279-80, 283, 432-3
cannot force men to obey, III 421
clauses examined, III 422
direct orders and, III 345
duty to Theosophical Movement, III 422
given to Masters' Lodge, III 345
Karma of disobedience to, III 421, 432-3
magnifies power of thoughts, III 274-5, 316
no gossip or slander permitted by, III 282
Pledge-fever &, III 274-7, 279-81, 282-3
purification required by, III 282-3
secrecy of signs & passwords, III 341
unchanged by H.P.B.'s departure, III 345
unexpended karma and, III 257, 279-80
on violation of, to secrecy, III 432

Polarity
of cells altered in mesmerism, II 37
of objects altered in apportation, II 313

Pole(s)
alteration of, II 318, 412
North, & Imperishable Sacred Land, II 24

Politics
T.S. avoids, III 203

Polygamy
on Mormon practice of, I 375

as taught in Islam, I 373
Poona Lodge
Judge visit of 1884, II 82-3
Pope
Tibetan, cp. to Catholic, II 155
Population
apparent increases, II 418
destruction by Nature, II 350
Porphyry (233-305?)
on "star-like" astral light, III 46
Poverty
not bad karma, I 21, 195-7, 484-5
is relative, I 242-3
on sympathy for, II 330
of T.S., I 111
Power(s)
See also Psychic Powers; Psychism
acquired by purity & knowledge, I 79; III 305
Adept never claims to have, II 446
on Adepts' help in gaining, I 106-7
can lead to death, III 306
evolutionary decree of new, II 305
knowledge and, needed to avoid illusions of Devas, I 148
misuse of, forbidden in E.S., III 305-6
needed to seize knowledge, I 79
over mind and matter, I 396-7
true, given to server of humanity, II 395
true, not for sale, I 23
Practical Occultism
See also Occultism
altruism & love needed for, III 438
stems from right mental views & philosophy, III 293
true ethics and, III 293, 298, 436-8
uses powers only for others, II 395; III 298
what is, III 264, 293, 298
Practical Theosophy
advice to new student, II 398-9
Pradhāna (Skt)
undifferentiated matter, III 368
Prajāpati(s) (Skt)
advice to sons, I 5
Brahmā-, as Vāch, III 338
as "Fathers" of physical man, III 295
Prakṛiti (Skt)
See also Matter; Nature
absorbed in the Unmanifested, III 55-6
evolution of, III 161
Purusha and, I 159; II 108; III 55-6
Pralaya(s) (Skt)
Dark Chohans preside at, I 475
evolution and, III 55
Great & Minor, II 224-5
Karma latent during, II 408
Mahā-, at close of Manvantara, III 253
matter during, II 225
as night of Brahmā, III 253
Nirvāṇa as a planetary, II 425
obscuration compared to, II 424-5
OṂ is silent in, III 338
periodic embodiment after each, II 345
plan for next Manvantara in, II 223
planets intact during minor, II 224-5
sleep & death as minor, III 253
when does it occur?, II 425
Prāṇa (Skt)
as aspect of Jīva, III 335, 367, 386
aspects of, III 320, 335
or breath, III 44, 189
derived from Sun, III 189
fashions physical body, III 335
as vital force, II 269
vitality in Eastern division of man, III 44
why considered a principle, III 386
Prasad, Rāma
on Ākāśa, III 359-60
Praśna-Upanishad
rebirth in, I 413q
Pratyeka Buddha (Skt)
Nirvāṇi reemerges as a, III 396
Prayāg Letter
authorship of, II 54-8, 215-17
Besant's view of, II 53-4, 217
Buddhism & Brahmanism the same esoterically in, II 55

Master's message to Brahmans of Prayāga T.S., I xlv &n, 470-5
Prayer(s)
Jesus on, III 404
is not justice, III 99-100
OṂ leads to true, III 404
OṂ should begin all, I 6
T.S. has no, or doxology, II 149
to Father "in secret," II 149
on true Occult, III 404-5
Preachers
materialistic and cowardly, I 32
Precipitation(s)
See also Phenomena
of Adept messages, I 391-8
Adepts on, of letters, II 300
astral light and, III 61
chemical & electrical, I 390
H.P.B. demonstrated, to Judge, I 398
H.P.B. on, I 309-10
imagination used in, I 308-10, 354-5; II 300, 307
medium a passive agent of, I 391
mediumistic, I 399; II 29
occult, rationale, I xlix-l
of pictures not uncommon, II 29
Predestination
Karma vs., III 71
not Theosophical, III 71
Pretas
worship of, in India, I 57
Pride
Lucifer's downfall, I 47
one who has, must fail, II 452
spiritual, of Hindus, II 113-14
Priesthood
admission of women to Buddhist, I 439
among all religions same, I 439
Primordial Substance
See also Mūlaprakṛiti
of our globe, II 239
Principle(s)
See also Ātma(n); Buddhi; Manas
Ākāśa as 5th universal, II 224
Boehme calls, "tinctures," II 109
of deceased sidereal body freed, II 234
distinct from plane it operates on, II 341
each, reflects every other, III 326
Eternal & unknowable, of Theosophy, III 233
four, & three aspects described, III 319-20, 325-7
higher, torpid after sudden death, II 303
Lodge helps in search for, II 304-5
of man, II 310
of moon, II 228
mysterious, hinted, II 239
omnipresent Infinite, II 296, 323
One, & its 6 vehicles, I 143-4; III 262
One, only, II 274
overlap one another, III 326
periodic manifestations of, III 233
planes of action and, III 416-18
sevenfold, II 137-8
seven manifested, 3 hidden, III 314
seventh, man's best teacher, III 452
seventh, present in other six, III 62-3
sheaths of soul &, II 459-60
on ternary & sevenfold, II 104-5
Universal Cosmic, & elements, II 224
Universal in Boehme, II 110
Unknown, Eternal, II 136, 323-4
Vāch & 4 highest, III 336-8
Prisons
never reduce crime or vice, I 5
Proctor, R. A. (1837-1888)
——— *Our Place Among Infinities*
on horary astrology, III 290
Progress
astral light and true, I 154-5
forfeited if claimed, II 446
natural & artificial, II 465-6
no one path for, II 465
pace of spiritual, III 65-6
sure path of spiritual, I 105
true, on inner planes, II 433
true spiritual, defined, I 50
unnecessary to know our inner, II 433

Propensities
converting the energy of, II 447
good and evil, II 447-8
Prophecy(ies)
about America, II 24-8
about Sanskrit, I 16-17
of Berossos, I 424
in dreams and clairvoyance, I 448
on Fraternity behind T.S., I 303
on future moral upheaval in U.S., I 17, 293-4
hunger for, I 495
a "lugubrious," II 436
in psychic Zodiac, I 423
pure motive in, II 367
on *S.D.* & future messenger, I 303-4
seismic, by astrologers, I 422
on T.S., I 10-11, 243-5
Prophets
false, I 112; II 192
ignoble schemes of U.S., I 112-13
Protestants
persecutions of, and by, II 144
Prototype(s)
of man in astral, II 225
pre-existence of, II 423
Protyle
a primordial substratum, I 209
Proverbs
on Solomon, I 305
Pryse, James Morgan (1859-1942)
biographical sketch, II 507-8
H.P.B. Press started by, II 508
printer for Āryan Press, II 507
Psychic(s)
Black Lodge fosters, growth, II 11
gifts are added after spiritual powers developed, II 356
inheritance in child, II 366-7
lineage of inner man, III 85
motive in, development, II 393, 416
realm to be entered from above not below, II 355
search for treasure, II 271
study confined to Psychical Research Congress, II 125-6
united endeavor &, work, I 90
Psychic Force
acts from without in, III 348
how cells propelled by, III 348
"Noetic Action" and, III 348
on psycho-molecular action, III 348
Psychic Powers
an abnormal development, III 38, 91-2
dabbling with, forbidden, III 92, 305-6
dangerous for selfish Americans, II 305
dangerous without altruism, II 11; III 92, 97q
inheritance of, III 85
selfish desire for, III 78, 91-2
Theosophy explains, III 67
training of, II 88, 246-7, 356-8, 416
in various types of precipitation, I 390-2
Psychic World
corresponds to Kāma in man, III 334
full of delusion, II 357
plane of interstellar atoms & cosmic dust, III 334
Psychical Research Society. *See* Society for Psychical Research
Psychism
allurements of, I 49-50
dangers & deceptions, II 247, 357-8, 416; III 423-4
for good or evil, I 90
growing in Western world, I 108
investigation of, II 357-8, 416
irresponsible, II 43, 246-7
latent in man, II 88
of left-hand order, III 258
overestimated, II 356-7
Psychology
of "glamour" in daily life, I 360
T.S. not a school of, I 318
Psychometry
cannot measure soul, III 119
definition, III 119
experiments can depict, III 120-1
experiments with Indian coin & seal, II 84

experiments with ostrich eggs, II 89
a form of mediumship, I 52
Prof. Buchanan and, III 265-7
proves soul's existence, II 91
Ptolemy, Claudius (2nd century CE)
——— *Tetrabiblos*, II 76
Public Opinion
on fear of, I 507-8
on rising above, II 397
Punishment
capital, reform needed, II 285
causes for, II 159-60
fondness for, increases evil, II 254
and Karma, I 138; II 284, 336
for reviling a righteous man, II 70-1
Pure-Land Buddhist Sect
Amita Buddha and, II 157
Doctrines of, I 86-8
vow of, I 438
Purification
effort needed for, II 236-7
and illusions of Devas, I 148
of motives and actions needed, I 148
sorrow & pain needed for, II 349
of thought as well as body, I 83; II 399
Puritans
little influence in U.S. founding, II 77
Purusha (Skt)
See also Spirit
body disappears when, withdrawn, III 290
definition, III 55
indrawn during night of Brahmā, III 55-6
interpenetrates all, III 56-7, 290
man overshadowed by, III 290
perfect consciousness of, III 57
and Prakṛiti, I 159
Purushottama and, III 55
spirit in man, III 155
Supreme Abode both, and Prakṛiti, II 108
Pythagoras (582?-495? BCE)
on music of the spheres, III 338
schools of, I 45
on world's emanation from Chaos, III 338

Q

Qabbālāh. *See* Kabbalah
Qualities
guṇas compared, II 109
Quotations
constant use not helpful, II 62-3
Qur'an. See Koran

R

Race(s)
See also Earth-Chain; Root-Race(s)
abandon globe when egos advance, II 424-5
Black Lodge seeks to wreck, II 11
both physical & spiritual, II 426
cataclysms indicate end of, I 206, 459; III 59, 66-7
cosmic environment densifies with each, III 20
dark & white, I 69, 318
dark & white in T.S., I 446
disappearance of, I 205-7, 459; III 181-2, 253
each, includes all ethnic groups, III 20, 253
European fifth sub-, II 25
evolution of, and Kingdoms, I 331-2
on four great Ages of, I 459-60; III 58
fusion of, in America, I 150, 480; III 21
future, much taller, II 26
human, develop in 4th Round, III 59
intermixture of, II 25-7
karma, national & family, I 336
Mahātmas above limits of, III 253
moment of choice for each, III 59, 65-6
new element to develop with fifth, II 368
new, in America, II 25-8; III 19-20

new senses developed with each, III 253
not from one common stock, I 161
overlap & vary through Yugas, I 459-60
on primary and sub-, I 459-60
Root, family & sub-, III 20
Root, sub-, & offshoots, II 422
seven great, in evolution, I 520; III 20
subject to cyclic law, III 59
Theosophical connotation of, III 20
white must help dark, I 318
why, die out, I 205-7; II 425-7
Rajah [Rāja] (Skt)
chaṇḍāla legend and, III 36
Rājanya (Skt)
line of sages, I 429
Rājas (Skt)
as bad action, II 109
pleasure leads to poison, II 379
Rāja-Yoga (Skt)
See also Patañjali
or culture of concentration, I 73
devotees of, in Hindustan, I 3-4
of fixing thought on high ideal, III 259-60
and Haṭha-Yoga, I 72-3; III 289
as higher yoga, III 308
on Mind as origin of everything, III 259
and pursuit of happiness, I 3
union of highest science & religion, I 3
virtue & altruism bases of, I 78
Rāja-Yoga Messenger (Pt. Loma)
on John H. Judge's visit to Pt. Loma, I xix
Rājputs (Skt)
or Kshatriyas, I 428
racial & spiritual traits of, I 428-9
Red, descendants of solar race, I 429
Raju
head of, I 550-1
Rākshasas (Skt)
astral beings, III 45
Rāma
God incarnate, III 105
opposed by Rāvaṇa, I 126, 440
as Savior, II 157
Rāmāyaṇa
Tulsi Das wrote version of, I 440
written in allegories, II 89
Rambo, E. B. (1845-1897)
biographical sketch, II 472-4
Pres. of Golden Gate T.S. branch, III 168
Ranade, Rao Bahadur Mahadev Govind (1842-1901)
on Founders of T.S., II 83
Rangampalli, Jagannathiah (1852-?)
biographical sketch, II 516-19
worker for T.S., I 443
Ransom, Josephine (1879-1960)
——— *A Short History of the T.S.*
ref. to Coues libel retraction, I xl n
Rāvaṇa
black magician-king, I 126
oposes Rāma, I 440
Ray(s)
only Adept recognizes chela of his, II 440
similar, among students, II 456
Reading
alone cannot produce self-knowledge, III 132-4
choice narrows as one grows wiser, III 315
of degrading literature, I 506
much, too little thought, I 151; III 87, 315
on passive, and skimming, I 151
Reason
intuition and, II 435-6
limits of, II 323
Rebirth. *See* Reincarnation(s)
Recollection
as hindrance to meditation, II 372
memory and, cp., II 281
Recording Angel
astral light cp. to, III 47
Reform(s)
all systems of, ineffective, III 160
of caste system needed in India, II 113-14

legislation cannot reap true, III 160
moral, versus political & social, II 285, 386
of physical condition not enough, III 161
pressing need for, III 159
as temporary cures, II 182, 285, 386
Theosophic truth will, humanity, II 185
Reformation
Luther's, & the Theosophical Movement, I 486
Reincarnation(s)
accepted in time of Jesus, II 160, 453
of Adept is voluntary, III 364
all have had numerous, II 419
all Nature experiences, III 127
allows karma to operate, III 71-2, 75, 99-100, 167, 169, 183-4, 245
ancients believed in, III 178-9
of animals, I 426-8; II 247
of animals found in Hindu folklore, I 426
astral light and, III 8-9
of Atlanteans in America, III 19
Ātma-Buddhi-Manas in, III 448
balance wheel, III 167
Bible references to, I 305-7, 419-21, 440; II 139, 141-2, 158, 159, 453
blind man and, III 155
brotherhood & evolution in, I 120
causes of, III 246-7, 364
of cells, I 118
charity to all now makes future, better, I 316-17
Church condemned, I 307, 422
clergy on, II 159
is common sense, III 176
creation of new souls not, II 419
cycle of 1,500 years, I 338-9; II 166
cyclic law in operation, I 519
desire for life one cause of, II 339
Devachan and, I 84, 337-9; III 42, 45, 245-7
Egos all in touch through, II 314
in every religion, II 160
evidence for, I 203
evolution requires, II 138; III 161-2, 176-8, 178-80, 235
explains inequalities, III 167, 182-4
faculties & character developed through, III 73-4, 180-82, 448
family tendencies accounted for by, I 203
of friends and relatives, III 40
in Gospels, III 110, 155, 177, 183-4
heredity and, I 93-6, 203; III 183
higher lamas may have immediate, II 450
Isis Unveiled did not deny, II 334
Jews believed in, I 304-5, 440
Jīvanmukta does not need, II 272
Judge's reminiscence of, I 571-2
Kāma-rūpa dissipated before, III 352-3
Kardec school on personal, II 334
Karmic tendencies, I 26-8, 276-9
Karmic ties relate to, II 314-15
Law of, not limited to man, I 114
of lives in our bodies, III 36, 178, 246
lost chord of Christianity, I 417, 422; II 160
of man as an animal, II 419-21; III 318
man's elevation requires, III 73-6, 161-2, 176, 180
mental tendencies cause, I 413
of monads, II 321-2
Mozart's early ability explained by, II 160
on need for, III 73-7
new personality essence of past, III 33, 34, 182, 397, 448
not for personal "I," I 132
on not remembering our, III 182-3
objections to, III 182-4
only an incident, I 33
past and future, within present, III 72
pre-existence of souls and, I 430
on proclaiming belief in, III 101-2
purpose of, II 267, 307-8; III 176, 178-84
racial evolution ensured by, III 75-6, 181-2

recognizing those from the past,
  I 83-4
reimbodiment or, II 138, 160
result of prior conduct, II 182
of Romans & Greeks today, II 352
sentimental objection to, III 183
sex and, II 249, 298-9
short, has purpose, II 307-8, 450
taught in early Christianity, II 138,
  158-60
of thoughts, III 127
twin doctrines of Karma and,
  I 156-7; III 6, 19, 35, 71-2, 94, 99,
  154, 235-6, 245-7, 252
types of, III 247
upper Triad basis for, III 364
vindicates Nature, II 138
vindicates sense of justice,
  III 99-100, 167, 176-7, 182-3
will and, after attaining Supreme,
  I 81
in *Zohar* & Talmud, I 418
Religion(s)
  See also Parliament of Religions;
    Wisdom-Religion
  all, had origin in truth, I 22
  bigoted, deaden conscience, II 343
  cycles of, II 167
  failure of conventional, III 67, 70,
    161
  God the source of, I 436-7
  highest, is Truth, II 203
  of India, II 50-2, 87-9
  keys to unlocking, II 157-8
  man's greater self is source of,
    III 217
  may hold man back, I 41, 42
  new, to be Theosophical, II 428
  no, higher than truth, I 35, 36, 57,
    436; III 154, 166
  no single, or sect predominates
    T.S., I 361-4
  One, behind all, II 154-5
  and Science, II 84
  Science and, should never be
    separated, II 135
  similarity of major, I 437-41
  T.S. foundation of future, I 318
  Theosophy is, itself, I 214

Theosophy reconciles science and,
  III 161
true, defined, I 35, 57
Religio-Philosophical Journal (Chicago)
  on astral light, III 135-7, 143-6
  attacks on Blavatsky, II 182-3
  editor of, witnessed séances, III 136
  on Hinduism & Theosophy,
    III 265-7
  letter to, on Kiddle incident,
    III 121-3
  mediumistic prophecies & "spirit
    lore," I 404-5
  regarding Gopal V. Joshee,
    III 127-8
Religious
  conflict with Science, II 84
  persecution & conscience, II 343
Reminiscence
  in Devachan, II 281
  as "memory of the soul," II 281
Remorse
  mantric nature of, I 89-90
Renunciation
  See also Sacrifice
  and crucifixion of Jesus, I 526
  the Great, I 526-7
Repentance
  constant, to be avoided, I 31
  of "sinner," I 56
Reservoirs
  of ancient India, I 451
Resignation
  total, mental, II 411
Retaliation
  implies a person, not a law, II 342-3
  Karma is not, II 341-2
Revelation
  on Book of Life, III 100
  Ezekiel's vision and, I 15
  on karma, III 111
  on man as incarnate God, I 421-2
  and mystery of "666," I 14
  rebirth implied in, I 440-1; II 141-2
  system of ciphers in, III 107
  on wonder in heaven, I 433
Reverence
  for H.P.B., II 60-2
  little, in our Age, II 62

Review of Reviews (London)
ed. examined spiritualism, I 360
Revue des Deux Mondes (Paris)
Émile Burnouf upholds T.S. in, III 165
Right(s)
Godmothers of, Living, I 24
rule that leads to, II 349
on so-called, I 504
on so-called equal, II 253-4
Ṛig-Veda
Gāyatrī quoted from, I 311
grander view of God than Islam, I 374
Ṛishi(s) (Skt)
above all systems of philosophy, II 56
Brahmans' view of, III 131
or Elder brothers, shield race, I 140-1
evolve into Planetary Spirits, III 56
great powers of, I 92
knew laws of nature, III 53
knew Sidereal cycles, II 234
Mahā-ṛishis and, as sages, III 53
once lived among men, I 567
as perfected or exalted men, III 5, 64
preserved knowledge of ages, III 5, 53, 64
Subba Row on, I 366
superior knowledge of ancient, I 413
unlimited knowledge of natural laws, III 5
Rites or Rituals
See also Initiation(s); Mystery(ies)
Egyptian, II 450
likeness of varied religious, I 438-9
Roman(s) and Greek(s)
as Atlanteans reborn, II 352
styles evident today, II 352
Roman Catholic Church
achievements of, foster dogmas, II 205
bloody history of, III 164
claim only true Christianity, II 169
doctrines and rituals borrowed, III 108-9
evolution not recognized by, III 103
forced Galileo to recant, III 106
mummery & dogmatism of, III 164
persecutions of, and by, II 144
rituals borrowed from East, III 164
Romans
on internal conflict, II 378
on lawlessness, II 337
Röntgen, Wilhelm Conrad (1845-1923)
discovery of "cathode [X-]rays," I 499-500
Roosevelt, Franklin D. (1882-1945)
Great Seal and, II 79n
Root
the "Rootless," II 323-4
Root-Race(s)
See also Race(s)
America to usher in Sixth, II 24-5; III 21
Fifth, includes Europeans, III 21
Fourth, developed man's present form, III 20
sub-races & family races, III 20
zones for development of, III 20
Rope Trick
Algerian, a hypnotic feat, III 172
Rosary
borrowed from Orient, III 108
used in ancient times, I 438
Rosenfeld, Sydney (1855-1931)
——— *The Stepping Stone*
play mentions Theosophy, III 153
Rosicrucian(s)
Adept influence in, order, I 273
claims to secret knowledge, III 27
Eastern sages differ from, III 27
as Fire Philosophers, III 447
on imitators of, III 443-4
mystics using Christian phraseology, I 273
ritualism mark of, III 27
theoretical as opposed to genuine, III 444
true, do not charge fees, III 444
true, serve Masters and mankind, III 443

Round(s)
all 7 planets traversed in one, III 387
animals get man's cast-off coating in 4th, II 322
anthropoids at close of 4th, II 230-1
Archetypal Man on Globe A in 1st, II 228
choice for good or evil in 5th, II 321
a cycle of the life-wave, III 387
difference between a "Ring" and a, II 422-3
each, has its own Dhyānis, II 225
Earth-Chain completed at end of 7th, II 424-5; III 387
element of ether in 5th, II 224, 237
evolution proceeds through 7, I 330q
evolutionary cycle of globes and, I 330-2
fire in preceding, II 237
Fourth, develops man, I 331-2; II 322; III 59
on interval between 2 terrestrial, III 387
kingdoms pass through lowest to highest, II 322
life in early, II 238, 321-2
man appears first in 4th, I 331q; II 322
meaning of one, II 422
model for future, set on 1st, II 233, 321-2
moon will dissolve by end of sixth, I 435
new element at end of 4th, II 224
no new human monads in 4th, II 314, 322
and obscurations, II 424-7
perfection realized at close of 7th, II 233
plan of monadic evolution alters in the 3rd, II 322
seven evolutionary, I 330-2
on stream of monads in first two, II 322
subject to cyclic law, III 59
Round Towers
allegory on keeping fires at the, I 541-4
once used by descendants of White Magicians, I 543-4
Row, T. Subba. *See* Subba Row, T.
Roy, Ram Mohun (1774-1833)
on OṂ, I 7
Royal Asiatic Society
on Buddhism, II 375
Rule(s)
of great teachers imply free choice, II 461
occult, re. claims of power, II 446
occult, re. "seventh seat," II 451-2
of secrecy abolished by T.S. in India, II 454
Rūpa (Skt)
influence in séances, II 353
Rūpa-Loka (Skt)
Arūpa-Loka cp. to, II 394
Rurik, Prince (9th century)
first Russian ruler, III 205
H.P.B.'s descent from, III 205
Russell, George Wm. (Æ) (1867-1935)
concerned over future of T.S., II 3
and Dublin Lodge, II 3
formed *The Hermetic Society*, II 3
Henry Wallace and, II 79n
Judge esteemed by, II 3-4, 5-6
poetic tribute to Judge, II 4
on W.Q.J. as adept in sacred lore, II 3
——— *Letters from Æ*
on Judge's writings, I xxix
Ryan, Charles J. (1865-1949)
——— *H. P. Blavatsky and the Theosophical Movement*
on Boston vote of American Section, II 431n

S

Sacred
Imperishable Land, II 24
syllable OṂ, II 406
Sacrifice
of lower to higher ego, II 461

spiritual benefit through, I 105
voluntary, on altar of Life, II 463
Saddharmapundarīka Sūtra
Nichi-Ren altered doctrine of, I 85
Sage(s)
causes for birth in family of, II 43
debt to great, II 106
definitions, III 53-4, 64
Eastern, carry indelible inner mark of Order, III 27
Eastern, in present cycle, III 53-4
Hindu accounts of Himalayan, III 227
on imitating Adepts and, II 405
live to regenerate world, I 218
T.S. can aid, of past, I 186
Saint-Germain, Count de (18th C)
a messenger, II 301, 366
Saint-Martin, Louis Claude, Comte de (1743-1803)
on Jacob Boehme, II 110q
a messenger, II 301, 366
——— *L'Homme de Désir*
widely read, I 274
——— *Theosophic Correspondence*
ref. to Boehme, I 274; II 112 &n
Saintship
on claims of, II 402
Salamanders
dwell in astral light, III 45
Salem Witch Trials
obey Mosaic Codes, I 286-7
Salvation
by faith, I 438; III 109
an illogical scheme, II 350
only in material existence, III 37
Zoroastrian, not vicarious, I 437
Saṃdhyā (Skt)
and Saṃdhyānśa, I 124, 125
Sāṃkhya Sāra. *See* Vijñāna Bhikshu
Saṃsāra (Skt)
wheel of, and karmic law, III 126
as wheel of rebirths, II 444
1 Samuel
on Saul, I 285q
2 Samuel
on wisdom, II 283
San Francisco Call
on Olcott carrying H.P.B.'s ashes, III 168
on Olcott's visit to S.F., III 168
San Francisco Chronicle
summary of Judge talk, III 166-7
Śaṅkarāchārya (509-477 BCE)
of Brahman caste, I 429; III 165
came to reform Hinduism, II 347-8
legend about, & Goddess of Love, III 179
——— *Shārīraka-Bhāshya*
comments on OṂ in, I 6
dwells on OṂ, I 6
——— *Vivekachūḍāmaṇi*
Great Ones regenerate world, I 218q
Sanmārga Samāj
founded on T.S. lines, II 518
Sannyāsis (Skt)
many, on path of error, I 475
Sanskrit
"Hindu Revival" goal to promote, I 442
language of the future, I 16-17, 102
more metaphysical than English, II 106, 324
use & beauty of, I 9
Sanyama [Saṃyama] (Skt). *See* Concentration
Saptaṛishis or Star Ṛishis
deflect development, II 250
not human but elementals, II 250
Sat (Skt)
Ego and, or Be-ness, I 213
Sat-Chit-Ānanda (Skt)
Brahman consists of, III 251
Satiation
doctrine of, I 495
Sattva (Skt)
on radiance of, & its obstruction, I 412
true action, II 109
Saturn
lead is sacred to, II 446
source of corporeal nature, II 111
Saul
necromancy and, I 285, 290
an obsessed medium, I 285-6

Savior(s)
Buddhist, before Christian, II 157
Jesus as a, I 439
man his own, I 31; II 157
in religions of India, II 157
sages &, in all religions, I 439
Schleyer, John Martin (1831-1912)
inventor of Universal language, I 456
Schliemann, Dr. Heinrich (1822-1890)
unearthed Troy, I 300
Schmiechen, Hermann (1855-?)
portraits of Masters by, I lxviii
portraits of Masters in W.Q.J. will, I lxvi
Science(s)
See also Occult Science
Adepts' attitude to, I 245, 319-20, 376-81
antithesis of Occult, I 379
atom not demonstrated by, I 173
axioms often unprovable, I 464
a book of Nature, II 90
brotherhood greater than, II 148
conflict with religion, II 84
conjectures of, III 13-14, 18
deals with intangibles, I 172-3
denies soul, II 90; III 161
life-force theory and, III 13
limitations of, III 10, 14, 102, 121, 161
modern, defective, II 87, 90, 322
modern, predicted by ancient, I 209
not based on philanthropy, I 377, 381
progress and, II 90; III 102-3, 121, 161
protoplasm of, not original matter, III 12
psychometry and, III 119-21
of soul has own rules, II 91
Theosophy is not a, I 214-15
true religion and, III 78, 102-3
what true, is, I 57
Scientist(s)
age of Man and, III 31-2
"coincidence" in terminology of, III 169
confirm theory of Polar shift, II 318
dogmatic, II 95
err on value of imagination, II 270
ignorant of true cycles, II 234
laughed at Theosophy, II 373
modern, is agnostic, I 208
no agreement between, III 14
psychometry ignored by, III 119-20
in Society for Psychical Research experiment, II 96
Seal
See also Theosophical Seal
Master's, not crucial to authenticate messages, II 48
Solomon's, I 14, 249-52; II 93
Séance(s)
See also Mediumship; Phenomena
ancient dead at, I 290
animals seldom appear in, I 427
astral currents aid phenomena of, III 146
attendance prohibited in E.S, III 331
"controls" of mediums at, II 458
danger of, I 409, 452-4; III 330-1, 445
deal with gross dregs, I 356
executed criminals & suicides at, II 303-4
explanation of, I 406-8
feats at, not unique, I 351
"Jim Nolan" reveals astral light in, III 136-7
Judge on attending, II 86
kāma-rūpa attracted to, III 330-1, 445
medium cannot control, I 308
Nāḍīgranthams at a, II 101
nefarious suicides at, II 280, 303-4
permeability of matter seen at, II 237-8
phenomena & Hermetic theory, II 331-2
phenomena explained, I 197-200
phenomena never classified, III 145-6

reliquiae of departed soul at, II 404; III 136-7
T.S never authorized, III 174
Secrecy
pledge published, II 434
rule of, in T.S. & its branches, II 454-5
Secret(s)
Mss. rediscovered, II 223
teachings of major religions are same, II 430
Secret Doctrine
atoms of, not those of science, I 212
Jacob Boehme a witness to, II 107, 109
Mahā-Pralaya part of, I 9
meditation on OṂ leads to, I 8, 9
older than Vedas, I 303
on responsibility of man for lower lives, I 120
synthetic view needed to master, II 109
The Secret Doctrine. *See* Blavatsky, H. P.
Sect
fear no faith or, I 22
Secunderabad (India)
Judge's visit to, II 85-92
second W.Q.J. lecture there, II 90
Seer(s)
Adepts are, III 11
and astral senses, II 43
untrained, II 39
untrained, and astral light, I 154
Self
See also Higher Self; Lower Self
acts through six vehicles, III 262
analysis & training, III 85-8, 262-4, 281, 436-7
as ātman, I 71
culture, II 462
culture can be selfish, I 70-1
examination as part of Kosmos, III 436-7
on forgetting lower, II 397, 429, 462
as friend & enemy, III 82-4
-ideation, II 274
Īśvara as, I 70, 71
its vehicles and the, II 274
its vehicles and the all-pervading, II 460
Judge served the One eternal, II 5
as Knower & the Known, II 317
lower, does not include body, III 304
"lower" must be merged in "Higher," II 460
as Manas-Buddhi-Ātman, II 317
no environment detrimental to, I 33-4
our Master is own, I 51
personal, must be mortified, III 443
proofs of hidden, I 448-50
raising the, III 82, 438, 447
or Real Ego at death, III 263
renunciation of, as occult practice, III 443
renunciation of, demanded in E.S., III 284, 422
study doesn't depend on conditions, II 386
subordination of lower, III 74, 284, 304, 436, 437, 447
thinning veil of, III 76, 263-4, 447
thought for others better than study of, I 18-19
transformation, III 447
within all, I 115
Self-Consciousness
aim of evolution, III 56
embodied, I 212
insects and, II 304
Self and, II 317
viewed from two planes, I 213
Self-Discipline
of all lower desires, III 64
cp. with "pledge fever," III 281
leads to Dhyāni stage, III 64
practical exercise in, II 429
self-criticism &, needed, III 436
trains spiritual will, III 442
Selfishness
always makes bad Karma, II 351
astral delusions deepened by, I 50
black magic triumph of, II 256-7
cause of misery, I 242; III 70, 72
death of, will uplift society, I 5
divine state blocked by, III 57

eradication of, III 64
inaction plants germs of, II 284
in magic arts usage, II 275
pursuit of Nirvāṇa and, II 327, 351
seeking seclusion a form of, II 454
"Self-culture" not always, II 462
Spiritual, III 328-9
taint of unconscious, I 379
wall of, bars truth, III 93
Selflessness
charity, & forgiveness of Adepts, I 502-5
develops spiritual will, III 442
leads to Divinity, III 452
speeds spiritual progress, II 441
vanity avoided with, I 77
Self-Reliance
central to Path, III 64-5
divine evolution requires, III 56
frames our destiny, III 71-2
in life & occult(ism), I 21, 104, 106
Selves
aspects of One principle, II 274
on the two, III 82
Semitic Race
bound to us karmically, I 524
Sensation(s)
delusions of, II 42
physical & astral, II 41-2
rebirth occurs unless overcome, II 325
Sense(s)
astral, II 36-7, 41-2
Sixth, II 237
Sensitives. *See* Mediums
Separateness
relates to personal self-assertion, III 316
self-vindication &, not for occultist, III 316
Sepharial. *See* Old, Walter R.
Septenary
constitution of man, II 137, 248-9, 310
cosmic differentiations, II 310
Serpent(s)
astral light to Initiates, III 45, 46
of evil, I 571-2
of evil in ancient legend, I 546-8
Hermetic symbol, I 13
as Karma-Nemesis, III 45
as Masters, I 250-1
power in ancient Ireland, I 546-8
swallowing tail, I 250
symbolism, I 12-13; II 267, 451; III 45
worship in Hindu religion, II 267
Service
path of, I 18-24
of Self hidden in Humanity, II 5
T.S. members and, II 170
true path is, not seclusion, II 454
Seven
colors & OṂ meditation, I 8
Ego connects to body at age, II 302
interlaced triangles &, I 14
kingdoms of nature, III 188
a perfect number, II 235
planes of manifestation, II 136; III 186
Worlds outlined, III 332-5
Sevenfold Division
analogy of prism for, III 187
of Boehme, II 109-10
compared with 10 divinities, III 313-14
constitution of man and, I 403-4; II 248-9, 310; III 168, 186, 187-9, 234-5, 367
in development of our globe, III 188
of Eastern system, III 44
in *Esoteric Buddhism*, II 104-5
of man, II 137, 248-9, 310
of man &, of Earth-Chain, I 369
mental deposits and, I 278-9
of nature, III 187-8
not rigid, I 143; III 62-3
one principle throughout, I 143-4
outlined, I 144
of spirit-matter, II 136, 310
Spiritualism and, I 351-2
triple division of St. Paul and, III 43
Sex(es)
how Ego chooses, II 249
no alternation of, II 298-9
no, on Spiritual plane, II 410

Shakespeare, William (1564-1616)
on fasting, III 255
inspired by Adept, III 9
Western Occultism and, III 451
——— *Julius Caesar*
on good & evil, III 9
——— *The Tempest*
we are "as dreams," III 186q
Sheath(s)
astral, after death, II 338
bodily & astral, II 41-3, 137
constructed by Soul, II 40
of the soul & principles, II 459
Shells
of gross persons & elementals, II 340
in séances resemble the deceased, II 331-2
Sherman Democrat (Texas)
S.D. review in, III 148-150
Shin Buddhism
doctrine of, sect, I 85-8
Shrine (Adyar)
Christian "investigation" of, curtailed, III 202
Judge dismantled Coulomb's, III 201-2
Shrines
major sacred, are spiritual centers, III 29
symbolized man's own nature, III 30
Shufeldt, Dr. Robert W. (1850-1934)
Coues and, III 127-8
Sibylline Books
of Rome, I 10
Siddhis (Skt)
See also Power(s)
occult rule on, II 446
Sidereal
body, & its principles, II 234
influences & Karma, II 273
particles (or atoms), II 420
Sidereal Cycle
exposes planets to interstellar space, III 12
known by ancients, II 165, 234
new conditions wrought by, III 12
Sight
Yogis can control, of others, I 411-12
Simla Eclectic T.S.
Master's letter to, I 69-70
Sin(s)
cause of all, III 70
in earthly vehicle, II 312
origin of, in mind, I 31
punishment and, II 159-60
repentance and, I 56
Saintship and, II 402
true, against Holy Ghost, III 66
washing away, II 155
why murder & suicide are, III 219
Sinnett, Alfred P. (1840-1921)
accuses H.P.B. of fraud, I 510
Adepts' letters to, investigated by the S.P.R., II 408
on "expiring Cycle," II 9
on 5th-Round "Rubicon," II 321
Judge criticizes words of, II 11
on Kāma-Loka, II 393
on letters from unseen Founders to, I 202
Masters' existence asserted by, I 386-7
Master's letters for his book, III 412-13
revealed only what H.P.B. taught, I 382
——— *Esoteric Buddhism*
confused on Earth-Chain, I 323-4
corrected by H.P.B., III 141
corrections in *S.D.*, I 342
distinctly Brahmanical, II 51
on early global periods, II 238
error on Devachanic period in, I 167, 336-8
from "Fragments of Occult Truth," I 362, 382
on highest development, II 278q
on human life-wave, II 238
key to, III 251-2
on later incarnations of Buddha, II 347
is mainly correct, I 324; III 95
on Mars & Mercury, I 368-9
new ideas in, I 324

not free of error, II 105, 261, 274
not textbook of Theosophy, II 456
one of our best works, II 265
"The Progress of Humanity" in, II 321 &n
sevenfold classification in, I 143; II 104-5, 274
on sevenfold constitution of man, III 44
title questioned, I 362-3, 382; III 250-1
——— *Incidents in the Life of Madame Blavatsky*
Cairo society failure, III 207 &n
H.P.B. on dangers at séances, I 409 &n
——— *Karma*
on astral spectres of dead, II 403-4 &n
——— *The Mahatma Letters to . . .*
on grossness of Western mind, I 327q
on handwriting of adepts, I xlix-l
on H.P.B.'s loyalty, I 511
K.H. & Kiddle in, III 122n
Masters copy nature, I 505
message to Prayāga branch in, I xlv &n
on occult powers, I 106-7
occult vs. physical science, I 379
on Olcott & H.P.B., I 64
on personal God worship, I 475
on untold evils, II 279
——— *The Occult World*
on Adepts and human progress, II 259q, 329-30
on Adepts and modern science, I 245q, 376-81
Adepts on retaliation in, I 503
appeal for Theosophy, III 81
on demand for phenomena, II 60 &n
K.H. on human nature in, I 378q
K.H. on India's destiny, I 478
K.H. on phenomenal display to masses, I 377q, 378q
K.H. on stifling magnetism of Hindus, II 115n
K.H. on true philanthropy, I 379-80
K.H. to Hume on thinking in grooves, I 327q
on need for practical Brotherhood, I 245
on Nirmāṇakāyas' influence, III 450
ref. to H.P.B. phenomena, I 307-8
T.S. not hall for Occultism, II 277q
value of K.H. letters in, II 48
West needs Asiatic psychology, I 245
——— *The Rationale of Mesmerism*
criticized by Judge, I 254-6
Śiva
in Hindu trinity, I 7
Skandha(s) (Skt)
as germs of future karma, III 236
Kāma & the related, II 302
magnetic force within kāma-rūpa and, III 334
the "remains" after life, I 485
return when we emerge from Devachan, II 315
Sleep
appeal to Higher Self before, II 261
brain impressions in, II 34, 397, 431-2
children's need for more, III 13
different organs function in, I 152-3
dreamless & with dreams, I 81-2
ego contacts Higher Self in, I 81-2, 152
fatigue is not cause of, III 13
frees soul from bodily cage, II 397
knowledge gained in dreamless, II 391
language of ego in, I 152-3
personality not conscious in, I 152
on phenomena of, III 13
Soul not in Devachan in, II 302
visions before, II 397
walking & astral organs, I 74-5
Smith, E. Delafield
Judge in law office of, I xviii
Smith, Ella M. (d. 1931)
wife of W. Q. Judge, I xvii-xviii

Smythe, A. E. S. (1861-1947)
on Judge & his character, I xxiv-xxv
president of Canadian T.S., I xxiv
Snake
See also Serpent(s)
poison experiments, III 192
Snake-charming
method of, I 310
Snell, Prof. Merwin-Marie (1863-?)
lectured on "Errors & Truths of Theosophy," III 163
refers to Coues' libel, III 163
speaks for Catholicism, III 162-4
Socialism
cannot legislate human nature, III 160
Society
any form of, may prosper, III 203
executed criminals affect Astral world of, I 488-90
unselfishness can regenerate, III 71
Society for Psychical Research
accusations against H.P.B., II 408
can't shake faith of Hindus, III 130
Harrison report of 1986 and, III 125n
Hodgson report and, II 408; III 123-5, 125n
Judge on alleged exposé, I 193
Olcott tried to prove Masters' existence to, I 386
on senile attacks by, II 61
on thought transference, II 96
Socrates (ca. 469-399 BCE)
despised in his own times, II 383
Solar
cycle, II 165
impregnation of Mercury, II 111
phenomena affect earth, III 118-9
phenomena and earth, II 279
Solar Biologists
"Adepts" of Hiram Butler, I 113
Solar Dynasty
and Kshatriya race, I 430
Solar Pitṛi(s) (Skt)
See also Kumāra(s); Lunar Pitṛi(s); Mānasaputra(s); Pitṛi(s)
as Agnishvāttas who impel intellectual evolution, III 361-3, 465
fashion inner man, III 294
Fire Dhyānis who reascend to Maharloka, III 463-4
or Fire Lords as progenitors of fire bodies, III 464-5
as Kumāras or Mānasaputras, etc., III 294, 462-3
Solar Plexus
controls organic life, II 457
Solar Systems
cosmic motion and, III 333
spring from Spiritual World, III 333
Solomon (ca. 1000-933 BCE)
buried wicked genii in the Red Sea, II 93
as Jewish sage, I 441
power in seal of, II 93
reckoned as an adept, II 93
Solomon's Seal
See also Seal
in T.S. Symbol, I 12-14, 249
Solon (638?-559? BCE)
corrected by Egyptian priests, I 459
Soma Juice
Buddha quoted on, II 277
Soul(s)
See also Buddhi; Higher Ego; Higher Manas
acts through seven sheaths, II 41, 459
after death not shell, I 356
ascending greatness of, II 227
character and loss of, III 381
character development and, I 73-4; III 180-2
conception of, lost, III 38
confused with spirit, II 370, 459
confused with spirit & "jīva," II 407
connecting bond with spirit, II 306
constructs own sheaths, II 40
creation vs. reincarnation of, II 418-19
Devachanic keynote formed by, III 43
Devachanic rest needed by, III 42
duality of Supreme, II 108
during concentration, III 261
earthly desires drag back, III 75

Egyptian belief in 5,000 year cycle of the, I 517-18
E.S. fired and energized, for future work, III 433
fall into matter, II 401-2
father of human will, II 393
on freeing the, II 391
as God, I 432
great goal for, III 16
heat of aspiration uplifts, III 447
how to open door to, I 18
idea in all religions, II 90-1, 154
immortality of, II 163, 306; III 10, 14, 29, 154, 178-9
longings of, for perfection, II 136
loss of, II 236, 306, 375
love or hatred brings, together again, I 84
Man is a, I 415; II 40, 90, 161; III 5, 10
manvantaric duration of, II 306
no special creation of a, I 160, 430-2; II 419
not permanent, II 306
number of, definite, I 160
object of, II 411
parentless, II 349
perfected, is Mahātma, III 5
pilgrimage of, III 29-30, 74-5, 154
as "pillar" when purified, I 422
powers of, can be dangerous, II 11
pre-existence of, I 430-2
progressed, helping man, I 129
qualities, II 161
recycles matter, II 43
reincarnation of, II 42-3, 138, 161, 334
remembrance of former lives, II 161
has rules of its own, II 91
seat of the, II 457-9
sheaths of the, III 44
in sleep, not in Devachan, II 302
"soulless" beings &, III 381
as Spectator, III 261-2
Theosophical Movement "a cry of the," II 6
Theosophists work for, progress, III 102
Theosophy the religion of, III 155
"Thread," II 334
transmigration of, II 420
value of unvexed, II 451
why so few great, living now, II 383-4

Soulless Being(s)
description and causes of, II 236; III 381-2
Divine Spark deprived of vehicle, III 66
does not refer to a "Dweller," III 381-2
Lower Manas divorced from upper principles, III 381-2
moment of choice and, III 65-6
more, than we think, III 406-7

Sound(s)
See also Vibrations
aspects of Vāch, III 336
awakening of pineal gland and, III 321
ladder of mystic sounds and, III 337
and Mercury acc. to Boehme, II 111
resolve into one harmonious tone, II 383
states of consciousness &, III 336-8
Tables on colors &, III 309-10
on tone, OṂ and, I 5-10
Vāch or Ākāśa, III 359

Source
great work of helping all to return to, I 14

Space
absolute abstract, II 296
bare subjectivity of, II 296
Dhyāni-Chohans guardians of, III 14-15
illusion of, shown, III 249
no idea of, in Devachan, III 42-3
parentless & eternal, III 15

Sparrow, John (1615-1670)
translator of Boehme, II 107n-8n

Spencer, Herbert (1820-1903)
on altruism, II 350
on social upheaval, I 423
"Synthetic Philosophy" a misnomer of, I 211

"Synthetic Philosophy" of, a method, I 207-8
——— *Principles of Ethics*
restates theory of Kant, I 220
Spheres
two ways to ascend to higher, II 391
The Sphinx (Leipzig)
cited for legal defense, III 142-3
conservatism of, III 142
German theosophical journal, III 142
K.H. quote in, I 319
Spinal Column
double, in future race, II 368
Spirit
See also Purusha
alone is, III 57
civilization regards not-spirit as, I 44
coeternalness with matter, II 238
conception of, lost, III 38
confused with soul, II 370, 406-7, 459
a differentiation of SPACE, II 238
diverse definitions of, II 324
Divine, overshadows man, III 57
existence in matter, II 255, 345
"Fall" into generation, II 232
father of true will, II 393
focalizes in man, II 136
immutable, eternal & indivisible, III 37, 44, 260
impresses Plan of evolution on matter, III 186
inseparable from matter, II 136, 227, 232, 238
knows no suffering, II 419
loss of soul from, II 306
of man is karmaless, III 37
and matter, III 186, 328
and matter co-eternal, II 232
never is seen, II 404
not a gas, I 39
not embodied in matter except in case of Mahātma, II 255, 406
One, in all, II 306; III 62
only real part of man, III 54, 260
only, reflects spiritual things, I 49
opposite pole of matter, I 119, 159; II 232, 238; III 186, 328
permanent & indivisible, III 54
presiding, is not modifiable, III 260
reascends to higher state, II 345
re-ascent to, II 419
reliquiae at séances, II 404
seeing what is not, I 49
six vehicles of, III 44
soul & body of Christians, II 137
St. Paul includes, in threefold division, III 44
of supersensuous regions, II 235-6
synthesis of all six principles, III 62-3
will is expression of, III 149
Spiritism
proper term for spiritualism, II 86
Spiritist(s)
See also Spiritualists
error of, I 52
writer of *Ghost Land* a misguided, II 451
Spiritual
advance may cause discard of old body, II 236
aroma assimilated by Auric Egg at death, III 363-4
aspirations, III 374
attainment & marriage, II 389
beings differ only in degree, II 298
consciousness, III 259
development cannot be judged, I 21
evil & three classes of useless beings, III 328
"gifts" a misnomer, I 104
knowledge & esoteric study, III 293
misuse of, endowment, II 467
Paul and James on, gifts, I 103, 104
perfection needed by lower man, not spirit, II 419
person must avoid illusions of Devas, I 148
pride & its danger, II 452, 467
progress, I 21-4, 50, 104-5; II 236-7; III 62-6
qualities & faculties, III 57, 64-5
quickening, progress, II 441

rationale of, development, III 64-5, 74-5
Self-consciousness, III 408
Spirit reflects, things, I 49
Sun & self-transformation, III 447
superior to psychic matters, II 355-6
things must not be materialized, III 294
training & perception, III 57-8, 64-5, 293, 442-3
war within, man, I 14
wickedness by deliberate choice, III 65
"wickedness in high places," III 328, 329
will and its development, III 442-3
wisdom, can't be sold, I 112
Spiritual Culture
ABC of, II 399
attainment of, III 57, 64-5
drugs & spirits obstruct, II 278
hindered by material gain, III 258
many rebirths needed for, III 74-5
meditation and, III 64
a misnomer, III 57
selflessness in, III 64-5, 293
Spiritual Scientist (Boston)
H.P.B. & Olcott and the, I 350
Spiritual Soul. *See* Buddhi
Spiritual World
plane of cosmic motion and Fohat, III 333
as source of solar systems, III 333
Spiritualism
See also Mediumship; Phenomena; Séance(s)
American expositions, I 57
ancient texts taught, I 285
astral light and, I 108; III 143-6
dangers of, I 393; III 190-1
explanation of, I 198-200, 351-6, 405-10, 452-6
genuine phenomena, not superstition, III 67
glamour in, I 359
H.P.B. hoped to reform, I 350
H.P.B.'s early investigation of, III 207
insidious form of materialism, III 174
"Jim Nolan" séances and, III 136-7
materializations in, via astral shells of the dead, II 331
and mediumship, I 51-2, 108, 353-7, 393, 399
modern, I 46-7, 197-200, 284-5, 290-2, 350-7
necromancy as term for, I 197, 285, 290-1
Nirmāṇakāyas & phenomena of, III 26
phenomena due to astral body, III 190
phenomena of, vs. spirit of enquiry, II 84
proofs of identity in, III 144
proves existence of soul, II 91
psychic deluge of, aided behind the scenes, III 26
utter emaciation of, III 145
Western, I 350-1
wonders of, in India, II 94
Spiritualists
assisted cycle of occult work, I 46-7
astral light unknown to, III 146
biased acceptance of messages by, III 144-5
cannot explain materializations, I 398, 408-10, 452
deal with elementals, II 94
dropped out of T.S., I 174
errors of, I 52-3, 285ff, 406-10
faith built on flimsy proofs, III 144
H.P.B. accused of mediumship by, III 22
intoxication with deceased, III 144
Judge parted ways with, II 86
need records from East, III 146
phenomena of, III 48, 136-7, 143-6
profit-seeking, I 285, 291-2
soul-awakening of former, II 354-5
Theosophists are not, III 155, 174
as tools of ill-disposed entities, I 393
worship the dead, I 197; III 174
Spirituality
loss of, in India, I 477-8

more important than psychism, II 355-8
true, not astral, I 49
vegetarianism is not, I 99-100, 468
Spleen
function unknown by Science, II 90
a seat of the soul, II 458
Spooks
as brain impressions, III 254
density of aura & resistance to seeing, III 254
on denying fact of, III 254-5
no blessing to "catch," III 254
soulless devils, I 356-7
spiritual knowledge not gained from, III 254
Srouthy, Sundaresvara
on sunspots & earthquakes, III 118-19
Stanton, Edward (pseud.)
——— *Dreams of the Dead*
on Kāma-Loka, II 333 &n
Star(s)
astrological, not a Planetary Spirit, III 402
compose man's astral spirit, III 334
distance of fixed, I 465
first are comets, II 234
influence us more than planets, II 15-16
Karma rules even the, II 273
magnetic attraction for cometary matter, III 334
small white, as thought remnant, I 109
within astral of this globe, II 391
States of Consciousness
confused with "planes," II 248-9
Stead, William T. (1849-1912)
examined spiritualism, I 360
Stevenson, Robert Louis (1850-1894)
how, stories were inspired, II 180
Stigmata
causes of, I 415-16
Stockton Mail (California)
sketch of W.Q.J. in, III 170-2
Stone(s)
of destiny, II 27
Druidic, I 572
magical sounding, I 544
Storms
sunspots & electrical, II 279
Study
devotion and, needed, III 379
Divine Wisdom not a subject for, II 398
good seeds from past lives revived by, III 134
Group, & fraternity, III 354-5
of karma & rebirth needed, I 156
more than reading & writing, II 386
not intellectual alone, I 78; III 354-5
not mere reading of books, I 132
OṂ should begin & end Vedic, I 6
of phenomena not, of Spirit, I 49
of Theosophy, III 65
thought for others better than self, I 18-19
unbiased, of Theosophy, I 131-2
work must accompany true, III 355
Subba Row, T. (1856-1890)
biographical sketch, II 480-1
Idyll of the White Lotus &, II 450n
on Mahātmas as Ṛishis, I 366
mastery of English by, II 106
on Nāḍīgranthams, II 101
questions sevenfold classification of modern Theosophy, II 104-5
——— *Notes on the Bhagavad Gita*
hints on Great Sacrifice, III 357
lectures now in print, II 481 &n
on Logos, III 333, 336, 359
on Logos as Kṛishṇa, III 358
on Vāch & its aspects, III 336-7
Sub-Race(s)
See also Race(s); Root-Race(s)
development, II 422
dying out of, II 425-6
European fifth, II 25
Success
no permanent, III 398
sense of failure is, III 398
Successorship
claims to, II 28-30
Succubus
and elementals, II 94

Suffering
  Adepts work to remove, I 320
  duty to relieve, II 405
  everyone a partial cause of world's, II 309
  on so-called unmerited, II 332
  on unmerited, II 335-6
Suffrage
  universal, criticized, III 160
Sufis [Sūfīs] (Arabic)
  mysticism taught by, I 375
  preserve inner doctrine of Islam, I 373
Suicide(s)
  astral personalities of, II 303
  based on belief that man is a body, III 218-19
  brings terror & despair to afterlife, III 220-1
  defeats Nature's design & harmony, III 219-21
  drawn into séances from Kāma-Loka, II 280, 303-4
  influences others to commit, III 221
  life-span completed in Kāma-Loka, II 303
  mediumship and, II 303; III 191
  remains in astral realm for rest of life, III 220-1
  soul cut off from life's pilgrimage, III 220-1
Sun
  Chaldean & Chinese astronomers on, I 140
  circulations of solar system &, III 313
  "cosmic dust" on, acc. to Science, I 136
  disciples' goal is true, I 140
  "Door of the," II 110
  draws earth into new spaces, II 165-6; III 11-12
  enormous orbit of, II 165 &n, 166
  first a comet, II 234
  heart of life, II 110
  heat from, I 135-6, 173, 464-5
  meditation on true, I 137
  of mystic, I 140
  mystical, is True, I 135-7, 311-13
  Nasmyth's discovery of photosphere around, I 136
  relation to planets, II 110-11, 234
  revolves around distant center, I 136
  revolves around its own center, I 516-17
  spots & electrical storms, I 136; II 279
  spots & "solar symptoms," III 118
  on ten Divinities within our, III 313-14
  theories of scientists about, I 135-6, 464-5, 516-17 &n
  true center & Dhyāni-Chohans, I 140
  True, within us, I 137
  unknown heat of, III 13-14
  visible, a reflection, I 136
  zodiacal cycle of, I 515-17
The Sun (New York)
  biographical sketch of H.P.B. in, III 204-12
  on Ceylon missionary work of T.S., III 117-18
  criticizes *Path* on T.S. prophecies, I 102-3
  Judge defended Theosophy in, III 115
  libel by Coues and, II 188-9
  makes retraction of Coues' libel, II 200-1; III 163
  prints Judge's defense of H.P.B., II 200
  T.S. criticized in, I 16; II 188
Sunday School
  Theosophists' children and, II 453
Supreme
  See also Absolute; Parabrahman; Paramātman; Supreme Soul
  Abode neither Purusha alone nor Prakṛiti, II 108
  Īśvara is the, I 35
  path to the, I 104; II 283
  principle is Ātman, II 274
  Universe itself is Karma of the, II 407
Supreme Being
  immortal portion of man, I 35

Supreme Self
humanity represents, II 9
Supreme Soul
environment not harmful to, I 33-4
Īśvara is, I 35
and its duality, II 108
and its sheaths, I 33-4
object of soul is union with, II 411
Sushumṇā (Skt)
on "fa" tone corresponding to, III 314
Sushupti (dreamless sleep) (Skt)
communion with Higher State in, I 81-2
deep sleep visions in, II 260
ideal impulses come from, I 182
ordinary man not conscious of, I 81-2
state of great purity, I 182
Sūtrātma(n) (Skt)
evil personality dropped from, III 353
thread soul as Auric Egg, III 337, 363-4
Svamiji K.B.
on H.P.B. to destroy Western materialism, III 419
on H.P.B.'s mission & T.S. destiny, III 418-20
high Chela, III 420
on meeting Himalayan Mahātma, III 419-20
Svapna (dreaming) (Skt)
dreaming as cp. to Devachan, II 302
state not consciously experienced by ordinary man, I 81
transition state between Jāgrat and Sushupti, I 81-2
Svarga (Skt)
heaven of Brahmanism, I 439; II 408
Karma draws us back to rebirth from, II 408
Svastika (Skt)
in Buddhism & Hinduism, I 253
Gnostic Cross or, I 14
meaning of, in T.S. seal, I 249, 253
"Wheel of the Law" and, I 253
Śvetāśvatara-Upanishad
on bridge to immortality, I 436
Swedenborg, Emmanuel (1688-1772)
in advance of his times, II 366
Devachanic visions of, II 308, 359
effects of affirming & denying, I 241
as seer of astral visions, I 154, 427
teachings of, sustained by Spiritualists, I 452
use of term "correspondence" by, III 312
——— *True Christian Religion*
on "lost word" in Tibet, III 130 &n
Sylphs
astral beings, III 45
Symbol(s)
in the Astral Light, II 412-13
of serpent, III 45
Symbolism
Egyptian scale of justice, I 12
Gnostic cross & Hindu chakra, I 14-15
interlaced triangles, I 13-16, 249-52
of number seven and T.S., I 11-12
and Numbers, II 226
origin of word, I 12
of temple guardians and cobra, II 267
of T.S. seal, I 12-16, 249-53
of winged globe, I 12
Sympathy
broad, for others, III 64
a disease for some, II 330
for spiritual loss of wrongdoer, II 253-4
true, derived from spiritual nature not desire, II 330
Synesius (ca. 373-414)
——— *On Providence*
on descent of gods, I 121-2, 127
Systems
of worlds, II 234-5

T

Tāj Mahāl
unrivalled beauty of, I 183

Tales
Occult, by Judge, I 531-71
Oriental fantasies not just fiction, II 92-4
of Red Sea in *Arabian Nights*, II 92-3
Talisman(s)
Ātman is, of white magician, II 94
cannot deter Karma, II 446
lead used as a, II 446
Talleyrand-Périgord, C. M. de (1754-1838). *See* Colmache, Édouard
Talmud
on reincarnation, I 419
Tamas (Skt)
indifferent action, II 109, 445
leads only to extinction, I 55
Taṇhā (Skt)
cause of rebirth, I 337; II 339-40
Tārā (Skt)
Virgins Dolma as, III 360
Tartary
Romish rituals in, II 155
Tathāgata-guhyaka
English translation of, III 164-5
esoteric Buddhist work, III 164-5n
or *Guhyasamāja Tantra*, III 164-5n
Tattva(s) (Skt)
Ākāśa emanates all other, III 359-60
elements comprising Universe, II 270
First, generates impulse within Atoms, III 360
study of, discouraged, II 270
Tatya [Padval], Tukaram (1836-1896)
biographical sketch, II 504-7
Tau
Egyptian, on T.S. pin, I 253
Taylor, Thomas (1758-1835)
——— *The Mystical Initiation* . . .
on principle of principles, I 214
Teacher
best, is within, III 452
will not pull one onward, I 21
woe for one who belittles, I 514
Teaching(s)
assimilation of, II 9-10
extinguished after 1897?, II 9-10
Telepathy
Blavatsky and, II 22
medium of, is astral light, III 47-8
Telephone
on ancient Hindu, I 447q
Tell, William (d. 1354)
high mountain and, III 228
legendary Swiss patriot, III 228
Temple(s)
man's body a, III 21-2
underground, guard sacred books, I 161
Temptation(s)
Jesus on, II 442
of occult student, II 450
twelve, of Egyptian mysteries, II 450
yearning for greater, when daily, not yet mastered, II 450-1
Ten
called perfect number in *S.D.*, III 314
Divinities of Sun, III 313-14
seven &, cp. with Pi ratio, III 314
Terunnanse, T. P.
on karma, III 33
Tetractys
on Divine, & lower Quaternary, III 326
Theosophical Congress
Report of Proceedings at World's Fair, II 125-8
selections from, II 125-34
summary of, II 168-73
The Theosophical Forum (New York)
correspondence class and, II 64
distributed free, II 253
The Theosophical Forum (Point Loma & Covina)
H.P.B.'s faith in W.Q.J. quoted, I xx &n
H.P.B.'s letter to Judge quoted, I xxxiv &n
on Judge document, III 250
Leonard Lester on Judge's Āryan T.S., II 439
letter of Harte quoted in, I xli &n
on spooks, III 254-5
Theosophical Miscellanies
existed before T.S., I 274 &n

Theosophical Movement
aspects of, I 485
basis for Unity of, I lii
"a cry of the soul," II 6
depends on unity & aspiration, II 217
distinct from T.S., I 485
for elevation of mankind, I 194
Émile Burnouf on, III 6
energy of human heart in, II 150
English language fostered Indian, I 479-80
E.S. core and promise of, III 284
existed before 19th century, I 270-5
first text representing, II 265
focused in West, III 458-9
Freemasonry as part of, I 486
genius of, II 380
great ideas of, II 12
greater than any T.S., II 204, 219
help to, aroused by belief in Masters, I 340-1
a human development, II 204
ideal of best workers for, II 60
"middle class" support for, II 373
neither Eastern nor Western, II 150
note of evolution voiced by, II 170
origins of, II 151
periodically made in each century, II 410
preparing the ground for, II 409-10
progress since 1875, I 496
reasons for founding in West, I 479
records of, in every age, II 301
returning Messenger of 1975 and, III 284
traces of, in U.S. before 1875, I 274
U.S.A. a result of, I 274
on unknown head of the, II 455
will of great Initiate behind, III 444
willfully misrepresented, II 91
worldly struggles of, II 19, 149-51, 373
The Theosophical Movement (Bombay)
reprints T.S. Branch papers, III 88, 98, 104
The Theosophical News (Boston)
on argument, III 244
The Theosophical Path (Point Loma)
on Time & Space, III 248
Theosophical Seal
explained, I 12-16, 249-53
origin explained, I 320-1
Theosophical Siftings (London)
Epitome quoted, II 375
Judge talk on karma in, III 98
"Topics in Karma," II 325n
Theosophical Society
Adepts and, III 28
Adepts did not leave, after H.P.B. died, I 201-3, 462-3
Adepts influenced spread of, III 28, 97, 284, 419-20
Adepts stand by, I 63, 201-3, 463; II 417
aim of, I 181
all may enter, I 55-6, 361-4, 371-2
all religions in ranks of, III 217-18
in America after split, II 217-19
American Convention Report, I lii q
American Section independence, I li-lii
Anglo-Indian proposed, I 63
Āryan lodge Headquarters, II 205
autonomy of branches & sections of, II 211-12; III 79, 216
avoids politics, III 77, 203
Blavatsky's death and, III 174, 344-6, 418-20
Branch activities, II 186-7, 429, 439
Branch independence, I 445-7
Branch news needed, II 199
Branch objectives, III 88-91, 94-5
Brotherhood chief object of, II 416-17; III 77, 157, 164, 168-9, 216-17
a "Brotherhood of Humanity," I 318
Burnouf on, I 149; III 165, 200
Cairo effort collapse, II 114n
chief objects of, II 87-8; III 77-8, 175, 210, 217, 237
"Closing Cycle" and the, II 9-10
Congress summary & reports regarding World's Fair, II 168-73
cornerstone of future religions, I 69, 318

correspondence class formed, II 64-6
cremation of Baron de Palm &, III 6
crisis passed through, III 439
cycle of, I 131, 462
danger of fast growth to, II 170
dangers to, II 206-7; III 457
degrees in, II 258, 439-40
diploma proves active in 1893, II 213-14
dischartered Gnostic branch of, III 7
discussion of side-issues in, II 382
disregards religious authorities, I 36
dogmatism would endanger, II 46, 60, 380; III 216-17, 376
doomed if E.S. fails, III 345, 433, 457
each member influences whole, III 89-91
Eastern craze in the, III 459
and education, II 152
in 1893, was worldwide, III 79
an elective body, II 30, 408
end of, & watchwords for, I 110
an Entity now, I 58
European convention addresses, III 98-103
first object of, II 42, 91, 416-17, 454, 461-2
on first object's possible removal, I 69, 501
founded in 1875, I 58, 64, 131, 174, 221-2, 297
founders' aim for, I 317
founding & objectives, III 5-6, 77, 153, 157-8, 175, 207, 216, 237
founding date discrepancies, II 208-13
free men's souls, III 153, 157-8
Freemasonry and, I 486
Fullerton's summary of its evolution, II 354-7
growth and influence of, I 149-50, 175-6, 298-300, 364; III 142-3, 153-4, 237
"Heathen," II 156
H.P.B. sacrificed herself for, I 58-9; III 391
H.P.B.'s office in, now extinct, II 29-30
H.P.B.'s vision of future, II 19
Hindus united by, III 153-4
historical data on, II 208-13, 354-7
inaugural address on T.S. aim, I 221-2
India and, I 149-50, 175, 479-80; II 84, 88-9, 210, 429; III 419-20
India and second object of, I 186
Indian, abolishes fees, I 111
Indian Section to follow different line, III 420
influence of, III 142
is international, II 50, 408
International Headquarters at Adyar, I 67
on Judge as co-founder of, I xix-xxii
Judge represents, at World's Fair, II 121, 133, 150-6
Karma and destiny of, II 58
Karma of, and its Branches, III 89-91
large funding would jeopardize, II 150, 206-7
list of first officers, II 209
Mahātmas and, III 5-6, 97, 283-4, 391-3, 418-20, 452
Master wants Olcott head of, until death, II 201-2
Masters on, I 155
Masters' program and, I 243-5
Masters uphold, II 10, 417
meant to be a selfless nucleus, II 20
methods of work in, I 204-5
mirrors state of the world, III 457
mission to India, I 479-80
must flourish on moral worth, not occult powers, I 245
must not deify Form of, I 487
mystical map of, III 7
national lines of work differ, III 412, 420
need for exposition of ethics in, I 280-1
needs martyrs in India, II 114-15

neutral to all religions, II 57
newspaper view of, in 1875, II 151
Nirmāṇakāyas linked with, III 452
no censorship in, I 371, 385-7; III 103
no claim to be a learned Oriental body, III 164
no dogmatic creeds in, I 111, 221-2, 385-7; II 46, 380
no doxology in, II 149
no one religion preferred in, I 361-4; III 174, 175
no private Branches, III 94
no salaries in, II 150, 151, 206
non-sectarian, I 363, 371-2; II 85, 130, 151-2, 203, 204
not atheistical, III 176
not bound by any system of reform, II 386
not Buddhist, II 57; III 201
not college or hall of Occultism, I 244, 379; II 277, 416
not forced to admit antagonistic persons, I 445-6
not school for psychology, I 69
obeys but makes no laws, II 152-3
objects explained, II 87-8
occult powers and, I 46, 155; II 417
Olcott's resignation revoked by, II 44, 201-2
organization of, II 204, 208-13, 354-6, 409, 457
Pantheists, Deists & Theists in, II 86-7
"Parent," non-existing, II 409, 456-7
philanthropy first object of, I 280, 319q
poverty explained, I 110-11
poverty, yet growth of, II 205
practical ethics and, III 94
preservation of Vedas by, II 52
primary purpose of, I 179, 245-6, 318-19
probationary period is passed, I 54
prophecies about, I 10-11, 193, 194, 203, 243-5, 463; III 28, 96-7q, 284, 344-5, 419-20
on psychic practices in, III 457
rapid spread of, I 149-50, 175, 298-9, 364; III 7, 142-3, 153-4, 237
recalled to original lines, III 391
recommended reading list of, III 79-80
redemption by E.S. hoped for, III 391, 433
as "reforming agency," III 68, 157, 217-18, 419-20
relation of *Esoteric Buddhism* to, II 265
Rosicrucian origins of, I 273
Russell's fears of 1922, may nurse black arts, II 3
science as a friend of, III 102-3
seal of, I 249-53
second object of, II 87
secrecy rule of, abolished, II 454
selection of name, I 67
service to, II 244
should work for Theosophy not rank, badges, etc., I 491
slogan of, III 154
sows seeds for future generations, III 78, 284, 419
sphere of influence, I 300
split during Boston Convention, II 430-1
stands for toleration, I 436, 467
supported by the few, I 188-90, 463
Third object of, II 88, 354-7
three great centers proposed, I 193
tract-mailing scheme of, III 68, 155
"tribe of heroes" founded, I 131
unites Science & Religion, I 57; II 133, 156-7; III 78
Universal Brotherhood its one doctrine, II 144, 151, 203, 455, 461-2
Universality of, II 87, 130-1, 454
is unsectarian, II 10, 57, 153-4; III 77, 103, 175-6, 203
vision for future of, III 344q
widespread, I 299; III 6-7, 153-4, 218
writers few in early days, II 502
Theosophical Society and Universal Brotherhood
on relation to the T.S., II 213

Theosophical Transactions
17th century effort for Theosophy, I 274 &n
old book of Dr. Buck's, II 301
Theosophist(s)
Adept message to London, I 147
admonitions to, I 467-8
advised on study, I 131-5, 151, 179; III 354-5
against dogmatic extremes, I 467-8
aims of true, III 60, 89, 93, 103
allow all methods of work, I 204-5
in America will prevail, II 19
American, aid Hindu, I 442-3
Anglo-Indian, propose change in leadership, I 63
are human, I 372
books recommended for, III 95
cautions for, I 371-2
center of light & hope for others, I 491
Christ principle believed in by, III 164
and Christian festivals, II 285-6
debate trivial questions, II 311-12
demons await, seeking clairvoyance, I 178
design in everything acc. to, I 174
Devas can "capture," I 148
doctrines of, III 154-5
duties of every, I 467; II 285, 373; III 203-4
"East" only India to some, I 477
encourage philosophical ethics, III 217
extend hand to dark nations, I 318
fail to recognize own ideas, I 249
fear of Dweller not needed by, I 98-9
follow path to Truth, I 34
fundamental unity in Masters, III 439
Hindu, II 112-14
how, should act, I 501
hypocritical views of some, I 218-19
intellect alone not enough for, III 101-2
laws of nature must be learned by, III 54
love must be expressed by, I 317
many lawyers among early, I 64
many Western, Atlanteans, I 130-1
meditation each day urged for, II 417
must apply doctrine of brotherhood, I 148
must be practical, I 491-3
need not be weak in convictions, I 385-7, 490-1
need to practice, I 319-20
no compilations when, gather, II 62-3
not free of superstitions, I 494
not mere professors of unity, I 502
not to condemn others, III 203
oppose hypnotism, III 214
"paper & straw," II 184
on path of true, I 17-24
practical, I 219-20
on practical advice to, I 156-7
practical presentation needed by, I 280-1
reciprocal influence between, III 88-91
seek perfection for self and all others, II 267
seek philosophy not mediums, I 351
social concourse of, I 506-7
some, wish to be Karmic agents, I 501
sought as earnest workers, II 20
struggle with nominal, II 19
Theosophical influence of each, II 170
thoughts of, must be elevated, I 83
true, belongs to no cult or sect, II 398
true, ignores self & helps others, I 18
various grades of students, III 54, 89
vicarious atonement not believed in by, III 164
what is needed by, I 135
work for future of soul, III 102
work for Theosophy not T.S. badges, etc., I 491
work in unity, III 354

work in unity needed by, III 90-1
The Theosophist (Bombay [Mumbai] & Adyar)
American Section requests Olcott to not resign, I xliv
differs from *The Path*, I 3
Five Years of Theosophy from, II 270 &n
Harte's policies as temporary editor of, I xx-xxi
Hindu contributions to, I 299
on Hindu group & T.S., I 442
Indian Sibylline Books article in, I 10n
Olcott thanks Judge for T.S. support, I xxxiii
Olcott's regard for Judge expressed in, I xxv-xxvi &n
only official T.S. organ, I 386
originated in Bombay, I 67; III 208-9
on Prāṇa, III 335
prosperous, III 143
publication noted by *The Sun*, III 117
published in Madras [Chennai], I 56
Theosophy
abstract yet practical, I 172-3, 491-3
for all classes, II 373
application of, in daily life, I 280-1, 315, 491-3
attraction to, II 466-7
basis of, II 202-3
as branch of Masonry, II 35, 225
cardinal doctrine of, III 70
changing public views toward, I 333, 467-8
common man and, II 373; III 101-2
compared to Christianity, II 452-3
cosmic vista revealed by, III 242-3
dabblers in, II 247
definitions, II 86; III 53, 175-6, 233-7
disdain for H.P.B. leads to end of, I 511, 513
East is primary source of, I 179
in esoteric Christianity, III 107
ethical system of, III 69, 94-5, 105
ethics of Christianity and, I 155-6, 493
ethics of, not new, II 139
etymology of, III 233
explaining & knowing, as a whole, III 93
few converted to, by phenomena, III 93
first concrete text on, II 265
fundamental ethics of, III 70-1
fundamentals of, III 54-5, 166-7
going beyond study of, II 398-9
how, is taught, I 274, 280-1
on intelligent representation of, III 203-4
key ideas not original, II 61-2
as knowledge of "God," III 53, 175-6, 233
leavens mind of the times, II 20
lifetimes needed to master, I 215
mechanical, negates brotherhood, I 493
morality given sure foundation by, I 526-7
more than a cult in India, III 129-32
Motto of, II 203
name originated by Ammonius Saccas, III 233
new wave of thought, III 157
no dogma or creeds in, I 214-15, 222-3, 467-8
no greater system of practice, II 399
no personal God in, III 14
no single criterion of, II 380
not a "cult," II 399
not a religion but in all, III 233
not against Christianity, III 104-6, 175
not heartless, I 219, 318-20, 492-3
not just for cultured, II 373
not materialism, III 173
not new invention, I 179
not one religion but Religion, I 214
not Spiritualism, III 166, 174
not to be confused with T.S., III 166
offered to all, II 260
old as the hills, II 86

only, has power to cure society,
  III 159-60
only panacea is, III 162-3
as perceived by Orientals, III 130-1
on perfectibility of the race, II 136
periodically revealed to men,
  III 233
and phenomena in France, II 22
problems explained by, III 66-7, 71,
  94, 101-2, 162, 166-7
proofs of, I 464
purpose of, I 46, 155-7, 218-19, 493;
  II 373
pursuit of knowledge and, I 18-19,
  315-17
reunites religion & science, II 135;
  III 176
science of divine things, III 132, 233
"scientific" fact-seekers and,
  I 59-60, 132
a scientific religion, II 156-7
shows cause of sin & misery, III 70,
  94, 99-100, 162
simplifying expression of, I 497
sounds note of human evolution,
  II 170
spreading, and influence, I 205,
  332-3, 467-8, 497
on studying, I 118, 131-5, 318-20,
  491, 497
teachings of Jesus and, II 452
theories of, from East, I 275
or Theosophia, II 391, 398
T.S. and, I 179-83
Theosophists work for, not T.S.,
  I 491
is true Reformer, III 161-3
true spirit of Christianity is, I 468
is truth behind all religions, III 174
types of workers for, II 59
unifier of diverse systems, I 442-3
Unknown Eternal postulated by,
  II 136
what is work for, II 244
widespread, III 237
wisdom of the Gods, II 380
is Wisdom-Religion, III 53, 166

Theosophy (Los Angeles)
  aphorisms on Occultism in,
    III 257-8
Theosophy (New York)
  new title for *The Path*, I 497, 505
Thinker
  man is the, II 138, 317, 385
Third Eye
  See also Pineal Gland
  connected with Karma, I 128
  an external organ once, II 368;
    III 380-1
  Eye of Śiva cp. with, III 380-1
  on location of, III 380
  on resurrection of, III 381
  as seat of soul?, II 458
Thomson, John Cockburn (1834-
    1860)
  tr. of *Bhagavad-Gītā*, III 39n
Thought(s)
  Adepts on importance of, III 8
  are things, II 346
  astral fashions are conditioned by,
    III 390
  astral light source of evil, III 45-9
  can be lost or deflected, I 109
  cause woe or bliss, II 138-9
  character of, and sex determination,
    II 299
  clarity of, and mesmerism, II 39
  coalesce with elementals, I 353;
    III 61
  concentration in, transference,
    II 96-7
  conform to law of cycles, I 44
  Devachan and, II 311
  on devoting, to Theosophy, I 118
  each, is an entity, III 61, 127
  earnest, needed for study of
    Theosophy, I 132
  E.S. Pledge magnifies power of,
    III 274-5, 316
  etheric form molded by, III 264-5
  evil, in left-hand magic, II 231
  evil, leads to evil act, I 81; II 293-4
  food of Ego, III 398
  freedom of, II 86
  issue as colors & sounds, III 379

of karma & reincarnation needed, I 157
life & after-life a result of, II 363-4
man enters Universal, III 263
man lives on, I 415
meditation on one, III 373
mental deposits & astral impressions, II 231-2
of mesmerist alters subjects' subconscious, I 255-6
motives determine quality of, III 263-4
must be on highest ideal, I 28, 31
narrow, bind one, I 23
often our, are not ours, I 52-3
only, has power to repair society, III 160
for others opens door to soul, I 18-24
outer self as puppet of own, II 399
pictures made by, I 352; II 346-7
plastic potency of Soul and, III 264-5
power of good, I 491; III 316
precedes Karma, I 504; II 162, 444-5
purification of, needed, I 81-2; II 399; III 127, 261-2, 263-4
reading, I 109; II 95-7, 395
reincarnates, I 118; III 127
results of angry, III 61-2
results of, on Theosophy, I 491
seeds of acts, II 347, 444-5
source of all our being, III 127
on "supersensuous," III 348
Theosophists need independent, II 62-3
has thinker's attributes, I 109
transference among children, II 95-6
transference from higher levels, I 52

Threshold
See also Dweller of the Threshold
mystery of, I 38-9q, 43q

Tibet
destiny of West even includes, I 480
H.P.B.'s training in, II 333, 335
influence in West, II 372
"pope" & rituals compared to Catholic rites, II 155

Tiger
in crystal experiment, II 89

Time
allegory of, I 548-50
allegory on synchronicity of, III 249
Devachan &, I 169
illusion of, in sleep, III 248
as Kāla, overpowers death, I 548
Mohammedan legend on, III 248
screen of, is "astral light," I 550
Space and, as māyās, III 248

Tingley, Katherine (1847-1929)
helps Judge, I lii

Tishby, Isaiah (1909-1992)
——— *The Wisdom of the Zohar*
consult, III 108n

Tobacco
abuse of, II 278
not protective in Occultism, II 278

Tone
letter & sound expressing, I 8
meaning of, I 6-9
OṂ, meditation, I 8

Topinard, Paul (1830-1911)
——— *Anthropology*
on colors in human organism, III 20

Torquemada, Tomás de (1420-1498)
headed Spanish Inquisition, III 164

Touch
sensations of, I 466

Tracts
and T.S. circulars, II 185-6

Trance
channels unfit as guides, I 256
on mesmeric, I 255-6; II 33-5

Translators
limitations of Western, II 89
Max Müller cited, II 87
of *The Theosophist* into Urdu, II 85

Transmigration
on corrupted ideas of, I 568-70
degradation of man's atoms as, III 318
of lives in our bodies, II 420-1

and metempsychosis cp., I 431
origin of belief in, II 420-1; III 318
of souls not taught by ancient Hindus, II 419-20
Triad
after-death state of, III 236
Higher, active in man, I 212
Higher, after death, II 281
Higher, represented in E.S. diagram, III 395
man's immortal, III 234, 236
Trials
meeting hourly, preparation for greater, I 118
Triangle(s)
symbolism of interlaced, I 13-16, 249-52
symbolism of man's Higher Triad, III 395
Tribhuvana (Skt)
lofty Devachanic state, III 42
Trinity
the real, in man, II 137-8
Trivialities
on discussion of, II 312
Truth(s)
all faiths had origin in, I 22; II 154-5, 170
alone remains, III 203
birthright of man, III 259
can be found regardless of conditions, II 386
common ideas point to, I 35
each sees only part of, III 86
of good and evil, I 19
idea of Universal Brotherhhood &, I 5
on individual views of, I 13
intense desire for, II 9
longing for, must be selfless, III 92
Masters help seekers after, II 329
no one creed exemplifies, II 170
no religion higher than, I 35, 36, 249; II 203; III 154
of Occultism for practical use, I 381
one, in beginning, II 154
open to all men, II 163, 386
Planetary Spirits strike keynote of, III 402-3
remains whatever outer veil, I 4
self-assertion prevents knowing, III 95
spiritual system grasps, III 57-8
sweeter than pleasures, II 379
Theosophic, and intellect, III 65
T.S. appeals to lovers of, III 77, 154, 203
T.S. motto on, II 203
Theosophists follow path to, I 34
Theosophy is essential, I 179
Theosophy is the one, III 104
as union of science with occultism, I 468
unproved, & theories, I 464-6
very simple, III 133
Tsong-kha-pa (1357-1419)
a reincarnation of Buddha, II 347
Tulku [sPrul-pa'i-sku] (Tib)
or Āveśa defined, I xxxiv
Tulsi Das (1532-1623)
version of *Rāmāyaṇa* by, I 440
Twentieth Century (New York)
on demagogues & universal suffrage, III 160
predictions on future in, III 159-63
Tyndall, John (1820-1893)
essence of matter unknown to, I 352
Typhos
signifies evil, I 126
tried to destroy Osiris, I 126

U

Uddalaka
advice of, to son, I 34
Umbrella
Buddhist & Hindu symbol, I 140
Unconscious
of European philosophy, II 296
Undines
astral beings, III 45
Union
of East & West, II 88, 190
Q & A brings closer, II 179
with divine, II 306
United States
See also America

birth of new race in, II 153
Black Magic in, II 345-6
Declaration of Independence & Constitution of, II 77
evolutionary plan &, I 149
forces for change in, III 18-19, 21
founders of, free thinkers, III 156
freedom of thought in, I 274; II 86
glorious future for, III 176
hope for liberty, truth & right in, III 157
individualism endangers, III 8
laws and people of, II 153
occult forces in, I 149
prophecies concerning, I 17, 423
as regarded by foreigners, I 148-9
revolution and Theosophical Movement, I 274, 486; II 77-9
sectarianism less rigid in, I 150
Spiritualism in, II 86
T.S. branches in, I 149, 175

Unity
Adepts represent love, spirit and, II 257
of all life, I 181-2; II 203, 226
of All should govern each act, III 259
common ground for all faiths, III 109
errors and study of, III 96
E.S., opens way for higher Force, III 354
of man on all planes, II 145-7
of mankind & moral life, I 181
meditation subject, III 454
non-separateness and, III 438
radical, of Ultimate Essence, II 226
of religion & science, II 135
Study, & Work, III 354-5
Theosophical view based on, I 502
underlying propositions of Theosophy, I 179

Universal Brotherhood
See also Brotherhood
aim of T.S. to form a nucleus of, I 179, 221-2, 279-80; II 20, 82, 139, 142, 151, 203, 416-17; III 5, 56, 78, 175, 329-30
base actions only on, III 259
common ground for all faiths, III 111, 175
denial of, dangerous, II 144-5
destroys idea of separateness, III 256
exclusion of unwholesome T.S. members and, I 444-6
a fact in nature, I 181-3, 280; II 143-8; III 89, 133, 181, 404
first step in Occultism, III 264
first step in true magic, III 134
goal of *The Path*, I 48
idea thought Utopian, III 8
Indian T.S. tried to drop, object, I 501
Masters of Light moved by, III 329-30
must be practiced, I 218-20; III 175, 330
not sentimental, III 175, 356
only doctrine with power to save, I 46
only saving power, I 46, 245
and original T.S. name, II 213
prevention of anarchy and, III 8
prime object of T.S., I 279-80, 318
reincarnation develops, III 181
requires emancipation from self, III 74-5
scientific, I 219
Sinnett protested T.S. object of, I 379
a theme of, at World's Fair, II 127-31
T.S. and, III 5
T.S. proposes to revise 1st object, I 501
true occultism needs, I 4-5
USA Declaration of Independence and, III 157
Utopia and, I 5
violated constantly, II 143

Universal Mind
See also Mahat
differentiated in human beings, III 260
immutable laws in, III 16
as State of Being, III 260, 261-2
Thought and, III 263-4

Universe
all, is Life, III 363
built by number, II 229
"Causeless Cause" and, III 55
conscious & intelligent, II 136
as Deity is one whole, III 55
Divine Resonance and, I 7
as egg, II 35, 225
evolving from Unknown, II 168
is "Karma of the Supreme," II 407
man is god of his little, I 119
no vacuum in, II 297
periodically manifests, III 55-6
single sound awakens, I 7
a vast ideation, II 336
as Will and Idea, I 400
Unknown and Unknowable
Absolute, II 225, 296
Principle, II 136
Principle symbolized, II 296
Universe, II 168
Unmerited Suffering
Devachan and, II 332, 336
there is no, II 335-6
Upādhi(s) (Skt)
See also Sheath(s)
term, preferred over "principles," I 143
Upanishad(s) (Skt)
See also Bṛihadāraṇyaka-Upanishad; *Gāyatrī*; *Muṇḍaka-Upanishad*; etc.
advise cutting away error, III 86
allegory of two birds, I 562
on death, I 115q
on "ether" of heart, I 40
European introduction to, I 275
Gāyatrī quoted from, II 464
on heart's knot, II 457
ideas on Self in, I 71, 115q, 163, 413q
India's literary treasure, I 185
Kshatriyas taught Brahmans once, I 429
on meditation, III 455
mystical genius ascribed to Rājanya race, I 429
on OṂ, I 6, 10 &n
quoted on true sun, I 140
on radiations from Great All, II 419
on rebirth & thoughts, I 413q
yoga based on, dangerous, II 246-7
youth should study, I 151
Urn of H.P.B.
American, designed by Judge, II 197
crafted by Herr Bengtsson, II 196 &n
description, II 194-7
designed by R. Machell, II 196n
Utopia(s)
Bellamyites, and T.S., II 152
not made in a day, I 5
Universal Brotherhood and, I 5

V

Vāch (Skt)
See also Sound(s)
as Aum or Praṇava, III 338
Brahmā-Prajāpati as, III 338
during pralaya, III 337-8, 360
female aspect of Brahmā, III 335, 359
four forms of, & corresponding principles, III 336-8, 360
Isis & Venus cp. with, III 335-6
Kwan-Yin and, III 359
Madhyama-, the light of Logos expressed, III 336-7
on māyāvic nature of, III 337-8
the "melodious cow," III 335-6
as mystic speech, III 359
Parā-, as subjective Light & Sound, III 337
Paśyanti-, Logos in the Cosmos & its latent light, III 337
Vaikharī-, basis for Mantric potency, III 336
Vaikharī-, sound, speech & its 4 modes, III 336
Vacuum
no, in Universe, II 297
The Vāhan
editorial policy by Mead, II 243
means "vehicle," II 243
Vanity
effects of, on ethereal body, I 77

Varāha Mihira (505-587)
——— *Bṛihatsaṃhitā*
on sun spots & solar color, III 118
Vaughn, Thomas (1622-1666)
obscured adept, I 128
Vāyu-Purāṇa
chapter on OṂ, I 6
Veda(s) (Skt)
authority of, I 36, 57
cp. to Buddhism on lawful warfare, II 376
gave rise to caste system, III 174
India's treasure, I 185, 437
Judge as devotee of, I 362
related to the mystic letters A U M, I 7
scripture of Brahmans, III 174
Secret Doctrine older than, I 303
sub-division of highest caste not sanctioned by, II 113
Vedāntin(s) (Skt)
sages reflect Gupta-Vidyā, III 327
Vedic Religion
has a warrior caste, II 376
Vegetarian(s)
Judge a, for 9 years, II 384
may subject themselves to disease, I 99-100
not sole possessors of nature's forces, I 100
think meat-eaters sinners, I 99
too self-watchful, II 371
Vegetarianism
alone cannot bring salvation, I 468
cautions on diet of, II 384
motive and, I 247
motives for, II 370-1
spirituality not dependent upon, II 385, 389-90
Vehicles
See also Sheath(s)
of man as aspects of Ātma, II 274
Venezuela
Judge's adventures in, I 532
Venus
elder sister of Earth, I 252
from Sun's effluvia, II 111
her old moons sublimated, II 229
peculiar bond to Earth, I 383-4
in Seventh Round, II 229
spirit of judgment &, I 384
Ver Planck, Mrs. Julia Campbell. *See* Keightley, Julia
Vestals
mediums for oracles, I 287
Vibrations
See also Sound(s); Vāch
on tone, OṂ and, I 6-9
Vicarious Atonement
no, in Theosophy, III 70-1
none in Karma, II 245
Vidyā-Nyaka (pseud. of Ohmart)
conspired with Butler in Esoteric College, I 113
Vijñāna Bhikshu (fl. 15th cent. CE)
——— *Sāṃkhya Sāra*
on Ākāśa, III 60n
Violence
effects of war or crime, II 276-7
victims of, after death, II 280
Virāj (Skt)
Brahmā and Vāch, III 359
Virgin(s)
and child found in Egyptian papyri, III 109
two, as dual nature of Manas, III 318, 360
Virtue(s)
See also Morality
altruism and, bases of Rāja-Yoga, I 78
both right philosophy &, needed, III 448
clarifies perception, I 153, 155
compared to wisdom, II 278, 283
knowledge will be lost at death without, III 448-9
life lacking, is vain, III 448-9
life of, builds merit, I 79
needed to build will, I 79
needed to develop astral, I 76-7
sages inculcate, III 260-1
unconscious growth of, cp. with flowers, III 395
Vishṇu (Skt)
See also Nārāyaṇa
chakra of, I 14-15
preservation aspect of Universe, I 7

Vishṇu-Purāṇa
on two ageless ones, I 429-30
Vision(s)
Adepts analyzed countless, III 11
in astral light dangerous, I 154-5
before sleep, II 397
at death, II 384
at death of past life, II 449
fatigue and, II 431-2
of night, I 152-3
of night & day, II 263
of night or dreams, II 260, 397
Thomas Paine's, II 78-9
uncontrollable except by occultist, II 397
Viśishtādvaitism
on karma, II 249, 407-8, 463
Vivisection
attack on, by Kingsford, I 500
Masters oppose, I 500
Voice
of "Bath-Kōl" & Mosaic codes, I 286
cultivation of, III 83
our own, not heard by us, III 83
Volapük (world-speech)
as universal language, I 457
Volatilization
of metals, I 390, 399
Vows
dynamic effect of holy, I 87
last for many lives, III 455
meditate on, or obligations, III 277
power of, changes Karma, I 335

W

Wachtmeister, Countess Constance (1838-1910)
biographical sketch, II 489-92
intimate friend of H.P.B., III 138, 141
——— *Reminiscences of H.P.B. . . .*
how H.P.B. wrote *The Secret Doctrine*, II 492 &n
on Tibetan training of H.P.B., II 335
W.Q.J. quoted on *S.D.*, III 238
Wallace, Henry A. (1888-1965)
Great Seal and, II 79n
Theosophy and, II 79n
War
effects on astral plane, II 276-7
ideal of Brotherhood &, II 144
lawful, of Vedic religion, II 376
Warner, Charles D. (1829-1900)
Editor of *Harper's Monthly*, II 180
on karma & reincarnation, II 180-2
Washington, George (1732-1799)
Adepts inspired, III 23-4
influenced Thomas Paine to write *Common Sense*, II 78
urged support for Paine, II 78
Washington Post (Washington D.C.)
cited Prof. Coues' expulsion from T.S., III 115
reply to Prof. Snell on Theosophy, III 162-4
on *The Hidden Way*, III 135
Water
Kwan-Yin symbolized by, III 358
mystical properties in Kosmos, III 319
Wealth
desire no greater, I 19, 21
Karma of giving away, II 350-1, III 162
rich must share, with poor, III 194
Webb, Alexander R. (1846-1916)
on Islamism, I 372
Muslim convert, I 372
on six doctrines of Islam, I 374-5
Webster, Daniel (1782-1852)
Great Seal and, II 79
Week
-days & colors representing them, III 291
on days of, & planetary correspondences, III 291
Weight
depolarized by astral hand, II 313
West
crest-wave of evolution is in, I 479
destiny of the, III 458-9
discovers treasures of the East, I 275; II 50, 87-9
material power of, I 479

must uplift "East," I 479-80
needs spirituality of East, II 106
new race to be born in, III 459
philosophy of India will conquer, I 184-5
preparation for next race in, I 479
selfishness of, II 113
Theosophical work began in, I 479
wave of progress now in, III 459
Western
appreciation for East, II 87, 89, 189-90, 371
bigotry & dogmatism, II 169
craze for India, II 371-2
few occultists among, people, II 416
fondness for staked path, II 7
grossness of, mind, I 327
materialism, I 293; II 82
mind not fitted for Yoga, II 416-17
nations foster notion of separate personality, I 31
new era in, Occultism, II 11
Occultism a hodgepodge, II 243-4
Philosophy on nature of soul, II 90
rājasika quality, II 115
religions cp. to Eastern, II 154-5
translations not always genuine, II 87, 89
Westminster Abbey
stone of destiny, II 27
Westminster Gazette (London)
Judge case papers printed in, I li
Wheel(s)
Ezekiel's, I 15
Ezekiel's, analogy, II 72
Wheel of Rebirth
Buddha's Wheel of Law and, III 45
ceaseless revolving of, III 45
Wheel of the Law
aim of true Theosophist to turn, III 45
and Svastika, I 253
Wheeler, Andrew C. (1835-1903)
on suicide, III 218-19
White Magic
Black Magic and, II 231-2, 275, 290
done for pay is Black Magic, II 275
in literature, II 180
motive determines, I 45, 47; III 92
spirit, unity and love is, II 257
White Magician(s)
beyond fear of destruction, II 94
Black and, cp., II 256-7, 414
need no talisman, II 94
Whitman, Walt (1819-1892)
on immortality, III 178 &n
quoted, II 451
Whittle, Dr. Mark (b. 1956)
——— *Cosmology* . . .
on sun & galaxy, II 165n
Will
acts according to desire, II 8, 289-90
behind, stands desire, III 35
control of vital currents by, II 269-70
Cosmic, unites infinitude of monads, III 351
direct way to illumination, II 236-7, 391, 395
disintegration & transfer of objects by, I 400-2
doctrine of Free, II 460-1
evolution and individual, III 56
expression of Spirit, III 149
force and imagination, II 269-70
free choice and, II 461
how to strengthen, II 8-9, 269-70, 395, 451
an impersonal, spiritual power, III 328-9, 442-3
little in our teachings on, II 8
mediums', can stop their obsession, I 90
in Occult phenomena, I 397
Occultism and true, II 277, 391
spiritual, cp. with ordinary, III 442
subjugation to God's, II 400-1
training of, III 431, 442-3
transforming human into Divine, II 392-3, 451
on true, II 392-3, 395
true, is God, II 393
universal & lacks moral quality, II 8
Universe is Idea &, I 400
virtue and self-knowledge needed to gain, I 79

way of peace is conforming to Divine, I 17-18
Willard, Cyrus Field (1858-1941)
testimony regarding Judge's borrowed body, I xxxv-vi
Winterburn, Dr. Charles
charged no fee for astrology, II 74
Judge on accurate astrology of, II 74-6
Wisdom
grows facet by facet, I 13
how to gain, III 373-4
life's struggles no barrier to study of Divine, II 386
love of, II 398
of nature is Theosophy, II 380
no, in too zealous personal loyalty, II 60
not obtained by phenomena, I 4
only steady effort leads to, I 18-19
supreme, and evolution of soul, III 76-7
Theo Sophia, II 398
virtue and, needed, II 278, 283; III 379-80
Wisdom-Religion
Adepts preserve the ancient, II 135
H.P.B. revived, in West, I 194; III 212
hierarchies postulated by, III 14, 361-3
India, America, and, I 150
knows man's prenatal & postmortem states, III 10
logical cp. to theological theory, III 10
never lacks a witness, II 107
no personal God in, III 16
only true science & religion is, I 57
outlines universal evolution, III 56-7
reason is authority in, II 135-6
Theosophy is, III 53
Witch of Endor
had familiar spirit, I 285-6
powerful medium, I 286
Witchcraft
Salem, phenomena, III 48
trials & Mosaic Codes, I 286
Wittgenstein, Prince Emil de (1824-1878)
family friend of H.P.B., III 205
joins T.S. by correspondence, III 205
Wizards
mentioned by Moses, I 290
Woman(en)
equal rights at World's Fair, II 127
H.P.B. chose incarnation as, II 320
in priesthood questioned, I 439
talking of, and Mercury, I 9
tendencies of, II 299, 400
T.S. not concerned with sex distinctions, I 372
Woman's Branch
T.S. and, at World's Fair, II 127
Wool
an occult protection, II 392
Word(s)
See also Sound(s); Vāch
or Logos, I 7; II 225
OṂ and tone, I 6-10
power of mantric, over forces of spirit, I 90
as seeds of Karma, II 444-5
use, only to help, I 507
The Word (New York)
account of high-mountain retreats in, III 225-9
on Judge in Paris, I xxiii
Laura Holloway cited on Masters' portraits, I lxviii
Work
evolution fulfilled by, for humanity, II 259-60
expression of brotherhood, I 505
fitting oneself for higher, I 22, 23
great, is helping all to return to the Source, I 14
great, needs will power, III 56
ideal of those who, for Theosophy, II 60
method of, for Theosophy, I 204-5; II 58-9, 244
not with body but mind and heart, II 406
Path is one of hard, I 18-20, 79
secret, of Adepts & chelas, II 440

World(s)
See also Globe(s); Plane(s)
all, governed by karma, II 256, 273
basis for illusion of, I 31-2
benefit, as Buddhas do, I 157
elevate one soul before helping, I 22
evolves just as man, III 36
interpenetration of, I 312
later, evolve from first model, II 233
law & conquest of, I 400
lifting Karma of, II 245
meaning of higher, III 332
needs ethics more than philosophy, III 448-9
objects in, keep impressions, III 120
other, in this globe, II 391
other, vary from our, II 368
Seven, described, III 332-5
on seven planes of consciousness, II 233
Suns cool down to, II 234
The World (New York)
criticism of *The Path* in, I 102
exposed Esoteric College of Hiram Butler, I 113
Ingersoll's ideas on suicide in, III 218
Wright, Claude Falls (1867-1923)
biographical sketch, II 496-7
describes death bed message of W.Q.J., III 222-4
on help from Masters, I 463
lecture tours of, I 333; II 218
popular lecturer, II 218
servant of silent workers, III 242-3
speaker at World's Fair, II 134
on T.S. work, II 149
Theosophists need no Pope, III 224
——— *An Outline of Principles of Modern Theosophy*
Introduction to, III 242-3
preparation for new civilization, III 243
Wright, George E. (1851-?)
biographical sketch, II 497-9
letter to, as head of Chicago T.S., II 125-6
reports on T.S. convention, II 126
Wright, Thomas (1711-1786)
——— *New Hypothesis of the Universe*
on galactic rotation, I 516n

Y

Yakshas (Skt)
astral beings, III 45
Yama (Skt)
as astral light, III 47
judge of dead, III 47
Kāla more powerful than, I 548
Yeats, Wm. Butler (1865-1939)
member of Dublin Lodge, II 3
Yoga (Skt)
See also Haṭha-Yoga; Rāja-Yoga
danger of, practices, I 230; II 246-7; III 327
highest, is union with all, I 13
mental-healing a sort of, I 230
Occidentals not fit for, II 416-17
Patañjali's system of, I 57; II 407
real, must have guide, III 327
Yogi(s) (Skt)
Algerian, performs rope trick, III 172
altruism must be motive for, II 416
as dabblers in psychic powers, II 246-7
dangers to Western, II 416
Devachan refused by few, III 449
disappearance of, I 410-12
on dynamo-spiritual forces induced by, III 337
feats of, I 402, 410-11
few among modern Hindus, II 371-2
few as guides to West, II 416
few true, brought by Hindus to West, II 371
Hindu, & genuine phenomena, III 48, 171-2
Maji a great woman, II 298
retired during "Black Age," I 410-11
Sabapathi Swami, etc., II 246
Young, Brigham (1801-1877)
prophet of Mormons, I 375

Yudhishṭhira
compassion of, I 341-2
dog of, I 101
stays in Hell for friends, I 101
Yuga(s) (Skt)
Adept on major & minor, III 17
compared to seasons, I 460
figures for each, apply to minor races only, I 459-60
four, in each Kalpa, III 58
four, in life of Brahmā, I 116, 123-6
major and minor, II 259q
man of this, has difficulty with sevenfold nature, II 105

Z

Zadok
one of Judge's pen-names, II 390
Zen Buddhism
origin of sect, I 85-6
taught self-reliance, I 86
Zendo [Chinese: Shan-tao (613-81)]
on sea of existence, I 88
Zirkoff, Boris de (1901-1981)
——— *Rebirth of the Occult Tradition*
on K.H. certificate to Hübbe-Schleiden, I 344n
Zodiac
ageless symbol, I 250
bearing of, on human evolution, I 465
calculation of Yugas and, I 460
Chaldean, inherited by West, I 132
constellations in, are moving, I 136
cosmic & microcosmic influences, I 162
on sun's passage through, III 12
Zohar
on rebirth, I 419
Zones
seven, and colors of Root-Races, III 20
Zoroastrianism
tenets of I 437

APPENDIX

List of Articles

Titles below in brackets were assigned by the compiler. In alphabetizing this list we have ignored initial prepositions, articles, and conjunctions. Biographical sketches from volume II of *Echoes* are indented, in page sequence, under their series title "Faces of Friends."

Abridgement of Discussions . . . . II 439
An Added Word . . . . III 147
The Adepts . . . . I 313
The Adepts and Modern Science . . . . I 376
The Adepts in America in 1776 . . . . II 76
Advantages and Disadvantages in Life . . . . I 483
Affirmations and Denials . . . . I 238
The Allegorical Umbrella . . . . I 140
Alone & Having Nothing — Astral Body & Spleen . . . . III 461
An American Experiment . . . . III 156
An Ancient Telephone . . . . I 447
Another Theosophical Prophecy . . . . I 16
Another View of Metaphysical Healing . . . . I 232
Answers to Correspondence [E.S.T.] . . . . III 377
Answers to Correspondence [E.S.T.] . . . . III 384
Answers to Correspondence [E.S.T.] . . . . III 394
The Antaḥkaraṇa . . . . III 302
Aphorisms on Karma . . . . I 333
The Application of Theosophical Theories . . . . III 125
Are the "Arabian Nights" All Fiction? . . . . II 92
Are There New Souls? Why Reincarnation? . . . . II 418
Are We Deserted? . . . . I 201
On Argument . . . . III 244
Argument for Reincarnation . . . . I 203
The Ashes of H.P.B. . . . . II 194
Astral Bodies . . . . III 444

By Astral Hand . . . III 222
Astral Intoxication . . . I 49
The Astral Light . . . III 135
The Astral Light . . . III 143
Astral Light Earth's Liṅga-Śarīra . . . III 317
An Astrological Question . . . II 15
Astrology Verified . . . II 73
Aum! . . . I 5
Authorship of *The Secret Doctrine* . . . I 342
Bases and Aspects — [Auric Envelope] . . . III 319
The Best Teacher . . . III 452
Beware [of Psychic Practices] . . . III 457
"Blavatskianism" In and Out of Season . . . II 58
Blavatsky Still Lives . . . III 138
Bogus Mahatma Messages . . . I 469
[Book Introduction] (*Modern Theosophy*) . . . III 242
The Brain and its Ventricles . . . III 303
"The Brotherhood of the New Life" . . . II 192
A Buddhist Doctrine . . . I 85
Care of Instructions — Inducing Persons to Join the E.S. . . . III 300
Cautions in Paragraphs . . . I 371
Chairman's Closing Address [European Convention 1892] . . . III 101
Chirognomy and Palmistry . . . II 97
Christian Fathers on Reincarnation . . . I 430
Cities Under Cities . . . I 300
Claiming to be Jesus . . . I 493
The Closing Cycle . . . II 9
Comets . . . I 481
The Coming of the Serpent . . . I 571
A Commentary on the Gāyatrī . . . I 311
[On Common Doctrines] . . . II 156
Communications from "Spirits" . . . I 452
Concerning Mr. Foulke's Claims . . . II 28
Conduct of Group Meetings . . . III 311
Considerations on Magic . . . I 44
Contemporary Literature and Theosophy . . . II 179
Convention of the European Section . . . II 43

[Conversations on Occultism] . . . . I 62
Correspondence . . . . I 322
Correspondence Group Questions & Answers . . . . III 289
Council for Eastern Division . . . . III 453
Culture of Concentration . . . . I 70
The Cure of Diseases . . . . I 281
A Curious Tale . . . . I 541
Cycles . . . . I 121
Cycles and Cyclic Law . . . . II 164
Cyclic Impression and Return and our Evolution . . . . I 514
Devachan . . . . I 167
Devachan . . . . I 336
Direful Prophecies . . . . I 422
Disappearance of Ascetics at Will . . . . I 410
Doctrine of Transmigration . . . . III 318
Dogmatism in Theosophy . . . . I 221
The Double-Page Diagram . . . . III 415
Duties of Group Presidents & Secretaries . . . . III 371
The Dweller of the Threshold . . . . I 96
The Dwellers on High Mountains . . . . III 225
Each Member a Center . . . . I 490
The Earth Chain of Globes . . . . I 323
East and West . . . . III 458
[On E.S.T. Headship] . . . . III 439
[E.S.T. Section Introduction — COMP.] . . . . III 273
Echoes from the Orient . . . . III 3
Editorial [*The Path*] . . . . I 3
Editorial [*The Path*] . . . . I 62
Editorial Note [*The Path*] . . . . II 182
End of Our Third Year . . . . I 109
Environment . . . . I 31
An Epitome of Theosophy . . . . III 53
Esoteric Buddhism . . . . III 250
[E.S. after H.P.B.] — E.S. — Order . . . . III 339
[E.S. Office Notices] . . . . III 370
The Esoteric She . . . . III 204
Ethics and Occultism . . . . III 465

Evolution . . . . I 157
Evolution . . . . II 421
Examination Paper I . . . . III 287
Examination Paper I, Remarks on . . . . III 294
Examination Paper No. 2, Correct Answers to . . . . III 361
Examination Paper No. 3, Remarks on . . . . III 402
FACES OF FRIENDS [Twelve Biographical Sketches]
Jirah Dewey Buck . . . . II 471
Edward Burroughs Rambo . . . . II 472
Major General Abner Doubleday . . . . II 474
Jerome A. Anderson . . . . II 477
Allen Griffiths . . . . II 479
T. Subba Row . . . . II 480
Bertram Keightley . . . . II 481
Dr. Archibald Keightley . . . . II 485
G. N. Chakravarti . . . . II 487
Countess Constance Wachtmeister . . . . II 489
H. Dharmapala . . . . II 492
George R. S. Mead . . . . II 493
Claude Falls Wright . . . . II 496
George Edward Wright . . . . II 497
Jasper Niemand (Mrs. Archibald Keightley) . . . . II 499
Tukaram Tatya [Padval] . . . . II 504
James Morgan Pryse . . . . II 507
Isabel Cooper-Oakley . . . . II 509
Emil August Neresheimer . . . . II 513
Ernest Temple Hargrove . . . . II 514
Rangampalli Jagannathiah and T. A. Swaminatha Aiyar . . . . II 516

A Few Words Personal . . . . III 460
Fiery Skies and Ancient Philosophers . . . . III 118
Fifteen Years Ago . . . . I 174
Five Years Finished . . . . I 191
The Four Basic Principles & Three Aspects . . . . III 325
Friends or Enemies in the Future . . . . I 315
Of Funds and Property . . . . II 205
On the Future: A Few Reflections . . . . II 24

The Future and the Theosophical Society . . . . I 243
Through the Gates of Gold . . . . I 36
A German Mystic's Teachings . . . . I 89
Give Us One Fact . . . . I 59
Glamour . . . . I 357
The Greatest Occult Truths . . . . III 433
Group Study . . . . III 331
Group Visits . . . . III 384
Habitations of H.P.B . . . . I 256
Haṭha Yoga Practices . . . . III 308
Have Patience with the Office . . . . III 414
The Headquarters at Adyar . . . . I 142
[On Healing] . . . . III 256
Hidden Hints in *The Secret Doctrine* [From *The Path*, 1891-2] . . II 223
"The Hidden Way" and Theosophists . . . . III 135
Hindu Theosophy and Professor Buchanan . . . . III 265
Hit the Mark . . . . I 163
An Hour in the Sanctum . . . . I 223
How She Must Laugh . . . . I 269
How Should We Treat Others? . . . . I 501
How the Society is Run . . . . I 188
How to Square the Teachings . . . . I 382
H.P.B.∴ — A Lion-Hearted Colleague Passes . . . . I 191
H.P.B at Enghien . . . . II 21
H. P. Blavatsky . . . . I 139
H.P.B. Was Not Deserted by the Masters . . . . I 509
H. S. Olcott versus H.P.B. . . . . II 215
Hypnotism . . . . I 413
Hypnotism and Theosophy . . . . III 212
Hypnotism — Mesmerism . . . . I 144
Hypocrisy or Ignorance . . . . I 218
Illusions of Time and Space . . . . III 248
Imagination and Occult Phenomena . . . . I 307
An Important Cycle — Study of the Instructions — the OṂ . III 283
Impossibilities Demanded . . . . II 198
The Impudence of Modern Philosophers . . . . I 220
India, A Trumpet Call at a Crisis . . . . II 49

India and Her Theosophists . . . . II 112
India a Storehouse for Us . . . . I 183
India's Wonder-Workers . . . . III 170
The Inner Constitution of Man . . . . III 186
Intellectual Gymnastics — There is an Age Limit . . . . III 460
An Interesting Letter . . . . II 46
[Introductory: World's Parliament] . . . . II 119
[Introductory Note to *Irish Theosophist* — COMP.] . . . . II 3
[Invocations] . . . . II 148
Ireland . . . . I 230
Is Heredity a Puzzle? . . . . I 93
Is Karma Only Punishment? . . . . I 137
Is Poverty Bad Karma? . . . . I 195
Is There a Soul in Man? . . . . II 90
Jacob Boehme and *The Secret Doctrine* . . . . II 106
The Kali-Yuga . . . . I 458
As to Kāma-Rūpa . . . . III 320
Karma . . . . I 24
Karma and Ethics . . . . III 168
Karma and Reincarnation . . . . III 245
Keeping the Rules . . . . III 324
About Killing Animals . . . . I 247
Koot Hoomi . . . . III 121
Law of Correspondences . . . . III 312
The Letter to the Brahmans . . . . I 424
Libel by Dr. Coues and the "New York Sun" . . . . II 188
The Light of Egypt . . . . II 193
The Lower Self . . . . III 304
Lunar Pitṛis . . . . III 462
Madame Blavatsky in India . . . . III 195
"Madame Blavatsky's Income" . . . . III 152
The Magic Screen of Time . . . . I 548
The Mahatmas as Ideals and Facts . . . . I 339
A Mahatma's Message to Some Brahmans . . . . I 470
As to Marriage . . . . III 302
Mars and Mercury . . . . I 368
Masters, Adepts, Teachers, and Disciples . . . . I 365

[Masters & the Eastern School of Theosophy] . . . . III 391
Matters Touching Theosophy . . . . III 127
Mechanical Theosophy . . . . I 491
Meditation . . . . III 453
Meditation, Concentration, Will . . . . II 7
Meditation — The Antaḥkaraṇa . . . . III 372
Mediumship . . . . I 51
[Meeting with a Mahatma] . . . . III 418
Mesmerism . . . . II 31
Mesmerism and the Higher Self . . . . I 254
Of "Metaphysical Healing" . . . . I 227
Methods of Group Study . . . . III 300
Methods of Theosophical Work . . . . I 204
Misunderstood Editorial . . . . I 269
Moon's Mystery and Fate . . . . I 432
The Moral Law of Compensation . . . . II 70
Mr. William Q. Judge at Hyderabad . . . . II 83
Much Reading, Little Thought . . . . I 151
Musings on the True Theosophist's Path . . . . I 17
The Mystery of the Moon . . . . III 306
The Nāḍīgranthams . . . . II 101
The Necessity for Reincarnation . . . . III 73
The New "Department of Branch Work" . . . . II 186
The New York Theosophical Society . . . . II 69
Nigamāgama Dharma Sabhā . . . . I 441
Nirmāṇakāyas . . . . III 449
No End and No Beginning . . . . III 152
Notice from H.P.B . . . . III 288
Notice to Inquirers . . . . II 179
Occult Arts . . . . I 390
Occultism . . . . III 258
Occultism for Barter . . . . I 112
Occultism: What Is It? . . . . I 146
Of Occult Powers and their Acquirement . . . . I 106
One of the Signs of the Cycle . . . . I 148
The Organized Life of The Theosophical Society . . . . II 149
On the Organs . . . . III 347

The Oriental Department . . . . . II 189
Our Convictions . . . . . I 384
Our Sun and the True Sun . . . . . I 135
Padmapāṇi . . . . . III 356
Papyrus . . . . . I 539
Papyrus —The Gem . . . . . III 267
The Pāramitās . . . . . III 305
A Parent T.S. Diploma . . . . . II 213
The Path of Action . . . . . I 54
The Path's Fifth Year . . . . . I 141
"Peace with Honor" or "A Scientific Frontier" . . . . . II 183
The Persian Students' Doctrine . . . . . I 567
Plain Theosophical Traces . . . . . I 270
Points of Agreement in All Religions . . . . . I 435
Practical Theosophy . . . . . I 155
Practicing Magic . . . . . III 305
The Prayag Letter . . . . . II 53
The Press and Occultism . . . . . I 102
Prince Talleyrand — Cagliostro . . . . . I 169
[On Probation and Pledge Fever] . . . . . III 274
Professor Max Müller on Buddhism . . . . . I 120
Proofs of the Hidden Self . . . . . I 448
Prophecies by H. P. Blavatsky . . . . . I 302
A Prophecy about Theosophy . . . . . I 10
Psychometry . . . . . III 119
Questions from *The Path* [1887-96] . . . . . II 389
Questions from *The Path* [cont.] . . . . . II 427
Questions from *The Theosophical Forum* [1889-95] . . . . . II 253
Questions from *The Vāhan* [1891-92] . . . . . II 243
Recall of the Instructions . . . . . III 428
The Red Rājputs . . . . . I 428
Regarding Islamism . . . . . I 372
Reincarnation . . . . . III 178
Reincarnation in Judaism and the Bible . . . . . I 417
Reincarnation in the Bible . . . . . I 304
Reincarnation of Animals . . . . . I 426
Relation of E.S.T. to the T.S . . . . . III 421

Religion and Reform From a Theosophical Viewpoint . . . . . III 159
Remembering the Experiences of the Ego . . . . I 152
A Reminiscence . . . . I 320
Replanting Diseases for Future Use . . . . I 294
Replies on Kāma-Rūpa . . . . III 352
"Reply to the Attack on Madame Blavatsky" . . . . III 150
Respecting Reincarnation . . . . I 83
A Review of *The Secret Doctrine* . . . . III 148
Rings, Rounds, and Obscuration . . . . II 424
Of Rosicrucian and Other Bodies . . . . III 443
[On Rule about Complaints] . . . . III 316
Sayings of Jesus . . . . III 255
The School & Correspondence Group . . . . III 375
The School Under Trial . . . . III 432
The Screen of Time . . . . I 494
The Screen of Time . . . . I 505
The Second Year . . . . I 47
About *The Secret Doctrine* . . . . III 238
The Secret Doctrine and Physiology . . . . I 387
Of Seeing and Not Seeing Spooks . . . . III 254
Seeking Occult Teachings Elsewhere . . . . III 423
"The Self is the Friend of Self and also Its Enemy" . . . . III 82
The Serpent's Blood . . . . I 544
A Servant of the Masters . . . . I 63
Seven Steps Forward . . . . I 248
The Seven Worlds . . . . III 332
Seven Years Gone . . . . I 332
The Sevenfold Division . . . . I 143
Seventeen Years Ago and Now . . . . I 297
Shall We Teach Clairvoyance? . . . . I 176
The Sheaths of the Soul . . . . II 40
The Signs of This Cycle . . . . I 292
Six Years Gone . . . . I 237
The Skin of the Earth . . . . I 557
The So-Called Exposé of Madame Blavatsky . . . . III 123
Some Answers about Kāma-Rūpa . . . . III 330
Something to Study . . . . III 430

About "Spirit" Materializations . . . . I 197
Spiritual Gifts and their Attainment . . . . I 103
The "Spiritual Will" . . . . III 442
Spiritualism . . . . I 350
Spiritualism: A "Spirit" Testifies . . . . I 405
Spiritualism Old and New . . . . I 284
Spiritually and Intellectually Evil . . . . III 328
The Status of the E.S.T. . . . . III 354
Stray Memoranda . . . . I 107
The Stream of Thought and Queries . . . . II 411
Of Studying Theosophy . . . . I 131
Suicide is Not Death . . . . III 218
Sundry Queries . . . . III 314
Sundry Queries . . . . III 321
The Synthesis of Occult Science . . . . I 207
Table of Vibrations . . . . III 309
Talk on Karma . . . . III 98
The Tell-Tale Picture Gallery . . . . I 553
Tenets of Theosophy . . . . III 163
Theosophic Diet . . . . I 99
Theosophic Duties . . . . III 203
The Theosophical Congress . . . . II 125
The Theosophical Congress & The Parliament of Religions . II 168
Theosophical Correspondence Class . . . . II 64
Theosophical Correspondence Class . . . . II 202
Theosophical Don'ts . . . . I 467
The Theosophical Movement . . . . I 485
The Theosophical Society . . . . I 194
The Theosophical Society . . . . I 361
The Theosophical Society . . . . II 208
The Theosophical Society . . . . III 77
The T.S. and Its Basis . . . . III 216
Theosophical Studies . . . . III 132
Theosophical Study and Work . . . . III 88
Theosophical Symbolism . . . . I 11
Theosophical Symbols . . . . I 249
Theosophical Theories of the Microcosm . . . . II 104

The Theosophist in Ceylon . . . . III 117
To Theosophists Willing to Work . . . . II 185
Theosophy and Capital Punishment . . . . I 487
Theosophy and Epidemics . . . . III 192
Theosophy and the Destiny of India (Bombay) . . . . II 80
Theosophy and the Destiny of India (Secunderabad) . . . . II 85
Theosophy and the Theosophical Society . . . . I 179
Theosophy as a Cult in India . . . . III 129
Theosophy as a Guide in Life . . . . III 69
Theosophy Defined . . . . III 233
Theosophy Generally Stated . . . . II 135
Theosophy in the Christian Bible . . . . II 140
Things Common to Christianity and Theosophy . . . . III 104
Thought Transference or Mind Reading . . . . II 95
Thoughts on Karma . . . . I 275
Three Great Ideas . . . . II 12
The Three Planes of Human Life . . . . I 80
A Time for Meditation . . . . III 394
Transmigration of Souls . . . . II 419
Tributes to W. Q. Judge . . . . II 4
True Progress . . . . I 153
The Truth about East and West . . . . I 476
The Turn of the Wheel . . . . I 561
Two Lost Keys: *Bhagavad-Gītā* — Zodiac . . . . I 161
Two Spiritualistic Prophecies . . . . I 404
Two Systems — of Lust and Sorrow . . . . I 91
Two Theosophical Events . . . . II 199
The Two Virgins Dolma . . . . III 318
Two Years on the Path . . . . I 56
Universal Applications of Doctrine . . . . I 114
Universal Brotherhood a Fact in Nature . . . . II 143
Universal Brotherhood and Admission of Members . . . . I 444
Upanishads on Rebirth . . . . I 413
The Use of the Word [OṂ] . . . . III 310
On "Vāch" . . . . III 335
Vast Works of the Past . . . . I 450
The Wandering Eye . . . . I 550

We Have Not Been Deserted . . . . III 411
A Weird Tale . . . . I 531
The West and What India Can Give It (Poona) . . . . II 82
What is Occultism? . . . . III 257
What Our Society Needs Most . . . . I 279
What the Masters Have Said . . . . I 317
What Theosophy Is . . . . III 166
Where the Ṛishis Were . . . . I 564
Which is Vague, Theosophy or Science? . . . . I 172
Who and What are the Masters? . . . . III 424
Why Races Die Out . . . . I 205
Why the Theosophical Society Is Poor . . . . I 110
Why Yoga Practice is Dangerous . . . . I 186
Will Masters' Help Be Withdrawn in 1898 until 1975? . . . . . . I 461
[W.Q.J. and the Press — COMP.] . . . . III 115
William Quan Judge: His Life and Work
(Compiled by Sven Eek and Boris de Zirkoff) . . . . I xvii
Wisdom of the Gods . . . . III 173
Words From Masters . . . . III 413
The Work Since May . . . . II 217
Would Universal Language Aid Universal Brotherhood? . . . . . I 456
Wrong Popular Notions . . . . I 464
A Year on the Path . . . . I 34
Yoga Practices . . . . III 327
"Yours till Death and after, H.P.B." . . . . II 16